Women in the
Church of God in Christ

Anthea D. Butler

Women in the Church of God in Christ

Making a Sanctified World

The University of
North Carolina Press
CHAPEL HILL

Designed by Heidi Perov

Set in C&C Galliard

by Tseng Information Systems, Inc.

The paper in this book meets the guidelines for permanence
and durability of the Committee on Production Guidelines
for Book Longevity of the Council on Library Resources.

Library of Congress Cataloging-in-Publication Data

Butler, Anthea D., 1960–

Women in the Church of God in Christ : making a sanctified world /
Anthea D. Butler.

p. cm.

Includes bibliographical references and index.

ISBN 978-0-8078-3117-5 (cloth : alk. paper)

ISBN 978-0-8078-5808-0 (pbk. : alk. paper)

1. Church of God in Christ. 2. Women in church work.

I. Title.

BX7056.A4B88 2007

289.9'4–dc22   2007002877

CLOTH   11 10 09 08 07   5 4 3 2 1

PAPER   11 10 09 08 07   5 4 3 2 1

for Oreo
. . . a faithful friend . . .
who would have chewed the book
up if he'd had the chance

Contents

Illustrations

Acknowledgments

I have many, many people to express my gratitude to for making this book possible. Without their help, whether financial, moral, academic, or otherwise, this book would not exist.

I owe a large debt to two agencies whose generosity funded this project. The Center for the Study of Religion at Princeton University, headed by Robert Wuthnow, granted me a postdoctoral fellowship in 2001–2. Thanks to Bob, Anita Kline, and Marie Griffith (associate director of the center at the time) for making my time at Princeton University productive and crucial to the direction of the book (despite 9/11 and anthrax!). The Louisville Institute, with Jim Lewis as executive director, and the board of the Louisville Institute graciously granted me a First Book Grant Program for Minority Scholars in 2003–4 that also helped tremendously in the completion of this book. Jim's graciousness and the input of board members helped in figuring out the "so what?" questions that are often most important to a book project.

Two other projects I was involved with during writing this book provided me with both the camaraderie and the theoretical framework that made this book possible. The Women and Religion in the African Diaspora Project, funded by the Ford Foundation was tremendously supportive. Leaders Marie Griffith and Barbara Savage, and the WRAD crew, were my "homies" on this long journey, and I appreciate their friendship and support. I am grateful for their advice, direction, and friendship. The History of American Christian Practice Project, funded by the Lilly Foundation and led by Laurie Maffly-Kipp, Leigh Schmidt, and Mark Valeri, gave me a space to work out the book's theoretical kinks. The much-needed working vacations we took over the span of the projects and the friendships that were built were of great support to me, especially the discovery of "Lapis"!

The opportunity to engage in these various grants and projects came about through the care and generosity of the Department of Theological Studies at Loyola Marymount University. It is a rare faculty that does its best to support junior scholars, and though I am no longer with them, their support was much valued and appreciated, and shows in this book.

To the woman who had a vision of what this book could be, my editor, Elaine Maisner, I give thanks from the bottom of my heart for having enormous patience with me! She is simply the best. I am grateful to her for all of her efforts and support. I thank Mary Caviness, manuscript editor, for her patience and hard work on making this book "sing." A special thank you also to Ruth Homrighaus, whose assistance with this manuscript in the initial stages was vital to maintaining my sanity!

To those within the Church of God in Christ who welcomed me into their homes, basements, and lives I owe profound thanks. I could not have completed this book without their assistance and input. Sherry Sherrod DuPree welcomed me into her home and let me accompany her on interviews. What she has done to prevent Pentecostal history from crumbling by the wayside has been inspirational. Her private collection and the collection given to the Shomburg Library in New York City provided much of the foundational work of this book. Thanks also go to Glenda Goodson, who provided me many of the pictures and convocation books mentioned, for her assistance and companionship on the road! Raynard Smith, founder and leader of COGIC scholars, graciously introduced me to many of the Saints on the East Coast, including Elder Gorham, who were instrumental in putting together some of the stories in the book. One of those Saints, Juanita Faulkner, was a source of great stories and insights, and I thank her very much for sharing herself with me. A special thanks also to Mother Phyllis Barnett in Los Angeles, Emma Clark, and state supervisor Mother Martha Parker of Nebraska, who also were of great assistance to me during the research and writing of this book. I could not have hoped to dress so well until Mother Barnett showed me how to shop!

There is one member of COGIC, however, who I must single out as the most important source for almost EVERYTHING in this book: Dr. David Daniels III. David and I have talked COGIC from Memphis, Tennessee, to São Paulo, Brazil, and every place imaginable in between! Without his vast knowledge of COGIC, this book could not have been written. I am profoundly grateful for his friendship and sharing his knowledge with me. I hope that the book is worthy of the time he spent in helping me to write and research the history of COGIC women.

Archivists also helped very much in piecing this history together. Several archives should be singled out for their special help and assistance: the American Baptist Historical Society, and specifically Deborah Van Broekhoven, Betty Layton, and Betsy Dunbar for their friendship and assistance. The staff of the Flower Pentecostal Heritage Center under Wayne Warner's leadership were of great help in the initial stages of the project. The staff at the Schomburg Library in New York and the Chicago Historical Society were also helpful. Finally, the archivists at the Moorland Spingarn Archives at Howard University were helpful in digging up a treasure trove of the COGIC newspaper *The Whole Truth* and other materials helpful to this project.

Many of my colleagues in the academic community proved to be excellent conversation partners, listening ears, and sources of encouragement when I felt overwhelmed or about to throw in the towel. They include Judith Weisenfeld, Lewis Baldwin, Victor Anderson, Darren Sherkat, Mel Robeck, Tim Matovina, Diane Winston, Heather Curtis, Dianne Glave, Katie Lofton, Leslie Callahan, Tisa Wenger, Daniel Ramirez, Suzette Lemrow, Kirsten Andresen, Jeff Williams, Paul Wilhelm, Barbara Holmes, Jane Crawford, Michelle Gonzalez Maldonado, James Pratt, Deidre Crumbley, Jean-Daniel Pluss, Walter Hollenweger, Fred Harris, Eric Williams, Suzanne O'Brien, Tim Kitchen, and Jack Sakmar. They all had my back, and I thank them for it.

To my parents, Jessie Butler and Willa Butler, and my sisters, Stacy, Kamala, and Keitha, I thank for their love and support during this time. Now I can talk about something else!

Finally, this book is dedicated to the faithful four-legged writing companion that did not make it to see the end of the book, Mr. Oreo, a rather scruffy but elegant black-and-white alley cat. His perch beside my desk where he would watch me write is empty now, and his playful distractions are sorely missed.

Women in the
Church of God in Christ

Introduction

*The "proper" place of women in the church is an age-old debate and from all appearances,
it seems that it perhaps will be an eternal one—for most mortals at least.*
Bishop O. T. Jones, D.D., in Pleas, *Fifty Years Achievement*

For many years now in the study of African American religious history, one statement has been believed as gospel: black women outnumber black men in the church. The reasons given to explain the imbalance have varied. Perhaps black men felt emasculated at church; perhaps the church was a women's space, even if there was sexism; perhaps women adapted better to Jesus, who seemed to answer prayer; perhaps it was a place to lay down the burdens of racism and a hard life and give them over to Jesus. Church, some argued, was the one place where the "mules of the world," as Zora Neale Hurston referred to black women, could lay their burdens down and become free. But what if there was something more behind black women's church attendance? What if they went to church not just to feel good or protected but to use their womanhood to become empowered, to wield power through a traditional office in subversive yet spiritual ways?[1] And what if that power, over the span of 100 years, translated into civic and economic empowerment for women?

I begin to answer these questions in this study of the Women's Department of the Church of God in Christ (COGIC). COGIC, an African American Pentecostal church, has origins both in the nineteenth-century Holiness movement and in the Pentecostal movement of the twentieth century. The church today numbers over 5 million adherents worldwide, and is the largest Pentecostal body in North America. COGIC's Women's Department, established by one of the denominational founders, Charles Harrison Mason, in 1911, is an organization of evangelists, missionaries, and church mothers who have led both the women and the men of COGIC. Unlike many of black women's sororities and clubs of the twentieth century, the Women's Department has included women from the upper and lower classes, light-skinned and dark-skinned women, women who were wives and mothers, and women who transcended the boundaries of motherhood to become spiritual mothers, or church mothers. These church mothers formed the backbone of an organization that has had only five women leaders since 1911. Reigning over morality in much the same way Queen Victoria did in the nineteenth century, the church mothers of the Church of God in Christ combined African-based spirituality, domesticity founded on scriptural principles, organizational savvy, and evangelical fervor to fuel a formidable organization that continues to exist today. Making use of a traditional role, motherhood, the women of COGIC carved a niche of spiritual and temporal power for themselves within a black patriarchy that continues to assert its leadership and authority over women by denying them ordination, yet allows them to have tremendous power and authority.

Perhaps it seems strange to attribute much power to church mothers. After all, the older women who lead songs, shout, and take homemade pies and dinners to the pastor are not those who we normally think of as policy makers or theologians. Look closer. Church mothers are the women who recall the history of their churches, who chastise the pastor when he has interpreted the scriptures incorrectly, and who set the cultural and behavioral patterns for their congregations. The church mother is a repository of both belief and culture within her religious communities. Although the antecedents of church mothers are unclear, their presence in black churches is linked to spiritual mothers within other religious traditions, to matriarchal leadership, and to fictive family relations. Within COGIC, church mothers are links to the past as well as a very present part of the church in the twentieth century. The church mother's role is as much of a fixture as the role of preacher, yet her life and work has been obscured by traditional roles of preaching and patriarchal leadership within the black church.

The title of "church mother," or "mother," given to older women within many black churches is the seed of leadership and eldership within the COGIC Women's Department.[2] From 1911, when the first women's leader was chosen, the role of mother provided the link between the ordained men of the denomination and the women they purported to lead, a role that led to the world and to the church, to education and to economic empowerment, and to the civic realm and to the spiritual realm. Within less than 100 years, COGIC women went from being leaders in Bible reading groups to smartly dressed, civically engaged, educated, and economically empowered women. Whereas the tradition in many African American churches was for the church mother to be a mere figurehead dressed in white, sitting in the front pew, COGIC church mothers established their own organizational sphere within the confines of their denomination.

But what salience, if any, does their story have for African American women and the broader history of women's roles in the African American church, and American religion? The importance of chronicling this history, I believe, lies in church mothers' negotiation of spiritual and temporal power, and their organizational acumen. Setting aside as incomplete other scholars' explanations for African American women's engagement in the church, which range from black women's quest for respectability and racial uplift, to their struggle for civil rights, to their need for faith to compensate for the harshness of their lives, I maintain that COGIC church mothers' quest for spiritual empowerment by means of "the sanctified life" provided the moral, spiritual, and physical fuel that enabled them to negotiate for and obtain power both within the denomination and outside it. Sanctification in COGIC is both theological and cultural, encompassing beliefs from the nineteenth-century Evangelical and Holiness movements that pushed followers to live a life of holiness, refraining from the sins and pollutions of modern life. In COGIC, sanctification was not an instantaneous process but a gradual one, requiring dedication to both spiritual practices and temporal obedience. Church members pursued sanctification through spiritual practices such as fasting, prayer, scripture study, and other disciplines, creating moral and spiritual authority. These practices enabled COGIC women to attain status within the confines of the denomination without being ordained. Their pursuit of sanctification was not simply a quest for personal meaning; it was also a pursuit to be shared with the world. Sanctified COGIC women took their sanctified bodies to street-corner ministries, to the front pews of country churches, to classrooms, and, soon, to the civic arena. Transformed from the mules of the world to sanctified women who shaped and changed it, COGIC women engaged both spirituality and culture in ways that have become integral to African American religious and social life.

Sanctification was also both public and private for COGIC women. Sanctifying self and others through practices such as fasting, prayer, and sexual abstinence bound the world of early church mothers, and those who were drawn to the sanctified world found themselves in an alternate reality of sorts, a sanctified world with its own prohibitions, practices, and familial allegiances. This first generation of COGIC women's leadership operated primarily to make the sanctified world an interior world, a world that was resistant to modernity under its first leader, Lizzie Woods Robinson. The next generation of women's leadership, under Lillian Brooks Coffey, would transform that sanctified world. Coffey's leadership of church mothers led the organization into an engagement with the outside world that allowed women to keep the practices of sanctification intact while making important social connections to the broader world of African American civic life. The history of COGIC women can be seen through the lens of how African Americans negotiated not only their religious lives but also the changes that modernity and progress brought to middle- and lower-class African Americans from the Reconstruction period to the advent of the civil rights movement. In moving sanctification from interior to exterior work COGIC women took what has previously been considered a fringe belief system into an engagement with broader social and cultural issues in American religious life. The negotiation of sanctification and its adaptation to the changing times places COGIC women's work into a broader arena of African American women's history.

On one level, most of what I have stated is not earth shattering to those familiar with the African American church tradition. After all, scholars have recognized for some time that black women's agency within the church has transcended the boundaries of ordination and has been deployed in ingenious ways, especially in the quest for civil rights. What is different about this book is its emphasis on how belief—in this case, belief in sanctification—acted as the impetus for what church mothers actually accomplished. I think that belief was and continues to be the foundation for many African American women's engagement with the church and the world. This is not to say that other issues were not important. African American studies have for the most part failed to significantly engage with how the power of belief has shaped black women's struggle for education, civil rights, and gender equality. This study challenges the traditional lacunae in African American studies by taking belief seriously, rather than treating it as a compensatory sideline to other issues, as did many of the early sociological studies of sanctified churches, from St. Clair Drake to Hortense Powdermaker and others.[3] Religion matters for black women, whether they are in agreement with it or in opposition to it.

Living the sanctified life helped to shape and define COGIC women's intellectual, spiritual, moral, and working worlds in such a way that their focus on sanctification became the catalyst for spiritual, social, and political change. COGIC women's tenacious focus on sanctification is thus a different lens with which to examine the religious and social worlds of African American women within and outside their religious tradition, one that provides a compelling alternative narrative to the traditional notion that African American women's beliefs were motivated by their desire to advance the race. This study also flies in the face of a narrative that we have lived with in African American religious history: that those who are concerned with sanctification and other types of religious disciplinary practices are not concerned with "this world." Described as accommodationist and otherworldly, sanctified traditions in black theology, sociology, and anthropology have been given short shrift because sanctified beliefs did not always translate into easily recognizable or measurable radical behavior.[4] My contention is that a historical look at how COGIC women negotiated beliefs regarding sanctification and how those beliefs about sanctification changed and modernized women's work reorients the notion that the sanctified churches were disengaged from the quest for social activism. On issues from education to civic engagement to war, COGIC women were vocal and active, supporting their core beliefs in sanctification while engaging with the broader issues of African American religion and life.

COGIC women's stories are compelling, then, not only because their beliefs about sanctification are interesting but also because of how those beliefs influenced their activities, and their negotiations of the boundary lines between authority and gender. At times, COGIC women affirmed the traditional roles of wife, mother, and homemaker, in line with nineteenth- and early-twentieth-century norms. At other times, they contravened gender roles by subverting both male and female authority within the church, transcending gender by appearing to be "sexless" and therefore set apart from traditional spiritual authority. These tensions are part of a complex historical narrative defined by the quest for purity and power. COGIC women sought purity through sanctification to transcend the physical body and its limitations, and to harness spiritual power to change the world. The negotiation of purity and power created tensions, however, among the women, their men, and outsiders. It caused outsiders to label church members "otherworldly" when their concerns were most definitely within the realm of conquering this temporal world. Purity and power became the underlying theme of many church mothers' lives, often in an uneasy alliance.

Power through purity also became a way in which COGIC women negotiated the continuing question of ordination for women. In American religious history, the struggle for women to have the right and authority to preach is a common theme that can be traced from Anne Hutchinson forward. What we have not asked as scholars is What about the women who do not seek ordination? How do they controvert, subvert, and supersede the ordained power of the male ministers? Why would any woman go along with the admonition not to preach? COGIC women struggled with the same questions, but their responses differed from the traditional narratives in which scholars have engaged in American religious history. There is the power of ordination, but there is a greater power in controlling the ordained, which is what COGIC women did; convincingly at times, not so convincingly at others. By using their charismatic authority and their organizational position that was outside, but alongside, the Episcopal structure, COGIC women were able to become power brokers both inside and outside of the church setting. This fact alone becomes very important when considering the fate of many churchwomen's organizations, such as the National Baptist Women's Convention, the Southern Baptist Convention, and the United Methodist Women. Whether missions-oriented or otherwise, women's authority to run their own sacred space and men's fears of women taking their pastoral authority have driven much of the organizational and strategic infighting in churches.

This book also has a very basic purpose. Secretly, this story is also a bit of denominational history. Yes, denominational histories are out of vogue, but when it comes to the history of African American church life, the dearth of scholarship in this area leaves a tremendous void. What I seek to do by writing this history is not only to tell the story of COGIC women but also to tell the story of a religious body in transition. Like all systems, churches must adapt to changing attitudes and mores while holding on to core beliefs and principles. The material on these types of organizational and cultural changes is well chronicled in American religious history for white Protestant and Catholic groups. African American religious history as a field, unfortunately, did not develop from this type of scholarship. Carter G. Woodson's *The Negro Church*, for example, omits a significant amount of noninstitutionalized, nonmainstream black church experience, a vital and important tradition. The common core of any history of black church bodies contends with the story of slavery and the struggle for civil rights. Cultural issues also abound in the discussion of black church life, but the organizational systems, belief structures, and practices that basic denominational histories contend with are sorely lacking when we move beyond the study of the African Methodist Episcopal, the black Baptist, and Christian Methodist Episcopal churches. The dominant narrative ignores the subtle and myriad ways in which adherents took their faith as both an individual imperative and a method to engage civic life while grappling with issues of modernity. That story in itself is one worth telling. Considering the rapid proliferation today of black megachurches, hybrid black Baptist churches masquerading as full gospel churches and emulating sanctified church practices and beliefs, it becomes even more important to understand the trajectory of history that allowed the traditions to merge together, when they were polar opposites at the beginning of the Great Migration.[5]

The history of the Women's Department of COGIC, then, can help us to understand some of the current tensions and cultural modifications that have occurred within the broader African American and American religious and cultural traditions. Perceptions of ecstatic worship, which was frowned upon in some black churches in the early decades of the twentieth century, began to change in the 1930s. The practices of sanctified life and worship originating with women in the sanctified church tradition infiltrated black church life. Looking at COGIC as a microcosm of this phenomenon can help us understand the broader cultural shift away from the politicized worship traditions of emulating civilized (read white) church culture and toward worship driven by bodies unbounded in worship yet bounded in behavior and appearance by beliefs about sanctification. Whether in dress, deportment, or fashion, COGIC church mothers and evangelists were in large part purveyors of a sanctified culture, and their public presence helped to bring vibrant worship into a cultural space that could be recognized and respected rather than reviled.

Most importantly, this study allows COGIC women's life stories to emerge from behind black men in the pulpit to the forefront of history. In writing about the women of COGIC, I have chosen to focus primarily on the period 1911–64, during which time the Women's Department was led by Lizzie Robinson and Lillian Brooks Coffey in turn. These women presided during a period of profound change for the women and men of COGIC, as well as for outsiders to the church. Spanning two world wars, a depression, and the long civil rights movement, this book about the lives and actions of COGIC women presents not merely their history but also the history of many African American men and women whose voices have been lost to us, although they lived not so long ago. Telling this story takes on even more importance now, when uncertainty surrounds the Church of God in Christ. The women of COGIC are beset by potential changes within the denomination that threaten to relegate them to an ancillary role, allowing men to make many of the appointments that have up to now been exclusively under women's purview. Sanctified churches' embrace of a softer, more feminized form of religion that is decidedly fashionable has reduced women's role to that of wearing elaborate hats, furs, and feathers, all of which would have been frowned upon by early COGIC church mothers.

Chronicling this story through research has been a hardscrabble project in many respects. There are no extant archives of the denomination, and when historical materials can be found, they are often in private hands. Much of this book is the result of my efforts to put together clues that were in well-worn denominational pamphlets and books that led me to newspaper articles, to records of the National Council of Negro Women, to tape recordings, to magazine articles, and to musty closets and bedrooms. Consequently, many of the records cited here are in my own private collection of materials purchased, found, given to me by erstwhile church mothers, and even literally rescued off of trash heaps. For the many who have waited patiently (and some grumpily) for this book to be finished, I encourage you to take heed of the fact that much of African American religious history is crumbling before our eyes. Research materials on Pentecostalism and much of African American religion do not exist solely in pristinely organized archives but in the homes of many senior citizens whose papers are daily thrown out by heedless relatives. Many times during research for this book, I was almost reduced to tears upon hearing of some cache of papers and pictures destroyed by relatives unaware of the history contained within.

In my quest to piece together this history, I interviewed older churchwomen and churchmen to help me understand issues of practice or belief that were not easily grasped by simply reading a text.[6] The reasons for particular religious practices and the meaning of several historical incidents became much clearer to me through interviews, which provided the "backstory" so often lacking in organizational minutes. I have sometimes obscured the identity of interviewees who were uncomfortable with being identified; some of the individuals I interviewed died before the publication of this book. I have attempted to present the fullest history possible, but I am also certain that many details have been lost to time, trash bins, and Alzheimer's disease.

What you will find, then, are seven chapters plus an epilogue that I hope present COGIC church mothers and their lives in the manner that they richly deserve. Each chapter has a one-word title that refers to the major theme of the chapter.[7] Chapter 1 begins with the life of Lizzie Robinson and her relationship with Joanna P. Moore, a woman who has been lost to the annals of history but who played a pivotal role in many African American women's lives in the post-Reconstruction period and into the twentieth century through her magazine

Hope. It was her relationship to Moore that provided Robinson with the foundational base for her organizational ideas and beliefs about sanctification.

Chapter 2 chronicles the establishment of the Women's Department (originally called the "women's work") by Charles Mason, one of the founders of COGIC, and the struggle to define a role for women within the denomination. It is here that one of the major distinctions of the black church—the distinction between "teaching" and "preaching"—came into play in the lives of COGIC church mothers, and it was here that the initial organization of the women's work under the leadership of Robinson began.

Chapter 3 focuses on the beginnings of the migration period and the church's struggle to define how sanctification would be modeled and taught to women who were joining the women's work and ascending into leadership. It also introduces two of the other women who had a major influence on the women's work in later years, Lillian Brooks Coffey and Arenia Mallory, whose friendship would later move the women's work into the modern age.

I regard Chapter 4 as a "lynchpin chapter," because it contains a deeper exploration of the practices of sanctification and how COGIC women struggled with being the modelers and enforcers of the sanctified life. During the crucial years of Prohibition, the toils of marriage, sexuality, holiness, and deportment shaped COGIC women's bodies and identities in such a way as to lock them into stagnancy that only radical behavior and education would eventually change.

Chapters 5 through 7 span roughly from 1930 to 1964, the years in which the Women's Department was transformed. The growth and impact of Saints Industrial School under the leadership of Arenia Mallory propelled COGIC women into interactions with the Depression-era presidency of Franklin Delano Roosevelt, with Eleanor Roosevelt, with Mary McLeod Bethune, and with the National Council of Negro Women. Alliances made in part to keep the denominational school afloat opened up the Women's Department to a new era of social and civic engagement that fundamentally changed the ways in which living the sanctified life was embodied and modeled by COGIC women, propelling them solidly into modernity and middle-class black life in America. Chapter 7 wraps up this history with the events leading to the death of Bishop Charles Harrison Mason and the impact of his death on the Women's Department. The epilogue, finally, brings the story forward with some thoughts about how church mothers' roles have changed within the denomination and some speculation about their future survival within COGIC structure.

In closing, I make no excuses for the fact that to some, this book may represent a challenge to the traditional ways of thinking about the supposed monolith of the black church, or women's engagement within it. In my estimation, the very fragmentation of beliefs, behaviors, and political and social engagements within African American religious traditions signals a vitality that scholars of the movement heretofore ignored because of the preoccupation with the themes of uplift and civil rights. I recognize their importance, but there are other stories that are clamoring to be told about African Americans and their religious lives. There is something of intrinsic value to placing these women of faith in their own context, a context in which they believed fervently in the eschatological hope that Jesus would make it all right. I like the women that I have written about, but I am also critical of the ways in which some women allowed the sanctified life to consume them to the point where they became abusive to themselves and one another. The church is not just about redemption; it is also about pain and subjugation. In spite of the pain, black churches are on par with the beauty shop as one of the few venues in America where African American women can congregate together, focusing their hopes and dreams on bettering themselves, their children, their men, and the world. Once you have read these stories, it is my hope that you will look a bit differently at older African American churchwomen the next time you find yourself in a restaurant on a Sunday afternoon. Beneath their hats and elaborate dresses lie compelling stories of perseverance and tenacity. It is to these women and in gratitude for their graciousness to me that I offer this book, a testimony to their many unsung labors.

1

Motherhood

> *What is a home without a mother? That was a motto written upon a wall.*
> Albertha McKenzie, in *Lifted Banners*

In one of her final letters to the Women's Department of the Church of God in Christ, Mother Lizzie Robinson reminded her able daughters of their role as mothers within their homes. A home without a mother would have been unthinkable to Robinson, a woman whose life spanned from slavery to World War II. When Robinson wrote this admonition in 1945, her vision of African American women's role hearkened back to a nineteenth-century domestic piety that would seem to have been seriously out of step with the reality of mid-twentieth-century black women's roles. Yet her idea of motherhood would form the core of the women's work that would eventually take COGIC women out of the home and into the world. To understand why Mother Robinson wrote what she did, it is necessary to consider the origins of her conception of women's role, found in a combination of her early childhood, the writings and works of late-nineteenth-century Baptist missionary Joanna P. Moore, and the beginnings of COGIC.

The enduring Christian symbol of the Madonna is etched in many people's minds as the prime example of a mother who cared for her child. But there are many different types of mothers: surrogate mothers, demanding mothers, aloof mothers, and others who represent different facets of motherhood. Yet there is one special kind of mother: she is mother to all; she exemplifies motherhood, yet her motherhood is rooted not in biology but in being a "Mother in Israel"—a woman with spiritual strength, fortitude, and a will to see the Christian life lived out among all of her children. Such "spiritual mothers," or "church mothers," as they are called in the African American church traditions, are women within the congregation who act as advisers to the pastors, as disciplinarians and leaders of wayward church members, and as spiritual avatars to the congregation.

Church mothers formed the backbone of the Church of God in Christ, an African American Holiness Pentecostal group founded in 1895 by Charles Harrison Mason and Charles Price Jones. The church mother in the COGIC tradition evolved from a honorary women's role into something more. Church mothers became a vehicle for women to remake their religious and social worlds within a framework of piety, devotion, and civic life. In a sense, church mothers in COGIC redefined motherhood numerous times in order to construct an identity that gave them an alternative to the traditional roles of African American women. The story of COGIC's three major women's leaders—Elizabeth "Lizzie" Robinson, Lillian Brooks Coffey, and Arenia Mallory—and those of the women they befriended, worshipped with, and trained provides an entry point for an investigation of how African American women's use of their beliefs gave them a place of authority, power, and community agency. In retelling the lost story of COGIC church mothers, the voices of women who struggled to fit their lives into a prescribed belief system that mandated them both to change and to renounce the world they lived in tell of shifting roles, identities, and relationships that spanned from the nineteenth to the twentieth century. Most importantly, the story of COGIC women provides a different lens through which to view African American women's religious agency. Tying together slavery and freedom, prohibition and deregulation, COGIC women brought to bear the fullness of their intimate religious selves in negotiating with a world that did not embrace their beliefs.

The first COGIC church mother, Elizabeth Isabelle Smith (later known as Lizzie Robinson), was born to Mose Smith and Elizabeth Jackson in Phillips County, Arkansas, on April 5, 1860.[1] Her parents may not have been legally married, since they were born slaves. Very little is known about her early life, but she revealed some tantalizing bits in an interview that was reprinted in the COGIC newspaper, *The Whole Truth*.[2] The overarching theme of the piece is the importance of her mother and of motherhood. Her account begins with a description of her early childhood, which she spent working in the fields with her mother and in the house of the white family who owned them. By the time she was five years old, the Civil War was over and her father was dead, which left her, along with her mother and her five siblings, with no choice but to continue doing backbreaking field work.

As a child, Robinson had an experience that later became part of her "testimonial" about her calling by God. "One day, while we were playing, I heard someone call me Liz," she recounted. "They called me three times, Liz, Liz, Liz. I did not know who it was that called me. My mother was in the field and when she came home I told her someone had called me. She said, don't answer when someone calls you like that or you will die, so don't answer. She did not know about Eli calling Samuel."[3] Robinson's mother did not want her to answer because of the generally accepted suspicion of the day—expressed in the spiritual "Hush, Somebody's Calling My Name"—that hearing the voice of God meant that a person was about to die or that God was convicting that person of sin and calling him or her to repent. Many slaves' conversion testimonies describe being outdoors and hearing a voice calling them to repent or "get right"; these stories also mention feelings of weakness, shame, or sickness accompanying conversion, as well as experiences of travail.[4] Since she was a young girl when she heard the call, Robinson's experience did not follow this template exactly. She did not understand the meaning of the voice until later, but the incident had a profound impact on her spirituality and left an indelible mark upon a young life destined for hard work and religiosity.

As a girl, Robinson sang hymns while her mother went to work, while preparing "breakfast at the white folks' house," and on her mother's bed in the middle of the night.[5] From the age of eight, she read scripture to her mother and her friends. Robinson's stories of her youthful spirituality highlight the importance of her mother to the formation of her religious sensibilities, particularly in the context of work, which would come to define her spirituality.[6] The death of her mother when Lizzie was fifteen, however, short-circuited her influence on Lizzie's spiritual life. Lizzie became her siblings' caretaker, and a few years later, in 1880, she married William Henry Holt, with whom she had one daughter, Ida Florence. Holt died a short time after, and she remarried, this time to William H. Woods. It was during this marriage that she joined the Baptist Church at Pine Bluff, Arkansas, in 1892.

Very little is known about this period of Robinson's life, but what is certain is that few options were available to her to learn how to be a wife and mother. Losing her mother at such a crucial time in her life prevented her from learning essential lessons her mother might have imparted to her as a young wife and mother. Other women who had been enslaved like Lizzie never knew their own mothers or were separated from them at an early age; the mother wit and traditions that their biological mothers carried were unavailable to them. How, then, did these young mothers cope with mothering? And how would they define their roles as mothers both in the home and outside of it?

Despite the fact that many African American women had long cared for both their own children and the children of others, there was a perception in the post-Reconstruction period that African American women lacked homemaking and parenting skills.[7] Mission boards and newly formed educational facilities for African Americans employed various methods to influence women's understanding of child rearing, housekeeping, and other uxorial duties. Leaders like W. E. B. Du Bois, Booker T. Washington, Nannie Helen Burroughs, and others focused on the home as the center of racial uplift and pride. They promoted "bourgeois respectability," as historian Victoria Wolcott has called it, fostering female respectability by indoctrinating African American women in the virtues of cleanliness and sexual morality—virtues that appealed to whites.[8] The improving literature of the day often also tied the theme of religious uplift to racial uplift, but it promoted a particular type of religiosity. Many of those who touted bourgeois respectability were appalled at certain types of African American Christian practices, such as shouting and dancing, and they strove to tie respectability to restrained religious fervor. The emotionalism of former slaves' religious practices did not fall in line with the bourgeois notions of respectability.[9] Those who favored what has been called the "politics of respectability" asked African American women to channel the energy they gave to ecstatic worship and the power they derived from it into motherhood. Religion was both promoted and domesticated to serve the uplift strategy. Domesticating religious fervor harnessed its potential transformative power to create women who had the potential to represent the race.

By focusing their attention on the external pressures on the African American community, like racial hatred, unemployment, and other social ills, however, reformers downplayed the very foundation from which the principles of motherhood, temperance, thrift, and service derived: the Bible. Christian endeavor, and the Bible in particular, provided many of the tenets of respectability that were pushed forward from the pulpits of churches on Sundays in the South. It was the Bible that most commonly introduced rural African Americans to ideals of "respectability." This was not a respectability focused on racial pride and the hope of impressing white southerners, however; rather, it derived from the desire to be pleasing and acceptable to God, and to obtain the promise of heaven while striving for perfection on earth. The desire to live "right" was, for many African Americans, much more important than living like whites.

The desire for right living was linked in many ways to motherhood, and this linkage opened up opportunities for African American women to lead. COGIC women like Lizzie Robinson, because of their religious beliefs and their focus on motherhood, would test the prescribed roles of mother, wife, and social leader to the utmost. Religious fervor, and Christianity in particular, empowered women like Lizzie Robinson to gain a measure of self-esteem that did not have its roots in respectability. It was rooted instead in Christian scripture, and the advent of Bible studies groups geared to the needs of African American women set the stage for a change not only in how women perceived their roles but in their ability to organize around a text as well. A small Bible study magazine, *Hope*, became the catalyst for that movement in the Church of God in Christ.

Joanna Moore and *Hope*

Hope magazine was first published in 1885 by Joanna Patterson Moore, a white missionary.[10] Moore, a prolific writer, is one of the lost lynchpins of the story of African American women's work, Baptist organizing, and the development of a Holiness network in the South. A Presbyterian-turned-Baptist, Moore parlayed her missionary zeal into the creation of a vital network of women missionary workers that had a profound effect upon women's organizing in both the Baptist Church and the Church of God in Christ. By promoting Bible reading, mothers' training, and home schooling in *Hope* magazine, Moore fostered the development of literary and religious fervor and of domestic tranquility among African American women. *Hope* was designed to introduce Bible study to women who were learning how to read and to teach them to organize Bible reading groups. Later, it was used to provide an in-home teaching program for children. Joanna Moore and missionaries like Virginia Broughton and Mary Sweet created the foundation for an organizational structure that still exists in COGIC churches and in black Baptist churches today. *Hope* and the "Bible Bands" that grew out of it gave Lizzie Robinson and many other southern African American women a way to conform to bourgeois respectability while shifting it to a very different playing field—the field of faith.

Joanna Patterson Moore, born and raised in Pennsylvania as a Presbyterian, had designs on becoming a foreign missionary. Moore's direction changed, however, when she heard a Baptist minister's speech on his home missionary activity at Rockford Seminary in Illinois, where she was training for the mission field. The Baptist minister told of his visit to Island Number 10, an island located in the Mississippi River that was fortified by Confederate soldiers during the Civil War and became a refugee camp at war's end. He painted a picture of suffering for his audience, telling stories of "1100 colored women and children in distress." The speaker told his audience: "What can a man do to help such a suffering mass of humanity. Nothing. A woman is needed, nothing else will do."[11] The message stirred Moore, and after settling her mother into a new, smaller cottage, she left with $4.00 from her Baptist Sabbath School and a commission from the American Baptist Home Mission Society, which provided her with no salary.[12]

Her mission to Island Number 10 launched an adulthood spent working with African American women in the South. Moore, who never married, was somewhat stereotypical of missionaries of the time period with her descriptions of the "poor benighted Negroes." Yet in at least one significant respect she was distinctly ahead of her time: she respected and befriended the African American men and women she lived and served with. In 1873, she became the first paid missionary of the Women's Baptist Home Mission Society, which began financially sponsoring her works in the South in 1877. Starting a faith home in New Orleans for former slave women and working in the bayou areas of southern Louisiana early in her career, Moore traveled from plantation to plantation teaching scripture, working with local pastors to promote temperance, and teaching young mothers and children to read and write. Poverty and backbreaking work cutting sugarcane made for hopeless living conditions in this part of southern Louisiana, and Moore, rather than staying apart from the people she served, lived in cabins with them, much to the consternation of whites in the area. Disturbed by the high levels of illiteracy she encountered among Louisiana's poor, she tried to devise ways to teach both reading and the Bible at once. To this end, she began what she called a "Bible Band" in 1884. The object of the organization, according to its constitution, was to "study and commit to memory the work of God; . . . to teach it to others, and . . . to provide the destitute with bibles."[13]

The Bible Bands became the core structure of an educational and entrepreneurial enterprise that encompassed black Baptists and, later, COGIC women's work in ways that Moore could not have foreseen. Bible Bands became an organizing tool for African American women that did not require a large investment of money and that used the communal nature of rural communities to

Joanna P. Moore. Courtesy of the American Baptist Historical Society, American Baptist Home Mission Society Group.

bind women together. The groups encouraged women to gather in homes to study scripture on their own, away from pastors, who often could not read themselves. Women began to study scripture autonomously and with a purpose in mind: to better their homes and their communities. Methodically, they mobilized around scripture reading.

As the Bible Band movement grew, Joanna Moore realized that it would not be enough for her to leave a few copies of Bible lessons behind for the groups to use. In order to meet the needs of women who were unable to obtain their lesson plans for Bible Band, she began *Hope*, a monthly paper which was to be used in conjunction with Bible Band meetings, in 1885. The first printing of 500 copies was distributed quickly within the area of Plaquemine, Louisiana, where it was printed. Moore's application to the postmaster in Plaquemine for mailing permits stated that "Hope was a paper dedicated to the interests of the colored women in the south and the dissemination of news and plans of work for their elevation and education."[14] *Hope* did that and more. It became central to a new spiritual and entrepreneurial enterprise that bound together African American women in a network that would eventually span most of the South and would play a large role in Lizzie Robinson's life.

The frontispiece of *Hope* had two guiding phrases printed upon it: "Love one another" and "Have Faith in God." Moore initially wrote most of the Bible lessons to promote educational and biblical literacy: she printed scripture citations rather than the text of scripture for her readers, for example, in order to encourage them to learn how to find cited passages.[15] *Hope* became an indispensable resource for the burgeoning Bible Band movement. By 1888, there were 90 Bible Bands with 1,683 members in the Louisiana area, and by 1889, 115 Bible Bands existed in Louisiana and other places in the South, such as North Carolina and Virginia.[16] Moore encouraged women to write to the magazine in order to report on the progress of their Bible Bands and to send in reports about how much money had been raised and how many Bibles were sold by their band. The letters brought together a network of women from varying social strata and educational backgrounds who had one thing in common: the Bible. These women, moreover, in time began to sell both *Hope* and Bibles obtained from the American Bible Society, creating their own entrepreneurial networks and fund-raising for their local churches and Bible Bands. Letters poured in to *Hope* about women's successes in selling Bibles door-to-door in their communities, as they canvassed for both sales and souls. Moore eventually added Fireside Schools to her training repertoire, which provided materials designed to "secure the daily prayerful study of the God's word in every home, with all the family together; and to put the appropriate books in our homes and see that parent and child read them together as far as possible."[17] She designed Fireside Schools to be a three-year correspondence program that would help promote interest in Bible reading, and the program became a vehicle for many of the materials that Moore produced, including such titles as "Peep of the Day" for children, "For Mother While She Rocks the Cradle," "Third Temperance Reader," "Kind and True," and "Black Beauty."[18]

Hope and the Fireside Schools provided an avenue for African American women outside of the canon of the "talented tenth" to obtain an education and cultivate self-esteem. In one sense, *Hope*, with its admonitions about house-keeping and child rearing, helped to accomplish what leaders like Booker T. Washington and W. E. B. Du Bois wished for African Americans in terms of respectability. But the education that *Hope* provided was not only about home-making and child rearing; it was also a spiritual education that gave identity and purpose to men and women who otherwise lived in the fields and doing manual labor for whites. Most important, perhaps, the Bible Band movement provided leadership roles for African American women who otherwise would not have had any opportunity to hold them, given the patriarchal structure of the Baptist networks. Although there were many fraternal orders and organizations that women could join, Bible Bands were a low-cost alternative that focused on everyday life and child rearing with a spiritual connection that pushed the reader toward "holy living."

Bible Bands and Black Women's Organizing

The emphasis on holy living embroiled many of the women who read *Hope* in a dispute among black Baptist groups about the theological definition of sanctification. "Sanctification," a term used throughout the history of Christianity but first articulated as a doctrine of "Christian Perfectionism" by John Wesley, is a theological term Wesley invoked to describe an instantaneous experience following one's conversion. The experience of sanctification, which Wesley described as "his heart being strangely warmed," ensured that the convert had experienced a second work of grace that allowed him or her to pursue the pathway of perfection, which was defined as freedom from sin in one's life and an infilling of God's love. Those who experienced sanctification began to call their shared experiences the "Holiness movement," a striving for Christian perfection that began to spread in evangelical circles of the nineteenth century.[19] Some Holiness movement adherents, seeking proof of their sanctification, eventually became Pentecostals, who claimed that the ability to speak in tongues was proof of the instantaneous sanctification that God had bestowed.[20] For black Baptist groups, sanctification and its meaning became divisive, affecting both men and women alike.[21]

The conversation about sanctification came to the attention of many black Baptist women through the pages of *Hope*. Joanna Moore's encounter with sanctification transformed her life's rationale, her missionary service, and her writings. Moore became sanctified at the age of twenty-eight, according to her account, after reading Holiness materials and attending a Methodist camp meeting.[22] A short time later, she discovered she had a tumor and, after some extended time of prayer, was healed. The healing experience solidified her sanctification experience.[23] Sanctification was believed not only to heal believers of their illnesses but also to cleanse them of desire for all the worldly temptations that pollute the body and the soul. Like most Holiness adherents, Moore viewed holiness as a total experience that unified the body and soul, enabling one to live a life worthy of God. One of her books illustrates this point in a list of instructions for those aspiring to holiness: "You will also be careful to eat only healthy food and be sure not to eat too much, for the drunkard and glutton are classed together. You will also be careful to keep your bodies clean, your clothes clean, your houses in order, because Jesus lives with you all the time through his spirit in your bodies. The women who receive the Baptism of the Holy Spirit are careful to keep themselves and their homes clean and in order."[24] Cleanliness, moderation in food intake, and abstinence from alcohol were all linked to the presence of Jesus within one's body, a concept derived from 1 Corinthians 6, which states that the body is the temple of the Holy Spirit and therefore that temple had to remain cleansed, in order for the Holy Spirit to remain within it.[25]

Joanna Moore encouraged readers of *Hope* to become sanctified, and she provided practical instructions for her readers about how to live a sanctified life. Both *Hope* and Moore's book *The Power and Work of the Holy Spirit*, published in 1898 to be used with the Fireside Schools, covered topics regarding sanctification. *Hope*'s concern with spiritual topics like sanctification and practical domestic issues touched a chord with readers, especially Lizzie Robinson. The emphasis on sanctification and the body, however, held special importance for former slaves like Robinson. The notion that God would inhabit a body deemed by whites to be inferior was a potent one for many African Americans. Among women and men whose bodies had been beaten and abused, this concept of divine embodiment through sanctification redefined the personhood of the individual.[26] Rather than pursuing cleanliness and abstinence for social reasons, many African American women were inspired to right living by scriptural admonitions coupled with the affirmation that Jesus lives within. By identifying with the divine within—Jesus—women like Lizzie Robinson could perceive themselves as special and set apart, despite what any white southerner could say.

Recounting her experience of reading *Hope* for the first time, Robinson claimed it made her realize that she needed a "deeper life." Robinson, who first joined a Bible Band in her hometown of Dermott, Arkansas, related how she became sanctified in 1901, at the age of forty-one, in a brief memoir about her entry into women's work: "I moved from Helena [Arkansas] to Pine Bluff in 1892, but, I didn't get in touch with Sister Moore until 1901. I was then a member of the Baptist church. I received my first *Hope* paper in the Bible Band of that church. I studied this paper until the Lord Sanctified me."[27] Robinson's correspondence with Moore between 1901 and 1909 in *Hope* shows both the effects of Bible Band participation on an African American woman and how sanctification became not simply a theological construct to be embraced but an identity-defining practice that gave women like Lizzie the fortitude and perseverance to engage in missions and organizational activity, all in service of biblical principles.

The first of Robinson's letters published in *Hope* gives insight into how important the magazine could be to the women who received it. At the time, Robinson was married to her second husband, George Woods, she was employed as a washerwoman, and she had one daughter, Ida. The letter, dated January 1902, stated: "*Hope* is my help in trouble, in sickness and in health. I will never forget the lessons in *Hope* about charity. Sister Moore, the Holy Ghost keeps me daily from my sins. Since reading *Hope*, I do not mind Satan, and I am happy in the Lord. Praise the Lord for this witness."[28] Woods relied on *Hope* to get her through the trials of mortal life. Her letter reveals how women thought about the sanctified life: sanctification meant that one could call on the Holy Spirit to keep one free from the desire to sin. For Lizzie, *Hope* gave her guidance by presenting scriptures related to the theme of sanctification. Her mention of "in sickness and in health" speaks to the fact that, for many adherents, sanctification and healing went hand in hand.[29]

Living a sanctified life was expected to change one's habits and tastes, as well. The immediate effect of sanctification and her embrace of *Hope* was to place Lizzie in a network of service and sacrifice that is traceable through the letters she wrote to Moore (and to *Hope*) from 1902 through 1909. Almost from the beginning, she pursued both Bible Bands and the sale of *Hope* with an amazing tenacity. One report about her read: "Sister Lizzie Woods, of Pine Bluff, has been doing some good work while visiting her sister in Brinkely. She sends us a club of Ten subscribers. . . . She writes: 'I never saw Hope until Sister Bailey showed it to me and encouraged me to subscribe for it. Now I would not be without it. It has stirred me up to my sense of my duty to God.'"[30] Duty and service, themes closely related to the practice of sanctification, were woven through the letters that she wrote to *Hope*. The letters also demonstrate her developing skill in becoming the organizational worker that other Bible Band workers had become. The following year, an update on her progress in service appeared in the August 1903 issue of *Hope*: "Sister Lizzie Woods, of Pine Bluff, had succeeded in securing twenty-three subscribers to *Hope*, and writes a very sweet and kind letter."[31] Robinson, like many women who participated in Bible Bands, found that Bible study and sanctification were not the only benefits of participation. Involvement with the bands also allowed women's latent entrepreneurial talents to arise.

From the beginning of the publication of *Hope*, Moore relied on women in the Bible Bands to sell subscriptions to the magazine, in part because of the constraints upon mailing out *Hope* to African Americans. Moore knew that in the South it was dangerous "for colored people to get papers through the mail," because whites feared that "some political scheme or something inside would tend to upset the established plans of society."[32] Selling *Hope* within the community was a much safer proposition, and one that required face-to-face meeting with other women. Bibles were also sold along with *Hope* to ensure that both scripture and the scripture lesson were provided—that there would be nothing lacking in the quest to promote both biblical and reading literacy. Robinson and other women skillfully combined evangelism and marketing to increase the number of Bible Bands and sales of *Hope* in their regions.[33] Subsequent letters from Robinson show the extent of her organizing activities on behalf of the Bible Bands. By 1906, she was engaging in extensive missionary work: "A Good Sister, Lizzie Woods, is scattering light in Lexa, Poplar Grove, and surrounding country in Ark. She has sold a large number of Bibles and secured subscribers to Hope. She says, 'Once I loved only to read novels and foolish trash, but now the Bible is to me the best of all books.'"[34]

In addition to selling subscriptions and distributing Bibles, Robinson was organizing Bible Bands and teaching women to read the scriptures: "Sister Lizzie Woods of Pine Bluff, Ark, is a very successful worker. She has supplied about thirty persons with bibles during the last few months, and taught them to read this book with the help of Hope, staying all night in homes and showing them how to have family worship and how to get time to read other good books with the children. She has the endorsement of the good people wherever she goes."[35] Robinson's zeal for the work was seemingly unstoppable. Two years later, Moore reprinted Robinson's report on her journeys:

Dear Sister Moore:

I have good news to tell. Have sold in this district 66 Bibles. Thirty-five Bible Bands reported. About 100 person's bought their Bibles and Hope. The pastors were with us and greatly pleased with this great bible work, I made 900 visits in homes in this district and had 500 prayer meetings. In my visits I read the lesson for the day in Hope and explained how to study it. Thank God, they are now studying God's word as never before, and as they see how God can and does take care of his children, they have come out of the secret societies and trust for help in God alone.[36]

One can infer from the letter that Robinson had more than embraced the Bible Band system: she had become a full-fledged home missionary worker. By this point, it would have been hard for her to continue her duties as washerwoman while visiting homes throughout the Baptist district. Through the sheer number of visits and prayer meetings that she conducted, with the help of others, over the course of a year, she carved out her own little niche of service. She was no longer a simple washerwoman; sanctification and Bible study had given her a purpose, drive, and vision for her life. Moore, of course, attributed it all to prayer, as she related at the end of the letter quoted above: "Lizzie Woods did not have a good chance for an education and she has passed through many trials. One day several years ago I visited her home in Pine Bluff; she was earning her living by washing; I knelt with her by the washtub and asked God to take her hands out of that tub and fill them with Bibles and send her from house to house to feed hungry souls with the Bread of Life. God has answered my prayer. Glory to his Name!"[37]

Only a year afterward, in 1909, Moore prevailed on the missionary society of the American Baptists to send Lizzie Robinson to school for two years at a Baptist training academy in Dermott, Arkansas. When she had completed her studies there, she was appointed matron of the academy. She later described her duties: "There I prayed and taught the children out of the Bible. I told them when we read the Bible God is talking to us. Sometimes in our prayer and bible reading the children would cry and refuse to eat their breakfast."[38] Bible Band participation had transformed Lizzie Robinson into a women's leader within her community. The ingeniousness of Moore's Bible Bands was that they created leadership roles for women like Robinson despite their condition in life or their social status. Connecting scripture, service, and community had the effect of empowering women like Robinson outside of the established educational and club networks, creating a women's leadership role that did not require a formal education. The promotion of what missions boards called "women's work" in the late nineteenth and early twentieth centuries created space for women who were social outsiders. The egalitarian nature of the Bible Bands and other women's work allowed lower classes of women to engage in activities that educated and upper-class African American women also engaged in during this period.[39]

Robinson's experience as a Bible Band woman illuminates the fact that in the traditional historical narrative of African American women's agency, roles for African American women between Reconstruction and the civil rights movement primarily lay in the realm of teaching or the club movements. Ida B. Wells Barnett, Mary McLeod Bethune, Mary Church Terrell, and others are often credited with having built organizations, but without reliance on a religious base, many of their endeavors would have failed. There were few areas of service available to African American women in the South who desired to put their social activism and their faith together within their communities. The "black church," patriarchal and hierarchical as it was, restricted women's participation to ancillary activities that centered on familial care rather than instruction and intellectual endeavor.[40] In contrast, Bible Bands provided instruction, organization, and some autonomy from the local pastor. The bands also created cross-community and even cross-state networks of women who would otherwise have been isolated in rural areas. Letters in *Hope* allowed women to connect, making them part of a "movement" despite not being geographically proximate to one another.

The Bible Band, in essence, trained women as leaders not just in their homes but in their communities. It provided its faithful with a pathway to leadership that did not rely on the most prominent role for African American women during this time period, that of teacher. It freed women to be able both to run their homes and to participate in organizational building outside of their churches, allowing them to gain a considerable amount of power within their local communities and across state lines. Furthermore, it provided an alternative to ordination that came to play an important part in the self-understanding of the Bible women who eventually followed Robinson from the Baptist ranks into the Church of God in Christ. The promise of the sanctified life purified these women and refined them to a such a degree that they were able to pursue the same concerns—temperance, thrift, industriousness, and education—as their more well-off sisters through *Hope* and the Bible Bands. Thus, even without the benefit of the club movement, women like Robinson were able to create their own organizational, entrepreneurial, and spiritual base through their connectedness to the text of *Hope* and the Bible, and through the women's work that they served and promoted.

Several important themes guided the developments of the women's work in the Church of God in Christ. The themes, broadly, are (1) service to home, family, and community; (2) concern for biblically based social reforms that translate into civic engagement, such as the promotion of temperance, purity, and good health and the amelioration of the ills created by industrialization and poverty; (3) focus on women's leadership without ordination; and (4) provision of educational opportunities for women to pursue personal spirituality and corporate good. Service to home, family, and community was based in biblical admonitions and the quest for a respectability that was not merely racially based but sanctioned by scripture. For COGIC women, these concerns would be supported both by the literature and teachings of the women's work and by auxiliaries focusing on training younger women to care for home, family, and community. Social reforms would from 1911 to 1945 involve mainly COGIC church mothers, but as COGIC women connected to women with like-minded ideals outside of the church, these reforms were rearticulated as both COGIC values and values of a broader Christian worldview. The role of women's leadership, framed by the role of church mother, would expand into its own organizational structure within the church and, while not specifically addressing the ordination of women, would apply rigorous standards to the training and support of women within the leadership. Questions surrounding ordination would continue, but the women of COGIC were savvy at applying other means of leadership to further their own ends. All of these issues, however, would benefit from the network of COGIC women promoting educational endeavors both through the denominational schools and through their educational publications focusing on sanctification, purity, and women's work. All of these principles would aid COGIC women to maintain a place of prominence in the building of religious networks and in upholding the spiritual "temper" of their churches.

Divisions and New Opportunities

Although all of this organizing activity through the Bible Bands seemed bucolic, there were tensions within local churches and associations regarding both the Bible Band work and sanctification. Bible Band work was a threat to the authority of black Baptist pastors who disdained the leadership of women. Virginia Broughton, a Bible Band worker and one of the first women's leaders of the National Baptist Women's Convention that was formed in 1900, related anecdotes about the tensions that surrounded Bible Band women in her memoir. One pastor who opposed the work stated that he would rather "take a rail and flail the life out of a woman than to hear her speak in the church."[41] Others openly condemned the women's work or attempted to limit its effectiveness within local churches. *Hope* articles alluded to these tensions when they stressed the importance of working with and respecting pastors within the local churches. Compounding the problem was the role Bible Bands played in promoting women's literacy, which offended some illiterate male pastors. Threatened by their lack of education, pastors sought to silence women who were literate in both reading ability and scriptural knowledge.[42] These conflicts played a role in the struggle to establish the women's auxiliary of the National Baptist Convention.

The other issue that threatened black Baptist stability throughout the region was the debate over sanctification and the burgeoning Holiness movement. Sanctification and its various explanations was a hotly debated topic among local and state Baptist networks in the area of Arkansas, Louisiana, Mississippi, and Tennessee. While *Hope* magazine addressed both the practical and the biblical defense of sanctification, Baptist pastors staked out their positions and engaged in creative "sheep stealing" in order to win Baptists to their way of defining sanctification. Holiness networks forming and camp meetings taking place throughout the South diffused differing formulations of what defined sanctification. Since Wesley's second conversion experience, sanctification had come to be seen variously as a definable experiential event that occurred after conversion, a theological position justified by scripture, a continuous process of cleansing, a state of sinless perfection, or simply part of the conversion experience.[43] These differing perspectives on sanctification had a profound affect upon teachings of sanctification and prompted many women and men to move out of the Baptist network, paving the way for growth of the Pentecostal churches. First, however, there was strife within the Baptist Church, and many Holiness believers were expelled from it. Although Baptists and Holiness proponents both believed in sanctification, the manner in which sanctification was attained differed profoundly between the groups.

Moore's affiliation with the Baptist networks through *Hope* and with state Baptist convention meetings placed her in proximity to those Baptists interested in holiness and sanctification. One such leader, C. P. Jones, became her dear friend and played a supporting role in the story of how sanctification and

Holiness beliefs came to divide Baptist groups. Jones became a Christian at the age of seventeen and entered into the ministry with black Baptists in Arkansas. He came into the Holiness movement through Joanna Moore, and they became lifelong friends. Moore encouraged Jones's spiritual quest, promising, "God is going to fill you with the Holy Ghost."[44] Moore's promise proved to be fortuitous, for it was the issue of the Holy Ghost that brought Jones and Charles Harrison Mason together; yet the Holy Ghost was also the catalyst for their eventual falling out.

Mason and Jones were part of a contingent of black Baptists who embraced Holiness teachings during the 1890s. C. H. Mason was born in Arkansas in 1866. Like many Pentecostals, he went through the trials of illness and received a miraculous healing at the age of fourteen, and he shortly thereafter answered the call to preach.[45] After receiving his license from the local Baptist missionary church, he married his first wife, Alice Sexton. The marriage to Sexton lasted for only three years, in part because Sexton did not want to be a pastor's wife. She left Mason, and Mason briefly attended the Arkansas Baptist College in 1893. After a three-month enrollment, he left the school. But a chance meeting with another Arkansas Baptist student—Jones—changed his life.

Encountering C. P. Jones at a local meeting in Mississippi, Mason joined him and his fellow pastors, J. E. Jeter and W. S. Pleasant, in study of the scriptures regarding sanctification. They all began to teach sanctification in churches in the Jackson, Mississippi, area, and soon many of the Baptist churches in the area were closed to them because of it. Jones gathered Baptists who believed in sanctification, organizing them into a fellowship known at first as the Church of God. At Jones's urging, Mason began traveling to preach sanctification. On one of his preaching journeys, walking down a street in Little Rock, Arkansas, Mason came up with the permanent name of the denomination: the Church of God in Christ. Mason's recounting of the story was that God told him the name of the church and that if the name was used properly by him that there would never be a building large enough to hold all the followers he would have. He shared this story with Jones and others in the fledgling fellowship, they accepted the name, and the first official meeting of COGIC was held in a gin house in Lexington, Mississippi. Jones proved to be a deft organizer, publishing a broadside called *Truth*, and the church grew in the tristate region of Tennessee, Mississippi, and Arkansas.

While Mason and Jones were breaking away from the Baptists, other Baptists and Holiness adherents were trying to figure out what being sanctified would lead to. Two men proved to be instrumental in the transition of be-

Charles H. Mason. Courtesy Flower Pentecostal
Heritage Center, Springfield, Missouri.

lievers in sanctification from the Holiness movement into the new Pentecostal
movement. Charles Parham, faith healer and founder of the Apostolic Faith
movement, was a noted healing evangelist who posited that sanctification and
baptism in the Holy Spirit were evidenced by speaking in tongues.[46] Parham's
travels throughout the South gained followers of his new iteration of Pentecostal doctrine, but it was a student of Parham's, William Seymour, who was
the catalyst for the explosion of Pentecostal fervor. Seymour, an African American former Catholic from Centerville, Louisiana, crossed Parham's path in
Houston, Texas. After entreating Parham to allow him to attend his segregated
Bible school to learn about Holy Spirit baptism and speaking in tongues, Sey-

mour went to Los Angeles in February 1906 to preach at a Methodist church. After giving a series of sermons on sanctification and baptism in the spirit and speaking in tongues, Seymour was barred from the church in March, and he began meeting with a group of African Americans at 216 Bonnie Brae Street who prayed for the experience of speaking in tongues.[47] A meeting on April 9, 1906, turned into a revival of sorts among the members, who began to speak in tongues. Word of the event quickly spread, and after one week, over 200 people were meeting at Bonnie Brae Street, culminating in a sweep by the Los Angeles Police Department because of zoning issues, as well as the newly baptized tongues speakers, having been overtaken by the Spirit, lying in the street. The group then found a property at 312 Azusa Street, and this became the seat of the ensuing Pentecostal revival, to which many people traveled to experience "tongues" in the place where, as many said, "the fire fell." Mason and Jones heard of that fire, and it was the beginning of the end of their church affiliation.

Mason, desiring what he called a deeper experience, asked Jones for permission to travel with Jeter and Young to Los Angeles to the revival. Jones agreed to the trip, and Mason left for Los Angeles in February 1907. Like most people coming to the revival, he did not know what to expect, and he had to "tarry" for a few days until the experience of speaking in tongues came upon him. He described the experience as "being filled with the glory of the Lord." He remained at the revival for five weeks before he returned to Memphis, but he did not immediately tell Jones of his experience. Jones discovered inadvertently that Mason had received the baptism though reports of a revival that Mason had held after his return. Jones disagreed with the notion that tongues speaking was proof of sanctification, even though he had given Mason permission to travel to Azusa Street. In the summer of 1907, Mason, Jeter, Young, and other members split off from the fellowship, and they subsequently sued for and won the right to use the COGIC name in 1909. Mason was elected head of the new church, and Jones renamed his faction the Church of Christ, Holiness.

Mason and Jones's story is not unique in the annals of Pentecostal history. In fact, many Holiness groups split over the issue of tongues speech. For many Holiness adherents, sanctification was an ultimate work of the Holy Spirit, and speaking in tongues was not sanctioned scripturally.[48] For others, the baptism represented by speaking in tongues was the proof of sanctification. The permutations of the Pentecostal experience produced a nearly endless number of theological camps, all of which engendered some type of vitriolic response from opposing forces. In the early years, Holiness, "finished work," and "Oneness" doctrines all tempted Holiness adherents and others to step over the lines of traditional religious experiences into the realm of the unknown. For Mason and others like him, the marriage between Holiness and the Pentecostal experience was the ultimate union of cleansing and empowerment, and the two could not be unbound. Yet it was that very experience that had unbound him and others, including Lizzie Robinson, from their Holiness moorings.

COGIC differed from other Pentecostal churches in its emphasis on sanctification as both a crisis experience and a constant striving to live a cleansed life; this latter element was at times even more doctrinally important in the church than speaking in tongues. Unlike in the Assemblies of God, a denomination started by some white ministers who left COGIC, Mason made sanctification an important teaching of his church. The manifestation of that teaching culturally and in religious practice prompted others to call churches like Mason's "sanctified churches."

In May 1911, General Overseer Mason conducted a meeting at the Baptist academy at which Lizzie Robinson worked in Dermott, Arkansas. It is unclear whether Mason was holding an evangelistic meeting or whether he had come to Dermott purposely to seek Robinson out.[49] Several accounts suggest that in his search for a woman capable of organizing the women of COGIC, he had heard Robinson's name mentioned by those who had heard her teach in the Dermott area. Others have speculated that Mason's unmarried state put pressure on him to find a leader for the women—a groundless speculation given that Mason had remarried in 1905.[50] Robinson later recalled their first meeting:

> I was sanctified in the Baptist School but did not have the Baptism of the Holy Ghost. Elder Roach was pastoring the Church of God in Christ at Dermott at that time and Bishop Mason came there to preach and came to the school. There was a teacher in the school who would go where Brother Mason was when he would come. . . . That time he came on a Saturday and it was the day I would always go down to pay my grocery bill, but I saw him coming and I didn't go, I sent an errand boy. When Brother Mason came in he asked me where was the other lady. They were upstairs. Mrs. Crow, Mrs. Jones, and Mrs. Cora came downstairs and he began to teach us, I told him that I had been living right for six years but I hadn't been baptized with the Holy Ghost. So, I received the baptism of the Holy Ghost that day, and Mrs. Jones, Mrs. Crow, and Mrs. Stewart looked on and were amazed.[51]

When Robinson received baptism in the Holy Spirit, it marked the end of her relationship with the Baptist school and with Baptist preachers. Reception of the "gift," that is, speaking in tongues, or glossolalia—meant swift expulsion from Baptist circles.[52] Robinson related that "two of the Baptist preachers said they would go down yonder [to hell] before they would let me stay in the school."[53] It was permissible for Baptists to be sanctified and to live a holy life, but not to speak in tongues. Finding herself disfellowshipped, Robinson returned to her child in Pine Bluff, Arkansas. By that time, her husband was dead, so she accepted an offer from Elder Frank O'Brien to teach in the Baptists' central district. When the Baptists heard that she had been baptized with the "Holy Ghost and Fire," as she put it, they explained that they were "so sorry," because "they hated to give [her] up."[54] The opportunity lost, she soon had another opportunity to use her abilities. It would be through COGIC that Joanna Moore's prayer for "getting [Robinson's] hands out of the washtubs, and into the bible" would be answered.

Robinson's life to this juncture was perhaps similar to those of many African American women in the post-Reconstruction period who sought to define themselves against the negative stereotypes of black women that permeated the dominant culture. Motherhood was one way in which that redefinition could occur. During Reconstruction, motherhood for black women was defined by caring for a white person's domestic space or children, deified in African Americans' quest to advance the race, or deemed a neglected skill set that needed to be taught. It was the religious sphere that allowed black women to embrace motherhood by adhering to Christian principles that emphasized both caring for the home, husband, and children and a higher calling through Bible study and service. The call to holiness and family service was one that women of all economic backgrounds could embrace through Bible Bands, as did Lizzie Robinson. Pentecostalism, however, upped the ante for Holiness women like Robinson, who were forced to choose between the power for service to the family and the power of the Holy Ghost, and many were propelled into new avenues of religious belief. For Mother Robinson, speaking in tongues was just the beginning of a whole new life that would ultimately take her and the women of COGIC far from the church lives they had known. It would change Robinson's role from a mother who remained in the home to a "mother in Israel," a church mother who could embrace her home, her church, and the world through living a sanctified life.

2

Calling

Jesus never called a woman's name. He never called a woman to preach.
Mother Robinson, in "Voice of Mother Robinson"

If the Azusa Street revival and the burgeoning Pentecostal movement had not caused enough upheaval, issues of gender and women's roles in the church caused even more. Pentecostalism provided African American women with both struggles and opportunities to advance in ministry. The issue of calling, in particular whether or not God had called women as well as men to the preaching ministry, was a source of contention not only within Pentecostalism but also for most of Protestant Christianity in America.[1] It was a certainty that men could be called, but women? For Pentecostals in the early days, the interpretation of the book of Joel, specifically Joel 2:29, sanctioned the calling of women because the Spirit was poured out on all flesh male and female. Despite the clarity of the scripture, the flesh of men was invigorated with opposition to women's spiritual advancement. Many African American men believed that women's flesh was not called for the pulpit, and many women subscribed to this notion as well, opposing their preaching sisters with as much or even more tenacity as men. More frequently than not, women who felt moved by the Spirit to preach often felt the sting of rejection made manifest in the hard seats of pews.

Several factors created formidable opposition to women preachers in the African American churches. Cultural accommodations, biblical literalism (as opposed to fundamentalism), and concerns about racial uplift all combined to keep women preachers at bay.[2] The environment of the Jim Crow South, with the ever-present threat of lynching, sexual violence, and other crimes against African American men and women, made the protection of womanhood as important for the African American community as it was to southern whites during the late nineteenth and early twentieth centuries.[3] Black pastors and other teachers, including Joanna Moore, stressed the importance of women being chaste and good homemakers who upheld the sanctity of femininity. The deification of southern womanhood and the vilification of black women and men pushed southern African American churches to design a role for black women similar to that of white southern women for the dual purpose of saving the race and promoting Christianity.[4]

Within the broader context of the struggles for women's suffrage and social reforms of the latter half of the nineteenth century, relationships between men and women were at times polarized. The prevalent idea that women's place was in the home was potent but poison for black women. The importance of women's homemaking was made more cogent when it was coupled with biblical admonitions for wives to be submissive to their husbands. Pastors behaved like second husbands to many churchwomen: pastoral admonitions that "wives to submit to their husbands" and that the "deacon must be the husband of one wife" contributed to the assumption that the black woman's place was in the home and not the pulpit.[5]

In the minds of pastors, pundits, and husbands, black women's submissiveness was linked inexorably to civilizing program that sought to substantiate the humanity, intelligence, and spirituality of African Americans against the prevailing racist norms. Women's proper behavior would combat the vilification of African Americans that was so prevalent in the early twentieth century. The strategies for racial uplift borne on the backs of black women served to mobilize both religious and social concerns in the quest to provide proof of black people's humanity and citizenship. Yet these attempts at inclusion also placed African Americans, especially Pentecostals, in a conundrum that pitted their social values against Pentecostal interpretation of scripture. Attempting to balance out conflicting views created what Evelyn Brooks Higginbotham has called a "metalanguage" of race.[6] For black Pentecostal women like Lizzie Robinson, the pathway through the tongues of men and of angels toward their calling required navigating interpretations in the seething torment of racial, religious, and cultural strife. It called for their own, unique metalanguage of holiness, tenacity, and women's rights.

"Teaching" vs "Preaching"

After Robinson's expulsion from the Baptist school and ouster from the Baptist central district meeting, a fortuitous event changed her circumstances. Elder R. E. Hart, originally a Christian Methodist Episcopal minister and lawyer, was the agent of Robinson's final move away from the Baptists to COGIC. A convert to Pentecostalism, Hart was instrumental in providing legal assistance to C. H. Mason during the COGIC split in 1907. Helping to reorganize the church in 1909 after the successful lawsuit, Hart pastored a COGIC church in Trenton, Tennessee, and traveled in the tristate area of Arkansas, Mississippi, and Tennessee on evangelistic missions.[7] Upon meeting Robinson in Pine Bluff on one of those trips, he invited her to join him for an evangelistic meeting at his home church. Robinson agreed, and she held services for integrated congregations under Hart's auspices. Her personal account of the meeting noted that twenty were saved and that some received the baptism of the Holy Ghost. Journeying on to Brownsville, Tennessee, Robinson conducted meetings there as well. Buoyed by her labors, she then focused her sights on traveling to COGIC headquarters in Memphis. Hart discouraged her. "Daughter," he told her, "the preachers will fight you there because they do not allow women to preach there."[8]

Robinson's reply to Hart's comment laid the foundation for an important historical distinction in COGIC thinking about women's roles and duties. Robinson later recalled, "Dr. Hart thought all teaching was preaching. I said to him, I am not a preacher. I have not been called to preach. In Mark 26, [Jesus] told the women to tell his disciples to meet him in Galilee. Judas killed himself but eleven were there and they came . . . in the last chapter of Mark, he told the Preachers to go into all the world and preach the gospel to every creature. [Jesus] never called a woman's name. He never called a woman to preach."[9]

Robinson's thinking about women and preaching was in keeping with the attitude of the Bible Band women with whom she had spent the last ten years. Women were allowed to be "teachers," not "preachers," and Robinson, even before being made leader of COGIC women, accepted the distinction.[10] By using the word "teaching," Robinson emphasized the educational function of biblical training and domesticity, rather than preaching skills. The antecedents of this differentiation lay within the interpretation of two biblical passages, specifically, 1 Timothy 2:11–12 and Titus 2:3–5, which read, respectively: "Let the women learn in silence with all subjection. But I suffer not a woman to teach, nor to usurp the authority over the man, but be in silence"; and "The aged women likewise, that they be in behaviour as becometh holiness, not false accusers, not given to much wine, teachers of good things; That they may teach the young women to be sober, to love their husbands, to love their children, To be discreet, chaste, keepers at home, good, obedient to their own husbands, that the word of God be not blasphemed."

Each of these scriptures would provide the foundation for scores of COGIC women to uphold the traditional patriarchal roles of black pastors while undercutting their influence and their authority. For Robinson, preaching was something that men were instructed in scripture to do. Women were to learn from men, as 1 Timothy 2 instructed, and remain silent, at least in the church. Where they were not to remain silent, however, was in teaching other women. Titus 2 would allow older women like Robinson to teach women the types of domestic duties outlined in *Hope* that would both be pleasing to God and assist in the quest for self and racial improvement. The distinction between "teaching" and "preaching" also highlighted the difference between helping people to learn the Word and actually proclaiming the Word. Robinson's leadership, then, could be couched in the Bible Band type of training for scriptural and reading literacy, not preaching.

The role of teacher, however, was not as simply constructed as it may seem. For African American women in the post-Reconstruction period, the role of teacher was a class-based position linked closely to racial uplift.[11] It was one of the few roles to which African American women could aspire that would spare them from subservient positions as houskeepers or laundresses, and it was also a way in which they would garner the respect of both the black and white communities. Unfortunately, it was also a position that illuminated the illiteracy of many black men, especially preachers, who were generally uneducated. For untrained pastors who relied on charisma and preaching skill in order to hold together their congregations, female teachers, and especially female teachers who could open the scriptures and expound on them, could be a serious threat to their authority. Bible Band work among women had exacerbated this threat, and even if Pentecostal beliefs mandated that the outpouring of the Holy Spirit affected both sexes equally, in practice that equality was interpreted in keeping with the patriarchal norms already entrenched within black churches.

Robinson's use of the word "teaching" rather than "preaching," therefore, foreshadowed the position from which she would later lead in her post in the Women's Department of COGIC: she seemingly acquiesced to social norms while also challenging the power and authority of the pastor. Teaching was a way to balance out the scales between men and women. It allowed pastors to be treated deferentially while giving women a voice that was pivotal in shaping

Elizabeth "Lizzie" Robinson. Courtesy Glenda Goodson Collection, the Center for African American Church History and Research, Lancaster, Texas.

the beliefs and behavior of church members. Teaching was a way to subtly re-define the locus of control in the dissemination of doctrines, beliefs, and prac-tices: the teacher could command respect without usurping the pastoral role. When the teaching role, which was analytical, methodical, and measured, was juxtaposed with the preaching role, which was affective and performative, the weight of spiritual authority came to be balanced between teacher and preacher, giving women like Robinson as much or even more authority than their pastors without visibly disrupting male leadership. Men remained uncomfortable with women's teaching role, of course, but Lizzie Robinson's strength rested on the fact that the most important man in the denomination, C. H. Mason, was satis-fied with her place as teacher, "rightly dividing the word." Mason would stretch

Robinson's ideas about women's teaching further by allowing her to teach both women and men within COGIC with his approval and authority.

After the meetings held with Elder Hart, Robinson contacted Mason via letter and expressed her desire to come to Memphis. He extended an invitation to her, and she arrived in Memphis, lodging with a Sister Georgia Westfield. Robinson began making house visits, as was her custom in Bible Band, and returning to Mason's church to teach. Her teaching mission in Memphis was received with considerably less approval than her previous evangelistic meetings had been. At one of her first teaching meetings in Mason's home church, the men in attendance, realizing that she would teach, walked out. "Forty-five or Fifty people went out of that house in a solid Prayer line," she later recalled. Mason asked her to teach morning sessions rather than afternoon sessions. But the first time she tried this, men who attended the morning messages left as well, taking their hats and shaking their heads. The next day, more men came, and when Robinson began to teach, they got up to go out. Mason, who had been watching secretly, came out and said, "Go back and sit down, go back and sit down and learn some sense, every one of you sit down, go back and sit down."[12]

Within groups like COGIC that professed Pentecostal beliefs, old habits died hard, even though the very foundations of Pentecostal belief challenged the gender structure and the baptism of the Holy Spirit empowered women and men not only to "preach the gospel to every nation" but also to prophesy. Both required speaking out, but women had to speak out over the din of men who did not want them in the pulpit. Many Pentecostal groups struggled with cultural and scriptural claims about men's and women's roles while attempting to make room for the charismatic gifts that the Bible and Pentecostals claimed fell upon women and men alike. How Pentecostal churches interpreted scripture and accommodated the norms of the prevailing culture (or not) determined what rights to leadership, if any, women gained in it. The Assemblies of God, for example, allowed women to be ordained but did not allow women to vote in the general assembly.[13] On the other side of the state of Tennessee, whites in the Church of God of Cleveland, Tennessee, offered the position of deaconess, as well as those of missionary and evangelist to women, but they soon revoked women's right to be deaconesses, excepting only those women whose husbands were ordained ministers.[14]

For African American Pentecostals, rules about women's roles were just as varied. Magdalena Tate, founder of the Church of God, Pillar and Ground of

Truth, sanctioned women's ordination, but after her death and in deference to her leadership, no other woman could be called "mother" in the church.[15] Ida Robinson, a member of the United Holy Church of America, claimed that she had a vision from God to "come out from Mount Sinai and loose the women." Starting her own church, the Mt. Sinai Holy Church of America, Ida Robinson extended ordination and the episcopacy to women.[16] But for many Pentecostal women, the contradiction between asserting the right to preach and complying with the wishes of men resulted in strained circumstances, as historian of Pentecostalism Grant Wacker demonstrates in his book *Heaven Below*. Wacker recites a litany of Pentecostal women who were divorced and ostracized for asserting their right to preach.[17] Given the backpedaling and splits over the myriad stances on women's right to preach, to be ordained, and to hold office among Pentecostals in general, the confusion and strife in COGIC was not surprising. The pragmatic need to carry on church planting, missionary work, and fundraising, however, did allow women to assume roles traditionally performed by ordained men, albeit without the proper sanctioning or the pay that men received.[18]

The former Baptists and Holiness adherents who populated COGIC churches in 1911 colored interpretations of women's role in the new denomination. For the Holiness adherents, the overarching thrust of the movement toward perfection and empowerment for service seemed on the surface to support women's right to take on ordained leadership roles. Other factors, however, mediated opinions about ordination for women. "Women's work," which focused on training women as homemakers and teachers, diverted some of the thrust for equality. Most Baptist converts to COGIC had an inherent bias against women preachers and knowledge of the struggles of Baptist women in the National Baptist Convention. Robinson may have been sympathetic with these women's struggle for a more expansive role, yet with Mason's support of her teaching leadership, she balanced her own calling to fit into the church she now belonged to. In order to do that, she took a hard line for herself and other women that set the stage for many years of struggle for COGIC women who wished to have a official leadership role in the church.

A meeting that Robinson attended with Mason at South Fort Pickering, Arkansas, defined her allegiance to both COGIC and Mason's leadership. The tenor of the meetings that Robinson led in Memphis gave only a hint of the ongoing battle between the preachers and women in the Memphis COGIC churches. The relationship between COGIC preachers and women leaders had became adversarial because the women had said that the "Man's time is out." Robinson's retort to that assertion was priceless: "If the man's time is out, why don't you quit your husbands?" Women in the church, at least in Memphis, were beginning to question the male leadership in general and the denial that women had the right to preach in particular. As they understood the Pentecostal hermeneutic of the time—that the Spirit could fall upon all flesh—there should have been no reason to prohibit women from preaching. In order to make some sense of the situation, Mason asked Robinson to come to South Fort Pickering with him to a joint meeting of COGIC men and women. While Mason attended to doctrinal issues with the men, Robinson addressed the women separately. She later recalled the controversial stance she took at the meeting: "The women were turned over to me and I asked, how many preachers are there? Thirty-two stood up. I asked, who told you to preach? I took them right down to the Bible. One said that God had spoken to her out of the cloud and told her to preach, out of the air, I said, well, the devil is the prince of the air and no one told you to preach but the devil. You are no Preacher. This is the way I started to work in this church. I began to teach. The saints need to be taught."[19]

The harshness of Robinson's corrective helps us to tease out the ways in which women leaders in COGIC subsequently navigated their situation within the seemingly male-dominated church. Robinson's appeal to scripture and her linking of the woman's spiritual experience to a demonic source was a brilliant assertion of her spiritual authority. By using the same scriptures that the women claimed validated their right to preach, she created uncertainty among the women, which pitted her teaching authority against their charismatic experience.[20] This confrontation indicates that in the early days of COGIC, some women understood their right to speak in the congregation as the right to preach, a claim in line with many early Pentecostal teachings. But Robinson, with her Baptist background, redrew the boundaries of women's role in her corrective, reinforcing women's right to teach while denying their right to preach. In her opinion, preaching implied leadership and ordained office, but a strict reading of scripture allowed no room for women to lead men. Emphasis on the saints' "need to be taught" affirmed her idea that the identity of women was one of homemakers and teachers, not preachers. Those who strayed from that line did not belong among the "Saints."

The altercation had implications for the future. As women's roles and duties became more defined within COGIC, both their freedom and their oppression could be attributed to Lizzie Robinson and the women she chose to lead alongside her; Robinson's adherence to nineteenth-century values meant that she chose women who resisted many of modernity's temptations. Her strict, unyielding nature became a staple in the stories women subsequently told about her leadership. Words like "strict," "stern," and "disciplinarian" all crop up in accounts about her, as her strictness permeated her leadership style. Her style of dress—a heavy, black, ankle-length skirt with a neatly starched white shirt, her hair pulled back in a bun—brooked nothing but respect. Perhaps she deployed harshness in her quest to remain true to her reading of scripture and, importantly, to make sure that no one would be able to usurp her authority. The women she appointed to succeed her had some of these same qualities, which enabled them to rein in other women when necessary.

Gender roles would continue to be contentious throughout the history of the denomination, and the women and men of COGIC alike had to take responsibility for the strife that ensued. But for the time being, tensions blew over, and the delegates returned to Memphis to prepare for the convocation of the denomination in 1911. Robinson's negotiation with the women in South Fort Pickering had not gone unnoticed, and Mason was prepared to bestow a church title on Robinson that would place her squarely in charge of COGIC women for some time to come.

Establishing the Women's Work

The convocation for the denomination was held yearly in Memphis, Tennessee, at 392 South Wellington Street, Mason's home church.[21] In keeping with the tradition of Holiness camp meetings, COGIC members were expected to attend the convocation, which doubled as the denominational annual meeting, at which prayer and revival meetings went on continuously for three weeks. Convocation was originally held from November 25 to December 14 of each year, following the fall harvest.[22] The convocation, the concept for which was taken from Leviticus 23:2–4, which calls for the "holy convocations which ye shall proclaim in their seasons," was a time of separation and consecration for church members. It was a time to pray, hear preaching, fast, and, most importantly, settle numerous items of church business with which the various state overseers had to deal during the year. The annual convocation drew COGIC members and spectators interested in the healing ministry of General Overseer Mason. Considered to be a sacred time, with emphasis on services, close quarters, and fellowship, it connected COGIC women and men in a sacred world of miracles and prayers.

Yet the sacred world also had to make way for the business of running a church. Even though Pentecostals resisted the creation of formalized church systems, the business of ordaining ministers, collecting funds, and mediating problems was just as important for them as it was for their more established denominational precursors. COGIC was no exception, and Mason found himself with not only a burgeoning church to run but also an increasing number of women who hoped to find a place where they could answer the calling they felt God had upon their lives. Judging from the contentious South Fort Pickering meeting, a mediator between the men and women of COGIC was needed. Mason's choice for that position was Lizzie Robinson. The position that he appointed her to was a new one, and a somewhat puzzling choice given Robinson's and perhaps also Mason's perception of women's roles. Robinson's new position was to undertake the role of general overseer of the "women's work," which eventually became the Women's Department. There are no extant records indicating how the appointment was handled at the convocation, nor is there any indication of how Mason made the decision. Mason also never explained how he came to the decision that the women needed a separate work; however, he would not have been ignorant either of the work the Bible Bands had been doing or of the National Baptist Women's Convention, which by this time had become a firmly established part of the National Baptist Convention. Some accounts have suggested that he had another woman in mind for the post.[23] Regardless of whom he initially intended to appoint, the creation of the position of "general overseer of the women's work" was itself a surprising decision. The term "overseer," used in the New Testament to designate a bishop, was bestowed on Robinson to solidify her appointment over all women's activities.[24] In effect, Mason made Robinson a bishop over COGIC women.

In the 1917 doctrinal statement of COGIC, overseers are linked to Acts 10:28, which states, "Feed the flock of God over whom the Holy Ghost hath made you overseers." The passage in the COGIC statement goes on to explicitly state, "while they [overseers] are not bishops in name, they are in fact."[25] In what was a common move, no gender differentiation was made in subsequent statements regarding the duties of overseers; their status was simply differentiated from that of the general overseer, who had authority over all overseers. So was the appointment as overseer of the women equal to that of an overseer of men? Looking at later COGIC histories of the Women's Department provides some clues to the power of the title bestowed upon Robinson. In *Fifty Years Achievement, 1906–1956: A Period in History of the Church of God in Christ*, Charles H. Pleas gave Robinson's title as "General Overseer of Women's Work," although he took pains to note, "That is what the National Supervisor of Women's Work

was called at the time."[26] Other accounts printed in various convention book-
lets gave her title as "general mother" over the women's work. These varying
accounts point to the title's inherent ambiguity. How could a woman who was
not ordained be appointed as overseer? Given these contradictions, perhaps
it is not surprising that the title did not last through Robinson's duration in
office. Nevertheless, the duties she undertook put her in the position of being
a "bishop" of the women she organized. Even more curious, the position of
Women's Department overseer set up an interesting dichotomy that continued
to exist for years between the department and the male episcopal structure. By
setting up a separate women's work, Mason had, wittingly or not, set up a parallel structure to the ordained track of ministry within COGIC.

The parallel structure of the Women's Department and the male episcopate
allowed Robinson and the women she later appointed an unprecedented degree
of autonomy within a framework of deference and discipline. The women's
work would grow to establish its own auxiliaries and missions, to appoint and
sanction its own leadership, and, most importantly, to provide its own financial base. By acceding to the cultural norms of deference and dependence by
disavowing the right of women to preach or be ordained, Robinson and her
workers were able to walk a tightrope between prohibition and freedom. As
long as the episcopate and preachers were given deference, they sanctioned the
work of the Women's Department.[27] Women could engage in all their traditional work—missions, teaching, evangelism—but from a different locus altogether. More than the National Baptist Women's Convention, COGIC women
had been given the right to establish a formidable women's organization that
was within the denomination yet solely under women's purview.

In the beginning, the title of overseer gave Lizzie Robinson the freedom to
speak for COGIC and exercise authority in her effort to organize the women. She
described her job as follows: "I have general supervision over all the women's
work, . . . to organize such activities as would be helpful to the work," and to
"evangelize and systematize the work among the women." The phrase "evangelize and systematize" summed up neatly Robinson's personal definition of
women's work, which was to organize the women and bring them into the
ranks of the church. She began her task with zeal, immediately leaving at the
end of the convocation to organize women in the states of Tennessee, Arkansas,
and Texas. At the time of Robinson's appointment, the women of COGIC were
meeting in two separate groups, Prayer Band and Bible Band. The Prayer Band
engaged in corporate prayer, usually in the early mornings. The Bible Bands

were reading *Hope* and were already well-established groups, many of which originated within their Baptist churches. On her first tour, Robinson brought the groups of praying women and Bible-study women together in the churches she visited, renaming their groups "Prayer and Bible Band." Her second task was to ensure that all groups were receiving the same instruction. Her third task— and this one would prove to be a bit more difficult—was to find women who would be able to help in leadership. Distance made it impossible for Robinson to correspond with all of the new Prayer and Bible Bands and to attend to every question about procedure or behavior. It was not only expedient but also necessary for her to delegate some of her authority. But to whom? The qualities of a good Bible Band member, who was generally a diligent homemaker who worked with only one group, did not necessarily make her a good candidate for a leadership role. The most logical people, already in place in COGIC and other local churches, were the church mothers, to whom church members and even pastors frequently looked for guidance and help.

Church Mothers

C. Eric Lincoln and Lawrence Mamiya define "church mother" as "an honorific title usually reserved for the wife of the founder or for the most experienced female members of the church." The phenomenon of the church mother, they claim, has no parallel in white churches: it is derived from the kinship networks found in black churches and black communities.[28] The most notable discussion of the role of the church mother is that of sociologist Cheryl Townsend Gilkes, who in a series of published articles examines what she terms the "dual sex roles" of the pastor and the church mother. She describes the roles of the church mother as follows:

> The Mother, while not the pastoral head, is the protocol leader for the congregation. She is the discipliner, enforcing good conduct and a dress code, as well as an instructor and counselor both for women generally but also, typically, young persons of both sexes. She may or may not be a voting member of the church board, but in either case her opinion is always consulted, and usually heeded. She provides cues or directions during the worship service, signaling how it should proceed. . . . The Church Mother also is the epitome of spirituality, providing a model for the women of the church. Whether she is scripturally knowledgeable, a prayer warrior, or a spiritual advisor, she has a "word from

the Lord" that is never to be taken lightly. She may speak in little sermonettes to the congregation. She is never ignored.[29]

Although both Gilkes and Lincoln and Mamiya provide cultural explanations for the role of the church mother, little information exists to help define what the role of church mothers has been historically. Robinson's deployment of church mothers as overseers of the Women's Department seems to have been unique. By formalizing an honorific position as part of an established organizational structure, Robinson gave church mothers the authority they needed both inside and outside of their congregations to engage in much of the same work that men were doing in the pastorate. More important, church mothers in COGIC redefined their role to be much different than what Lincoln and Mamiya suggest it generally is. For COGIC women, the church mother became the pathway to power through perseverance.

In order to understand how the role of the church mother changed, it is helpful to look at the first church mothers Robinson appointed. These women became both modelers and enforcers of the sanctified life within COGIC. For the fledgling women's work, church mothers were the bricks and mortar that Robinson used to build the women up. Robinson's first trip as overseer took her to Arkansas and into Texas, where she appointed Hannah Chandler to assist her in organizing Bible Bands throughout the state of Texas. Mother Chandler, as she was called, became the first appointee to the position of overseer of women in Texas in 1914. Chandler had originally belonged to the Methodist Episcopal Church and had converted to Pentecostalism in 1910. Ostracized by her former church, Chandler joined COGIC and apparently drifted about for a few years before she was hired by the deacons of Mason's church on Wellington Street in Memphis to become its janitor.[30] Like many of the first women that Robinson chose, she was not wealthy, but she was eager to work. In Chandler's case, as in Robinson's, titles were important. Chandler referred to herself as "mother," even though in print her title was listed as "state overseer." But regardless of her title, Mother Chandler was enthusiastic about her appointment in Texas. Robinson recalled: "Mother Chandler was one of the first to get up while I was talking about the Bible and declared I would never have to say more about it to her. She said I am going home to organize Bible Bands, and you will know about them when you return."[31]

Bible Bands, important for both scripture training and literacy, took on a new role in COGIC, as they came to be used to teach new members the principles of sanctification and tongues speaking. Given the multiple splits among various Pentecostal denominations, Bible Bands were an effective tool for disseminating the particularities of COGIC's doctrinal take on Pentecostal beliefs. Church mothers were the initial teachers who imparted doctrine to the membership. For a time in the early years of the Women's Department, Bible Bands were also used as a training ground for fledgling men to obtain their preaching credentials in COGIC.[32] Thus, although the denominational focus was on those who preached, the church mothers were the front line of defense against erroneous teachings and doctrines.

The opportunity to do Bible Band work motivated many women like Chandler to join the ranks of the Women's Department. During Robinson's initial trip around the three states, she used the Bible Band method of referencing a specific scripture, in this case Jeremiah 9:17–20, to bring the women together:

> Thus Saith the Lord of hosts, consider ye, and call for the mourning women, that they may come, and send for the cunning women, that they may come, and let them make haste and take up a wailing for us, that out eyes may run with tears, and our eyelids gush out with waters. For a voice of wailing is heard out of Zion, how we are spoiled. We are greatly confounded, because we have forsaken the land, because our dwellings have cast us out. Yet we heard the Word of the Lord, o ye women and let our ears receive the words of his mouth, and teach your daughters wailing and everyone her neighbor lamentation.[33]

The scripture Robinson chose echoes a familiar refrain from the nineteenth-century Holiness movement, and it set up the template for the women's work: commitment to prayer and service, along with commitment to perfection to eradicate sinfulness.

Robinson's early goals were largely organizational, yet the structure of the organization she built suggested that she had broader-reaching spiritual goals. In keeping with the ideals of the nineteenth-century Holiness movement, women were the ones who brought holy living back to their families and communities. Calling women to prayer and repentance set up a rigorous program of spiritual fortitude and placed them within a structure administered by church mothers. These practices of prayer and Pentecostal living instilled a specific character and identity within the women. Linking piety with preparation for leadership set the stage for local spiritual avatars to direct women, organize them, and lead them to sanctified living. Most important, it gave church mothers and the women following them charismatic power. Their temporal powers, explicitly less powerful than those of pastors, nonetheless gave COGIC women a spiritual authority more powerful than ordination. The charismatic authority of the appointed church mother coupled with the fledgling organizational structure soon became a formidable force for ordained men to contend with in the church. Where the male episcopate during the years of 1912–30 had room only for overseers and pastors (with elders in local churches), Mother Robinson, within the confines of the women's work, established other auxiliaries: the Sewing Circle and the Sunshine Band. These auxiliaries enabled church mothers to consolidate women in groups that showcased their talents.

Sewing Circle was inspired by the story of Dorcas in Acts 9:36–40.[34] Originally called "The Daughters of Zion," Sewing Circle members belonged to a small, organized group within some COGIC churches that attended to the uxorial arts of sewing. Many of the members were domestics or washerwomen, like Robinson. Like its precursor, the school for mothers, Sewing Circle was used to train women in sewing, knitting, making patterns, and crocheting. Much of the handiwork created by the groups was used for fund-raising, and the proceeds were sent to the local or national COGIC church. In the minutes of the 1916 convocation, the women were praised for their industrious work: "The women as heretofore had on hand some of their handiwork, showing how they are still working with their hands to the glory of God."[35] But Sewing Circle was more than just a way for women to engage in household duties; it was essential to the comfort of the church members during convocation. Jim Crow laws limited housing space for members traveling to Memphis. Thus, local church members and the enterprising blacks of Memphis opened up their homes to the visiting COGIC members and provided housing at a nominal cost. Clothing and bedding materials from the Sewing Circle groups was distributed to members arriving without their own. Also, proper attire was handmade and sold to rural COGIC members at prices lower than those charged for merchandise at white-owned stores; this practice was a way of empowering church members while at the same time ensuring that they were properly dressed in accordance with holiness.

Another of the domestic duties important to Robinson's vision for the women of COGIC was child rearing. Once again, Robinson used the material by Joanna Moore to supplement the education of her fledgling organization.[36] The Sunshine Band, an in-home Sunday school for children, originated with Moore as a school in which to teach children between the ages of five and twelve to read and memorize scriptures and to learn COGIC doctrine.[37] Sunshine Band operated in lieu of an organized Sunday school in the early years of the church; a Sunday school was established in the first COGIC church in Lexington, Mississippi, but it did not begin to publish quarterly periodicals until 1916.[38] In addition to functioning as a children's version of the Prayer and Bible Band, the Sunshine Band taught children hymns and sponsored a children's choir and a mini-playhouse that featured events stressing biblical themes, holiness, and pure living. Not content with merely reaching the youth, moreover, Mother Enora C. J. Johnson, one of Robinson's appointees, created a "purity class" for teens in 1926 as a direct offshoot of Sunshine Band. The advent of flapper fashions and "questionable moral behavior" prompted COGIC mothers to found the purity class for adolescents, male and female, between the ages of twelve and fifteen on the principles of "preserving in Christian youth a high moral standard of living." Equipped with a creed and a song designed expressly for the purity class, the mothers endeavored to instill in their young members, who were called the Puritans, the basics of a sanctified lifestyle: modest dress, abstinence from sex and alcohol, and pure speech.[39]

The purity class was actually a way for COGIC women to discharge one of their most important responsibilities: teaching the principles and lifestyle of sanctification. For COGIC members, sanctification was in some senses more important than speaking in tongues. Sanctification meant the Holy Spirit would work to cleanse the sin away from a person's life, and that cleansing produced visible signs that a believer's life was free from sin. Conquering desires to engage in ungodly practices like snuff dipping, smoking, drinking, fornication, and wearing immodest dress provided the outward hallmark of the sanctified life. Prayer, fasting, Bible study, and an overall attitude of Godliness helped one to attain the sanctified life, and such practices were expected of all who participated in Bible Band, Sunshine Band, purity class, and Sewing Circle. Sanctification was the core teaching of each of these groups, and it was reinforced by the church mothers' comportment and deportment. An individual woman's personal emphasis on sanctification and sanctified living helped to identify her as someone who was available to lead within the Women's Department.[40] Women who had worked to become sanctified, practicing personal sacrifice, cleansing themselves, and consecrating their lives to service to the church and to God were those most likely to become church mothers.

All of the first auxiliaries of the women's work had their foundation within the pages of *Hope* and Joanna Moore's other works. The time that Lizzie Robinson spent reading *Hope*, selling it and the Bible, and organizing Bible Bands was directly useful in her work as overseer in COGIC. Had it not been for her involvement with Bible Bands, it is quite doubtful that the tight organizational structure of COGIC women's work would have come into existence. Each one of the early auxiliaries integrated domesticity with religious concerns, enabling less-trained women to enter into the ranks and participate just as much as the growing leadership of church mothers. The structured, family-centered thrust of the auxiliaries created an interesting organizational culture that set the foundation for the manner in which COGIC men and women would interact as a religious group and corporately as a people.

The Church Family

It was important, then, that the women in charge model this familial organizational structure, and even Robinson found time to attend to familial concerns. Her relentless travels during the first few years of establishing the women's work brought an unexpected bonus: a husband. Meeting a COGIC minister, Edward Robinson, Lizzie Woods adhered to her admonitions about family and married her third and final husband. He worked for the railway, and because of his travels Robinson moved with him and her daughter, Ida, to Omaha, Nebraska. They began a COGIC church there in a converted chicken coop, and, most likely as a result of her husband's job, Robinson traveled extensively by train to do the organizing work of gathering overseers and women for them to lead. Based on the virtues of happy and wholesome family life, the Women's Department of COGIC blossomed even as Mother Robinson began her third round of married life. Family, of course, was important to her, and given the ability of the women she organized to bring in and sustain members by teaching the importance of the family as the core of sanctified life, it was also important to the church.

Familial roles also found their way into the everyday relationship between church mothers and pastors. Because of the use of the term "church mother," pastors, and in particular C. H. Mason, were sometimes referred to as "fathers," or, in the case of Mason, "Dad Mason." A COGIC publication made the importance of the familial connection between church mother and pastor explicit: "The role of the local church mother is indeed one of great importance and a 'must' for a growing church. She is to a pastor in the local church what a wife is to her husband in the home. The day has far past for a pastor to teach from the pulpit things that women should know. It was never proper, but accepted because of the time. . . . There should be a pastor–church mother relationship going on at all times."[41]

Describing the role of the church mother as a "wife" to the pastor makes the relationship between COGIC church mothers and pastors much clearer. The working relationship was expected to be a familial relationship or, to use an anthropological term, a fictive family relationship. This family was related not by blood ties but by a much more binding tie for COGIC members: belief. In this sense, COGIC was very much like many early Pentecostal churches of the day, in which members referred to one another by familial terms such as "brother" or "sister," "mother" or "father." The familial manner of address among Pentecostals had it roots in biblical admonitions, and it helped to bind people within the movement as a family over and against those who ridiculed it. For those in COGIC who had been ejected from their homes merely because they attended a sanctified church, the comfort of calling one another sister, brother, mother, or father must have been palpable. To be able to call a church mother "mother" must have been even more affecting, especially during the migration period, when families were split apart in their quest to gain a better life materially and spiritually.

Even COGIC songs extolled the virtue of familial relationships, fictive or otherwise, in the church. Their song lyric "This is the Church of God in Christ. . . . You can't join it, you have to be born in it" speaks to the importance of family within the church.[42] The song is still sung in COGIC churches and annual meetings today. It may put many converts to COGIC on edge, but the way to be born into COGIC is to embrace the familial manner of address and allow those who are your mothers and fathers in the faith to have an important role in the formation of your spiritual and temporal life.

The fictive familial relationships of COGIC members not only held the organizational structure together but also ensured that members could be identified by their manner of addressing each other. COGIC church mothers and pastors were expected and encouraged, moreover, to take on the traditional expectations and duties of mothers and fathers. COGIC motherhood, however, developed a bit differently from the traditional roles of mothers during the period in which the Women's Department expanded.

Understanding the duties of the church mother and father within the COGIC church family can help us to clarify the structure of the organization. The church mother acts as the disciplinarian, teacher, and enforcer, while the father (the pastor) exhorts, amplifies the teachings and doctrines that the church mothers have already imparted, and legitimizes these teaching and doctrines by means of his personal authority. More often than not, the pastor and the church mother were not married to each other, and thus power was not usually concentrated in one household.[43] By modeling the "ideal" gender relations of their time, the church mother and the pastor together created a fictive church family in the midst of unstable family conditions created by migration, sharecropping, and racial violence. Within the enclave of the spiritual and fictive family, COGIC women used the female-dominated, male-sanctioned, shared gender space to further their admonitions about the sanctified life, as well as their control of the congregation.

Contrary to descriptions of COGIC as a dual-sexed system, the department as it initially developed formed an entirely separate organizational entity that existed within the church yet was not formally under the aegis of the male episcopate. It could not, in fact, have fallen under the dominion of a male episcopate because the fully formed episcopate did not appear until the 1930s. In its absence, it was left to Robinson's appointees to assist in its formation by creating the fictive family. That family would multiply through women's insistence and assistance in spreading the church.

Planting Churches

Mother Robinson's relentless travels drew a coterie of women into the family of COGIC. Appointed by Robinson to assist with the task of training women as overseers over their respective states, these women were unknowns, but some would distinguish themselves with their service. By 1916, the women appointed as state overseers were as follows: Mother Robinson, Arkansas and Oklahoma; Sister Margianna Kelly, Georgia; Eliza Hollins, Louisiana; J. Watson, Mississippi; Katherine Hutson, Tennessee; Lucinda Bostick, Missouri and Illinois; Lillie Early, Kansas City; and Hannah Chandler, Texas. Though most of these women have been lost to obscurity, some, like Lucinda Bostick, were key to the growth and development of the women's work. Along with her husband, Daniel, one of the first COGIC male overseers, Bostick established COGIC churches in the Saint Louis area. She was highly regarded by the church as a great fund-raiser and organizer, but she also engaged in church planting, one of tasks that would prove to be important in the development and entrenchment of the women's work.

Church mothers and other, younger women would often establish evangelistic street ministries in new areas, some of which led to the creation of new churches. Younger women who worked alongside church mothers in the ministry in an official capacity were assigned the title of "missionary." The first thirty-two missionaries, whose names were listed in the minutes of the 1916 convocation, worked in cities throughout the United States. From their home states of Tennessee and Arkansas, they traveled to and from various COGIC churches, teaching and evangelizing in places that did not have a formal COGIC congregation. These missionaries were most likely women that Robinson was familiar with, long-standing members of COGIC who were steeped in denominational doctrines and beliefs. Alongside church mothers like Bostick, they engaged in the "digging out" activities of preaching—or "teaching," as they referred to it—on street corners and of setting up tents to hold revival meetings.

Church mothers' and missionaries' task was to draw in new members and "dig out" a church for a male to pastor. When the tent meeting or street preaching had produced a number of converts, church mothers like Bostick sent a letter back to Memphis that a pastor was needed, often suggesting the name of a man whom they were familiar with. The following is a typical account:

> Mother Lucinda Bostic[k] and Mother Hattie of St. Louis erected a tent at 1430 Colas Avenue as a Mission for the Church of God in Christ. The tent burnt down the first year. Then, with Elder Bell as pastor, the brothers and sisters worked hard, gathering money and building materials. During the day, the ladies and their children washed down the brick used by the Black brigade to be used in the structure of the "First" COGIC in East St. Louis and Southern Illinois. The women also made home-cooked dinners which they sold for 35 cents each. . . . Mother Lucinda Bostic[k] was instrumental in securing Elder A. W. Webb as pastor.[44]

Women were hard workers in the establishment of COGIC churches. Like Mother Bostick and Mother Hattie, they conducted street meetings and raised their own funds. Manual labor in the service of the church was also service to God. Women were expected not only to work as evangelists but also to perform the domestic duties, such as cooking dinner or producing needlework for sale, that were necessary to keep the newly planted churches alive. The work in Saint Louis progressed so well that the Bosticks were able to hold their first statewide convocation in 1914, although the church that they established did not have a permanent building until the 1930s.

Not all church-planting activities initiated by women went so smoothly. Opposition to them came in various forms, as the following example illustrates: "Brothers Mathis and Sisters Fugett, Elija, Prescott, and Warren who were saved under my ministry in 1914 in Waco, Texas, were there [in Tulsa, Oklahoma] trying to raise up a work for the master. They had quite a struggle because of those ministers who claimed to be saved but had not the Spirit nor the vision of God. These faithful women on this work were doing their uttermost to help the brethren get the work established, but every time they would get anything started these visionless, Godless ministers would tear it up."[45] In the case of the sisters involved in Tulsa, the perceptions of women's roles in the ministry played a large role in the opposition of preachers to their evangelistic work. Such opposition was endemic in many Pentecostal denominations. Tent ministries were some of the most dangerous activities to be engaged in: those who ridiculed or disapproved of the holy rollers would shoot into tents, pelt meeting participants with rotten eggs, or attempt to cause melees when tents were erected. One state mother, Mother Mary Magrum Johnson, lost her father to a bullet fired by a heckler, who shot into a meeting tent where her father was holding a meeting.[46]

Because of these external battles and the internal struggles between men and women, missionaries and fledgling church mothers had to be hardy and re-sourceful. Perhaps, at times, they were more headstrong than the men liked. In the minutes of the 1916 convocation, the women were admonished to be more obedient: "Mothers [and elect ladies] are exhorted to be obedient and hear their Overseers."[47]

In some ways, Mother Robinson had done too good a job of organizing the Women's Department. The increase in numbers of COGIC women may have exceeded her expectations. Her efforts coincided with the beginnings of the great migration of African Americans northward and westward, and thus many women without spouses—a ready source of converts—were available.[48] In the surviving minutes of the convocations of the years 1910–19, admonitions for women to "be obedient and hear the male overseers" suggest that the growth of women's participation in COGIC was perceived as a threat by the overseers. It also threatened the delicate working balance between Robinson and Mason. A system of checks and balances was put into place so that the authority and power of the women would not usurp that of the men. A statement from the 1924 convocation suggests that the male leadership, in fact, attempted to dic-tate what the women's work might entail: "The woman's place in the church[:] whereas the woman have proven to be of Great help to the church general and are great help to and among the pastors and evangelists with whom she works[, . . .] that it shall be left with the state overseer and pastors to guide her sphere of work and that each pastor will be granted the power to direct any woman worker in his congregation[,] both the pastor and the woman being subject to the state overseer."[49] This statement is interesting for its recognition of the importance of women to the work and growth of COGIC. But despite the laudatory tone, the stipulation that men were allowed to guide women's sphere or work was an attempt to make sure that women did not usurp male authority. The statement outlined the manner in which women were to "submit" to the male-led episcopate. The male state overseer and pastors could guide a woman's work, as could the state mother and the national mother: overseer Robinson. Women's leadership appointments had to be sanctioned by both the state mother and the (male) state overseer. They, in turn, were accountable to General Overseer Mason and to Mother Robinson. It would seem, then, that the mothers did not have much leverage against male interference in their realm, at least after 1924.

But that was not the case. While temporal authority had been given to the men, the mothers held the spiritual authority. Women like Mother Robinson who were great "teachers" possessed significant charismatic authority that was not easily assailable by men. To enforce their charismatic leadership, the women could call on the male episcopate to back up their decisions. In time, this strategy would be used to rein in women who attempted to subvert Robinson's authority. Women's oversight, however, helped to ensure that the primacy of male authority within the episcopate did not overwhelm the women's work.

While some scholars have argued that the Women's Department was an autonomous space in which women defined their own destinies, it is more accurate to think of power within the organization as shared by men and women at times and autonomous at others. All of the auxiliaries that were set up by Mother Robinson and later mothers were autonomous and were able to run under their own jurisdictions, even though the local pastors and state overseers were consulted. What resulted, then, was a denomination within a denomination, one that was made up entirely of women who were subject to the rules and doctrines of COGIC yet who dominated their own affairs with strength and tenacity. That strength was evident, for example, in 1917, when the Women's Department gave the denomination its first bank account, containing $168.50. The fact that the women, and not the men, established the account is telling.[50] C. H. Mason, receiving the funds from Robinson, put part in white banks and part in a black bank, explaining, "Now Sister, you have given me a standing with the banks, now we can build."[51]

—☓—

The Women's Department of COGIC was conceived by Mason, but the midwife was Robinson, who helped to birth the department by using her experiences as a Bible Band woman in Arkansas. Targeting women in churches who had already been involved in Bible Band and other types of missions activity,

Robinson ensured that she would have a steady stream of women workers who would be enthusiastic both about the denomination and about working for God. Building on the foundation laid by nineteenth-century Bible Band work into the twentieth century enabled Robinson and the women she brought into the fold to expand the work, always under the watchful eyes of the COGIC men, who approved of the fruits of their labors. The COGIC sisters may not have been as well organized as their Baptist counterparts in the early days of the church, but time and opportunity ensured the rapid growth of the women's work, particularly during the Great Migration. It was in this context that COGIC women began to redefine the role of church mother and of Pentecostal womanhood itself, creating a formidable force to sanctify the cities and far-flung locales in which they found themselves.

Migration

Many people ignored us; considered us as southerners, who did not have good sense.
Mary Magrum Johnson, *Life and Labors*

For the women of COGIC who ventured beyond the South in search of a better life early in the Great Migration, the cities of the North and West provided opportunities for advancing their message of the sanctified life, but they also posed tremendous challenges to it. The Great Migration redefined how African American men and women shaped their worlds within the confines of urban space and in many ways fundamentally changed the nature of the African American religious experience. The urban space, with its secular entertainments in close proximity to sacred space, focused and sharpened the messages that were transmitted to African Americans about holy living. Migrants' religious practices, deemed backward and unprogressive by many urban dwellers, had to be reshaped by enterprising individuals who were able to bridge the divide.[1]

The challenge for COGIC women in this environment was to be faithful and to adjust to urban life. For women trying to make their way in the city, the streets and pews held temptations, snares, and tremendous opportunities for spiritual and social leadership. Migrant women's stories not only illuminate the lives of COGIC church mothers as agents of change but also tell of African American women's roles in changing the trajectory of African American religious life. Women who ventured out into the streets, preaching on street corners and opening storefront churches, opened a new avenue of religious service that did not rely solely on the power of the pulpit. The ability of COGIC women to carry their unique blend of African American, southern, and Holiness culture to the streets of the cities placed them in a unique position of authority that did not rest on traditional avenues of power within the African American church. Becoming "cultural entrepreneurs," COGIC women expanded the roles and identities of church mothers by establishing rural religious practices in an urban setting.[2] Women like COGIC mother Lillian Brooks Coffey were an important force in tying southern religious practices and beliefs to a new form of religious life in the urban North and West, transforming the urban landscape into religious worlds uniquely their own.

Change and Conflict

If Lizzie Robinson was the model of nineteenth-century leadership, Lillian Brooks Coffey was the epitome of the twentieth-century COGIC woman. Coffey, who ascended after Robinson's death in 1945 to become leader of the women's work, is said to have been C. H. Mason's initial pick to lead the Women's Department. Unlike Robinson, Coffey cleverly used both her long-standing friendship with Mason and her forward-thinking expertise to enhance the organization of the department. Possessed of great style, wit, and energy, Coffey won the admiration of many men and women both within and outside the denomination.

Little is known about her early life. Lillian Brooks was born in Paris, Tennessee, on March 29, 1891, to Jerry and Lula Brooks. Her grandfather, a Baptist minister, was an acquaintance of Mason's when the future COGIC founder was still involved with the Baptists in Arkansas.[3] Visiting young Lillian's home from time to time, Mason made an impression upon her when she was still a child, and Coffey attended Sunday school in the church tent adjacent to Mason's church prior to his reception of the Pentecostal experience. Recalling her conversion under Mason's preaching, Coffey clearly revealed that her lifelong devotion to Mason began while she was still young:

> As time went on after the establishment of the Sunday school, Brother Mason came in one Sunday morning and taught us about Jesus in a childlike manner. He told us stories about Jesus as a little boy, how He would make little things like other little boys . . . how Jesus loved his playmates and how he would pick them up and wipe the tears from their eyes when they would get hurt. He talked

on and on until he got to the part of the story where Jesus grew up and when He became a man his friends killed him. I felt so sorry in my heart that friends would do good Jesus that way. . . . I began crying and said to brother Mason "I won't do him like that, I want Him to love me." That morning, the Lord touched my little tender heart and saved me. I have been in this church under Bishop Mason ever since.[4]

Coffey's conversion during Mason's Sunday school appearance linked the two of them together for the rest of their time in COGIC, which spanned over sixty-five years. Few men would be able to say that their friendship with Mason lasted as long. Yet "friendship" is not the most appropriate word to describe the relationship between Mason and Coffey. More accurately, perhaps, Mason was more like a mentor to Coffey, and at times Mason's attempts to groom Coffey in every area of her life could be called "Svengalian." Unlike his relationship to Robinson, which involved mutual respect and admiration, Mason took in "Little Lillian," as she was called. She cared for his children during the Mason family's summer vacations in Lexington, Mississippi, and in her teen years she traveled with Mason and other, older churchwomen on his evangelistic tours, singing and reading the Bible for him as well as assisting the women.[5] She may even have accompanied Mason on his trip to Dermott, Arkansas, on which he met Robinson for the first time.

The relationship between Coffey and Mason, much like those between church mothers, pastors, and congregants, was familial in nature, but it was not a sibling relationship; Mason shaped Coffey's life like a possessive and somewhat domineering father. Mason made sure that Coffey not only engaged with her schoolwork but also did her Bible studies under his strict tutelage. As Coffey recounted,

He knew that I was interested in his welfare and the welfare of his family. He would tell me about the work. During those days he would not allow me to be too idle. He often had me reading the Bible even while he slept in the office. I would complain at times for as the other youngsters I wanted to go down into the Basement and laugh and talk with the folks. He would often say to me "Watch yourself for your future. Someday you will lead the Women of this church and anything you do now will could [sic] weigh heavily against your leadership. Now I cannot say that I was always too willing to obey, for I was young and full of life, but I put aside my will and heard what Bishop Mason had to say."[6]

Coffey may have chafed under Mason's scrutiny, but their relationship remained close: Coffey once remarked that Mason became her "earthly father" when her parents died in 1912 and she and her siblings were relocated to Chicago. It is interesting that Mason would devote so much time to a young woman's spiritual and temporal life when he almost certainly could have mentored any number of men. But, as Coffey recalled, Mason had chosen her for future leadership of COGIC women. His protection and oversight suggests, perhaps, that the women's work was integral to his ideas about where the church would go in the future. For a man to have a relationship to a young woman in her teens might now be viewed as unseemly. Yet the communal aspects of African American culture, coupled with the fictive family relationships prevalent in both COGIC and the Pentecostal movement, during this time account for the closeness of the two.[7] By folding Coffey into his fictive family, Mason both legitimated her eventual claims to leadership and ensured her loyalty to him and to the church's teachings. Even after she married in the 1920s, Mason's admonitions continued to influence her life, and after she divorced, she chose not to remarry in keeping with his wishes.[8]

When Coffey first moved to Chicago, her relatives, concerned about her immersion in the sanctified church, tried to limit her connections to it. It helped their cause that there was no organized COGIC church in Chicago at the time. Working as a hotel maid, Coffey tried to acclimatize herself to the urban life, but the transition proved difficult for her without the support of a church. Coffey's need for religious fellowship was so great that she began a small storefront COGIC mission. Like many of the church mothers, she "dug out" the church, which became W. M. Roberts's temple in 1917. Coffey requested the pastor for her church by name, asking that Roberts be sent from Memphis, where he served as Mason's assistant pastor. Roberts made his way to Chicago, and there, at Coffey's instance, what later became the formidable church organization (and women's work) of COGIC in Chicago began to take root.

For many COGIC women like Coffey, starting a church met the biblical injunction to spread the gospel and provided a way to combat the social and religious ostracism experienced by southern women and men who migrated to the North, Midwest, and West. Southern practices, religious or otherwise, were looked upon as backward outside of the South, and many migrants were ostracized. Moreover, whereas Jim Crow had been the prevailing law of the South, the North's racial repression came from whites and African Americans in equal measure. In many of the larger black churches light-skinned blacks were segregated from darker-skinned blacks. In addition, the larger black churches that

Lillian Brooks Coffey. Courtesy Glenda Goodson Collection, the Center for African American Church History and Research, Lancaster, Texas.

moved into the spaces in transitional urban areas formerly occupied by white churches continued to be bastions of exclusivity even with black pastors at the helm and black congregations in the pews. COGIC women who encountered such discrimination appropriated the southern revivalist traditions of outdoor preaching and canvassing from door to door for converts, and these techniques bore fruit in the urban locales to which they had migrated. Coffey herself eventually went on to help found eleven congregations, and she is credited with being the first COGIC official to have founded churches north of the Mason-

Dixon line. COGIC women who simply wanted to re-create familiar religious environments, then, effected the proliferation of COGIC storefront churches, simultaneously redefining the urban religious landscape in the process.

Mother Mary Mangum Johnson was among the women who helped to re-shape urban religiosity. Johnson, a former state mother of Michigan, wrote her memoirs some time after she began her evangelistic work in Detroit and throughout the state of Michigan. It is not clear what compelled her to tell her story, but the text is a fascinating piece illuminating her life—and perhaps also the lives of many other religious black women who migrated north. A member of COGIC since 1901, Mother Johnson lost her first husband to tuberculosis. Some time after she married her second husband, Brother W. G. "Ting-a-ling" Johnson (nicknamed for the sweetness of his singing voice), Brother Johnson handwrote a message in an unknown language after a Church of God in Christ prayer meeting. Ting-a-ling took the writing to C. H. Mason, who interpreted it as call for the Johnsons to move to the state of Michigan to preach. Mary re-sisted the message, but then she, too, felt compelled by the Holy Ghost, in her case while she was doing her household chores, to write down a similar message in an unknown language. The message was interpreted again, this time by her husband, as the call for them to move to Michigan. Johnson remained uncon-vinced until she attended the following Sunday's church service, where, while praying, she came to have a feeling of peace about the move.

Leaving their much-prized mule in the front yard for a prospective buyer to retrieve, the Johnsons set off for Michigan.[9] Upon their arrival, Mother John-son's first official "digging out" enterprise was held on Elliot Street in front of a house called a "Bear Trap . . . because of the class of people who lived within." In Detroit, bear traps were boardinghouses that charged tenants low rent; they were havens for illicit activities such as prostitution and gambling.[10] Rather than avoid these areas, COGIC members sought out bear traps and boarding-houses as places rife with potential converts and evangelistic opportunities. Johnson remarked that her husband "preached" and she "spoke" from the sixth chapter of Romans.

Mother Robinson's distinction between preaching and teaching on the one hand and speaking on the other was often invoked by COGIC mothers. But the distinction proved to be problematic in urban areas. Women would begin evan-gelistic meetings, starting a tent congregation or a small storefront church, and then would be expected to turn over control to ordained men as soon as a con-gregation's numbers increased. In Mother Johnson's case, this was perhaps less difficult than it was for other women, because she turned the congregation over to her husband. Ever cognizant of the southern gender norms, she remarked in her memoir, "I was my husband's helper, stayed in my place, and let God do the work." By following biblical admonitions and upholding traditional gender roles, COGIC church mothers could present an example to their neighbors and conform to the expectations of traditional churches already thriving in the community.

For other COGIC women, however, turning over the fruits of their digging out work to male pastors rankled, unless they were able to bring men into the new church who were related to them by blood or by sanctified kinship, as Lillian Coffey did. Asking for W. M. Roberts to come and pastor in Chicago in 1917 proved to be a shrewd move on Coffey's part. Roberts was a champion of Coffey's ministry, and he stood resolutely by her throughout her tenure as second-in-command to Mother Robinson in the Women's Department.[11] Other women were not as fortunate as Coffey, and their replacement by male pastors sometimes caused feelings of anger, irritation, and even bitterness. Mother Millie Crawford from Texas and Mother Martha Armstrong, for example, two intrepid street missionaries who gathered up converts, started a mission in a tent at Fourteenth and Woodson in Los Angeles, California. Services there started at 9 A.M. and continued all day long, stopping for lunch and resuming in the afternoon. The southern-style revival preaching fared well in the temperate climate of Los Angeles. Men were also involved, but the women "[stood] out as beacon lights" in the leadership of the group.[12] No matter their brightness, Mason sent Elder Eddie Driver to Los Angeles to pastor the work the women had started after Driver had a vision in which the "Lord told him to go to California." Described as having a "strong personality," Driver soon had a run-in with the women who had dug out Saint's Home through their tent ministry and who found it painful to watch their work be taken over by a man.

The migration period was one of change—sometimes painful and sometimes exciting—for church mothers. Previously, they had served the church by occupying pews and encouraging the pastor and congregants. Baptist church mothers had slightly modified this paradigm with their involvement in the National Baptist Women's Convention and in home missions work. But COGIC church mothers, out of necessity, became roving home missions workers and street evangelists. Traveling to support the fledgling women's work, migrating in search of a better life, and working the streets teaching and evangelizing, these church mothers began perceptibly to change their traditional roles. The mothers could reach into enclaves of women through work and home visitations much more easily than pastors could, imparting both religious and domestic advice that brought them into contact with many southerners who yearned for a bit of home, even from someone they did not know. Bible Bands and Sunshine Bands met during the week in small storefronts organized from street ministries and helped to reinforce COGIC teachings. Church mothers became, during the period of the Great Migration, both the public face of COGIC and the best representation of what it meant to live a sanctified life. What people thought about sanctified people during the migration was inevitably shaped by their witnessing of church mothers and other COGIC women in public places doing very public things that subverted both the southern and the elite African American ideal of womanhood.

Sometimes COGIC women took their new leadership roles further than the church would accept, sparking conflict. Mother Emma Cotton provides a poignant example of a COGIC woman who felt thwarted in her desire to take up her calling. Born in Louisiana and healed of cancer during the Azusa Street revivals, she described herself as a "walking drug store." The healing she experienced compelled her into the ministry, and after moving back to Louisiana for a time, she was appointed assistant state mother of California by Lizzie Robinson. She returned to California with her husband sometime between 1916 and 1919, and they served as missionaries and pastors in Northern California. Yet Mother Cotton was not satisfied being "Mother Cotton," as an anecdote told by a visitor from Texas shows. Elder McKinley McCardell, who boarded at Mother Cotton's home after arriving in Oakland from Texas as a young migrant, remarked, "As I approached the door, there was a sign, Elder H. C. Cotton, Pastor and Mrs. Emma Cotton, Assistant Pastor; that startled me—looking and thinking; because I had just left a state where women did not pastor churches."[13]

McCardell was right, but distance from Memphis and southern life allowed women like Cotton to challenge the gender norms that Lizzie Robinson had carefully passed on to COGIC women. Cotton and others like her posed a unique challenge to the expansion of the denomination. Though their representation of the denomination helped the church to grow, C. H. Mason and especially Lizzie Robinson wanted these women to comply with its expectations and rules. Enforcement of church bylaws was a subject constantly revisited during the migratory period. Statements like "Women are to respect their overseers" and "Women should not usurp the authority of the man" crop up consistently in the minutes of COGIC meetings from this period.[14] Unruly women like Cotton both reinforced and rebelled against the stereotypes of women's roles within COGIC and other African American churches. They supported the

Henry and Emma Cotton, 1939.
Courtesy Flower Pentecostal Heritage Center, Springfield, Missouri.

idea that COGIC church mothers were concerned with the lives of those around them, but they did so by taking to the streets and pastoring active ministries.

Though Cotton disappeared from the roll of church mothers sometime in the 1920s, her ministry continued: she eventually opened her own church in Los Angeles and held services with another noted Pentecostal women's leader, Aimee Semple McPherson.[15] A small advertisement for Cotton's ministry in the *California Eagle* announced she had opened a church while her husband was still pastoring in San Diego. The Pentecostal Gospel Mission on 4709 Central Avenue in Los Angeles was touted as having meetings "every night at 7:30 P.M., and the purpose of the meetings was to save sinners and have believers receive the baptism of the Holy Ghost, and the Sick healed."[16] The Reverend H. C. Cotton, meanwhile, made the San Diego news column in the same newspaper. A three-line statement read: "Rev. H. C. Cotton, pastor of the Church of God in Christ, has gone to Los Angeles for an indefinite stay."[17] Rev. Cotton never returned to San Diego, and he once again began to pastor alongside his wife in Los Angeles.

Sanctified Living

Other women approached their ministries as church mothers and urban missionaries in ways that were less confrontational but no less innovative. Mother Johnson made the storefront church she and her husband dug out in Detroit into a haven for homesick migrants. In true southern homemaker style, she used percale material from Memphis to cover the pulpit and had her husband "gather chicken giblets, heads, and feet" on Saturday nights from the butcher, which she prepared with dumplings for dinners served to the visitors to the Sunday service. Replicating the southern-style church service by providing food and long services on Sunday was a way to bring urban dwellers into the church family. But Johnson also lamented the loss of her southern comforts:

> Since this rented store front had to be both our house and church, Elder Johnson erected a partition within the building by means of a post, and some of the cotton material we had bought from Memphis. We had in our little "home-made" room, a roll-away bed, a monkeys-stove, which we used for both heat and cooking purposes. . . . Although I had given up and left a comfortable and well furnished home in Memphis to do God's will in Detroit, there were no rugs on the cold floor of our room, until I made a rug of burlap cloth which was generally used as a wrapping for bulk of cloth material. This piece of burlap was sold to me by a man for the price of seventy-five cents.[18]

Her description presents a cogent example of how southern practices helped to win over both transplants and lifelong urbanites. The homey touches she added to the storefront space strengthened the bonds among the members of the domestic family of God. The connections Mother Johnson made between the work of the Lord and the creation of a neat home reflected the strong connections southern women made between domesticity and spirituality. It was not enough simply to have a space in which to live and worship; she wanted a space that would be pleasing to the eye and to God.

To outsiders, especially middle-class African American churchgoers who watched the migrants from the South enter their cities with trepidation; domesticity was seen as a means both to impart racial pride and to control the masses. Sanctified church members spoke improper English, had southern accents, left their hair unprocessed, wore plain dress, and seemed not to have the common manners that accompanied urban living and a "respectable" lifestyle. They sang spirituals and, later, gospel music, which was gaining a foothold in Chicago and Detroit, embracing the sounds of drums and tambourines, much like those coming from juke joints. Worst of all, women were upsetting traditional gender roles, and their leading worship, street preaching, and shouting all branded them as unrespectable and wholly unacceptable. For many northern African Americans, these masses of southerners represented the antithesis of uplift and racial pride.

In this context, storefront churches did not escape criticism. Despite the success of the Johnsons' church, for example, Detroiters attributed its "strangeness" to the Johnsons' "backward" southernisms—activities like praying in the street and eating the leftover parts of chickens. The attitude toward the storefronts was at times brutal and unforgiving: when a visiting preacher, Elder W. G. Johnson, was in the pulpit of the COGIC church on Saint Antoine Street in Detroit, disgruntled people threw bottles and rotten eggs at him. Historian Victoria W. Wolcott notes in her book about Detroit that "all of the African American church leaders and members of the Detroit Urban League lumped all storefront churches together as a cohesive and reprehensible group." But the reality, Wolcott skillfully demonstrates, was that the churches provided stability to migrants to the city.[19] Church mothers were not only missions workers but also "mothers" to those displaced from their families, re-creating their fictive COGIC families in the cities. Saint's Home in Los Angeles, for example, designated a small area built in the back of the church for church mothers and other women who found themselves homeless, and some of the churchwomen made dinners to sell to members who lived in single rooms without kitchens. Others made room in their homes for migrating church members, and churches took in those who had recently converted to the fold with the expectation that they too would reach out to others once they were on their feet.

The church's emphasis on living a sanctified life as a Saint held great appeal for young women who were displaced and without spouses. Such a cohort provided a ready source of converts for the women's work of COGIC. It was no accident that COGIC church mothers targeted the slum areas of the major migration cities like Detroit, Philadelphia, and Chicago. Unemployed women, young women without families, and abandoned "women in trouble"—their conditions often created or exacerbated by migration itself—all became potential converts.[20]

Even something as seemingly minor as the mode of address among COGIC members could be a life raft to those entering the church in the cities. The members of COGIC, in addition to calling each other "brother" and "sister," in the Pentecostal manner, referred to other members as "the Saints." In COGIC terminology, "Saint" is used as a form of address or greeting, signifying a sanctified individual or group, as in "Praise the Lord Saints." The term refers to someone who has made a personal commitment to living the sanctified life, someone who has gone through all the stages of the sanctification and exemplifies it, as in "She is a model Saint."[21] A Saint models his or her attainment or desire for the sanctified life in dress, belief, and behavior, and the title of Saint sets a person apart as a member of a Sanctified or Holiness Pentecostal church. Comments such as "There goes a Saint" or "The Saints are here" recognize the behaviors of like-minded church members often identifiable by plain dress, lack of makeup, and decorous behavior. The term "Saint" became particularly important at a time when African Americans were often called "Boy," "Mammy," or other derogatory, generic terms rather than their given names.[22]

Sanctified women's agency in the interwar period grew out of their pursuit of new, urban lives that reflected their religious values of purity and holiness, the qualities of a sanctified life. Their pursuit of sanctification involved many of the outward signs of respectability, namely, proper dress, homemaking, education, and respect for gender norms. But the activities that sanctified women engaged in, such as street preaching and ecstatic worship, clashed with the class-based religiosity of the urban African American churches and social organizations. Organizations like the Urban League and churches like the African Methodist Episcopal (AME) Church and the Baptist Church sought to instill in the African American community a strong work ethic and respect for gender norms in the service of racial pride and uplift, but sanctified women wanted all of that and more. Their concern with living right for God rather than living right for upper-class blacks and whites led to behaviors that drew a great deal of criticism.

For COGIC women, the goal was not to present a respectable public figure but to remove the sin from their lives in order to move in the power of the Holy Spirit. That power meant release—the freedom to move freely through society knowing that one belonged to God. Although others have explained away sanctified beliefs as "otherworldly" or, more importantly, as part and parcel of the "deradicalized church," it is incorrect to argue that sanctified worshipers did not engage with social concerns. Carefully negotiating the boundaries of what women "ought to be and do," COGIC women took to the streets and ministered in rough parts of town, in direct opposition to the social norms promoted by middle- and upper-class black women. COGIC women's concern for living holy and living right, rather than living like whites, made their belief in living sanctified a subversive exercise that gave them access to lower-class women that their Baptist and AME sisters did not have. This difference has made it easy for scholars to write off sanctified and storefront churches as unrepresentative of African American religious belief because of their apparent opposition to structure and indifference to temporal concerns. But the presence of sanctified women and churches in the urban environment provided an alternative route for women's leadership that would ultimately overtake that of the traditional women's groups within the National Baptist Convention and the local churches.

This transition happened in large part due to the ministrations of women like Mother Coffey and Mother Johnson. Relying on their beliefs in sanctification and the sanctified life to impel and compel themselves and others to dress modestly, keep their homes in good condition, and be active churchwomen, they made themselves visible in the urban landscape, challenging the encroaching "modern" styles of the twenties. The women's work of the nineteenth century was carried forward into the storefronts. Their regulations helped to provide shape and form to women's lives and presented both an invitation and a challenge to churchwomen trying to make the urban space a "sanctified space" in which they could live and practice their Pentecostal beliefs. The women's lifestyle regulations also set boundaries between the sanctified and outsiders that made attracting new members and sustaining current membership a continuous challenge.

COGIC religious practices became a hallmark of the church's presence within the cities. Both attracting and repelling participants, the sanctified life required COGIC women not simply to study but also to model correct behavior for other religious women in the urban sphere. Given the proliferation of Spiritualists, Pentecostal denominations, Garveyites, and others crowding the cities between 1910 and 1950, church mothers were, to the casual observer, just another manifestation of the peculiarities of black urban religious lives. COGIC spiritual practices, however, placed women's bodies at the crossroads of belief and identity. The traditional southern practices of tarrying, fasting, prayer, sacrifice, and self-denial helped to ensure that new members were fully aware of what sanctification meant, how to get it, and, most importantly, how to keep it.

Church mothers reinforced the steps necessary for sanctification: consecration and cleansing. Consecration functioned to set apart the Saint for service to God. For many converts, this was the first step they took after a church mother ministered to them in a street or tent ministry. Mother Robinson's admonitions to the women about consecration began with Jeremiah 9:17–20, mentioned in Chapter 2. Prayer was one of the foundational practices of the women's work, and, like the professional mourning women referred to in the passage, COGIC prayer "warriors" were expected to engage in protracted prayer services designed to increase their personal spiritual discipline and communal focus. These communal prayer times, called "shut-ins," replete with groaning, prostration, and scripture recitation, were usually held overnight at the church, starting at dusk and breaking up early the next morning. COGIC members believed that these extended periods of prayer curbed the worldly desires of the flesh and yielded spiritual benefits such as healing, financial and spiritual breakthroughs, and answers from God.

The corporate prayer times were accompanied by a period of fasting that began before and continued throughout the shut-in. Three days of fasting with no food or water to pass one's lips was a usual prescription. A COGIC text described the power of fasting:

> Fasting is another powerful offensive spiritual weapon. Without this weapon you are not fully equipped for battle. Just as we have been equipped with the weapon of prayer, God wants us to be equipped with the weapon of fasting. Prayer and fasting go together to penetrate and to break through every resistance that the enemy has built. Fasting strengthens and intensifies our prayers. As you begin to use your spiritual weapon of fasting, as you humble yourself through fasting and prayer before God, you will break through enemy territories and claim victory in every circumstance.[23]

The combination of prayer and fasting was used to create the right ground for consecration to the work God had called one to do. For the women of COGIC, fasting was an important element in the sanctification process. It was thought to purge one's body of impurities and prepare it for the cleansing work of the Holy Spirit that took place during the prayer shut-in. The disciplines of fasting and communal prayer intensified solidarity among the women and made those unwilling to discipline themselves in order to be consecrated easily identifiable.

Since there was not an established process for ascending to the position of church mother, missionary, or evangelist, moreover, consistent consecration practices of prayer and fasting helped to identify which women were potential leaders. Monitoring women's participation in prayer and fasting regimens, Bible study, and attendance at Prayer and Bible Bands helped identify who was prepared and spiritually mature enough to take on leadership duties. Within urban confines, these practices became an important way for church mothers to scrutinize the readiness of women for increased recognition and responsibilities. Many times, the shut-ins included "tarrying services," at which participants waited to be baptized with the Holy Spirit, although these services were intended only for those members of the congregation who had long since forsaken their worldly practices. Speaking in tongues, though valued and important, was the culmination of the sanctification process, not the sole reason for it. Consecration prepared members to be cleansed of the impurities of the world so that they could live *in* it while not being *of* it.

Cleansing also addressed the outward manifestations of worldliness. Dress, hairstyle, and bodily discipline became important in navigating the nexus between body and belief. One's body had to manifest the beliefs of sanctification and appear pure, unlike the urban bodies that were sculpted to fit the new urban lifestyle. The advent of Madame C. J. Walker's hair products brought about profound changes in hairstyles and beauty culture for African Americans.[24] Women with hair that was coarse and kinky could aspire to a new look that placed them in the mainstream of changing fashion styles and the shifting meanings of race and sexuality for African American women. Women's entrepreneurial endeavors as beauticians were soon prodigious, and black newspapers touted all sorts of hair care and beauty products. These changes in style hardened church mothers admonitions and teachings about proper dress.

COGIC women's manner of dress stood out in stark contrast to styles popular among most African American women. Mother Robinson's call to "dress as becometh holiness" became important to COGIC women in the migratory period. They were expected to wear plain, modest clothing. Mother Robinson's traditional traveling attire—a heavily starched, long-sleeved white blouse and a stiffly starched black skirt that stopped at her ankles—was favored. Pants were off-limits to women, and hats were expected to be plain, with no ribbons, bows, or feathers to adorn them. Patterns in the Sewing Circle handbook instructed COGIC women in how to "change pants into skirts" and sew up the splits in skirts deemed too worldly.

Prohibitions regarding dress had their antecedents in Holiness dress codes of the nineteenth century. Wesleyan Holiness women and women in other Holiness sects followed a rigid code of dress in part to show their inward holiness to outsiders and as a means of setting themselves apart. Unprocessed hair, plain dress, and modesty made COGIC women stand out in urban areas. By making the bodies of women conform to what the ideal Holiness woman looked like through dress, the identity of the Women's Department was shaped by its interpretation of what Holiness meant. The women's plain dress allowed them to be "in the world, but not of it." In the sanctified world, women were most attractive when their beauty was natural and they did not draw attention to their beauty with adornment. This individual and corporate attitude toward beauty and dress was codified in doctrinal statements and beliefs about Holiness. The first dress code appeared in the rules for the women's work in the early 1920s. A short example suffices to give its flavor: "Rule #4. All members and missionaries must not wear hats with flowers or feathers nor Short Dresses, Split Skirts or Short Sleeves. . . . Rule #5. All members and missionaries must dress in modest apparel as becometh holiness, professing Godliness with good work."[25]

For the women who preached on urban street corners, dress helped to portray their ideal of the sanctified woman. Lucinda Bostick, cofounder of Bostick Temple in Saint Louis, famously wore ankle-length dresses when ministering with her husband in the city. Numerous admonitions and teachings from the Holiness movement were incorporated into the COGIC Pentecostal understanding of the pathway to sanctification. The beliefs worked both to admit those who were willing to accept them and to exclude those who would not commit to their embodiment. COGIC women used their dress code not only to differentiate themselves from other urban groups but also to broadcast their own particular definition of what it meant to live a life apart, sanctified to God and free from temptations, in the midst of urban vice.

The peculiarity of COGIC members' worship and dress attracted outsiders who came to observe and ridicule members. Many passersby would watch the storefront services with disdain and amazement, the peculiar practices both impelling and repelling them. But quite a few members of COGIC joined the church after being driven by curiosity or the hope of entertainment to investigate it. One such person was Arenia Mallory, who attended a service in the hope of getting a laugh and ended up becoming an important leader in the women's work. Born in 1904, Mallory was brought up in a relatively privileged environment. Her father, Eddy Mallory, an entertainer, traveled around the country with his brother, Frank, performing comedy routines and opening up for musical acts such as Bert Williams, the famous comedian and entertainer.[26] Mallory's father married her mother, Mazy Brooks, and settled in Jacksonville, Illinois, establishing a business that sold musical instruments, antiques, and real estate, among other things. Since both her parents were involved in entertainment and music, Arenia was given piano lessons in the hope that she would become a concert pianist. Her visit to a tent revival meeting of COGIC members in Jacksonville pushed her to use her talents in an entirely different venue. As her biographer, Dovie Simmonds, related her conversion story, the seventeen-year-old listened to the message, came forward for the altar call, and "rolled around the floor in her brand new dress." Her claim to have spoken in tongues upset her mother, who forbid Arenia to go back to the tent. She returned a few days later, nevertheless, and requested that she be allowed to travel with Elder and Mother Carter, COGIC missionaries. Her mother, in turn, gave Mallory an ultimatum: Stay home or live with the Carters permanently. Mallory chose the latter.[27]

Renewal

Practices such as plain dressing and prayer attracted the occasional convert at the same time that they helped to order the lives of COGIC women during the inter-war period; these practices were connected to southern life through the influx of migrants to the cities and through the annual convocation in Memphis. For many COGIC members, the Great Migration was not a one-directional move away from the South but a process of shifting back and forth from the North and West to Memphis each year. At the annual convocation, COGIC women re-connected to their southern way of life, heard from Mother Robinson, and got the directives they needed to withstand life in the cities of the North.

The convocation was also a time to remember what had been left behind, including Jim Crow, segregated railway cars, and meager housing. The poor treatment of African American women on public transportation necessitated their careful comportment and modeling of holiness through dress and demeanor; thus, the annual convocation reinforced the southern Holiness and Pentecostal practices that made COGIC members stand out in the urban setting. And it was important for the women to be present, as many of the details of the convocation were entrusted to them. Because of the lack of rooms for rent in the black sections of Memphis convocation attendees often stayed in the homes of COGIC members in the Memphis area. Attendees slept in eight-hour shifts, and the convocation ran services almost twenty-four hours a day to accommodate the unusual sleeping schedules. Women attending the convocation were asked to "send along bedding, as the meeting is still growing larger each year, and the demand for more cover is necessary."[28] Convocation attendees had to be fed, as well. Food was served mainly at the homes of members in the years from 1915 to 1920s; the cooking, of course, was handled by the women. Lelia Byas, daughter of founder C. H. Mason, remarked in an interview that the "members depended on the praying Church mothers to take care of the needs of the sick, poor and indigent."[29] The church mothers who had money and other resources took care of those who came to the convocation in need of food and a place to sleep. Homemade soup and cornbread were served to all of the Saints, and the cooking was done in various homes. Over the years, increasing attendance and food service needs necessitated bigger facilities.[30]

But despite all of the intricate planning involved, COGIC members looked forward to the convocation, which immersed them in fervor, prayer, fellowship, and rest for a protracted period. Pentecostal practices of fasting, protracted prayer, lengthy services, and testimonies were integral to the marking of sacred and secular time. Scripture was used to both justify and set the tone for the convocation, as did the following excerpt from a COGIC publication: "Blow the Trumpet in Zion, sanctify a fast, call a solemn assembly. To sanctify means to set apart for God—a fast to consecrate ourselves for the work He has given us to do, to humble ourselves before God, and to repent of all sin and disobedience in our lives."[31]

C. H. Mason claimed that he wanted to have a church meeting that was focused on "sacred and sanctified gatherings for the Saints" where they could "have communion with one another."[32] It was also a way to make sure that the practices of sanctification were reinforced in a communal setting, as they were for the women all year long. Members rushed to Memphis to participate in the first three days and nights of the convocation, which were devoted to prayer and fasting. The stringent fasting ritual acted as a cleansing process, allowing members to focus clearly on garnering spiritual strength and subduing their flesh, with its carnal desires. The practice of fasting, prayer, and repentance was believed to allow the Spirit to enter the services. Members expected, in the words of Bishop Mason, "that the presence of the Lord was great to bless and heal." Women and men alike packed the convocation services to encounter miracles and healings. Within this charged environment of continual prayer, singing, shouting, and fervor, power encounters of various kinds occurred on a regular basis. Mason's ministry of healing by prayer and the laying on of hands was critical to the convocation services, so much so that nonmembers attended the convocation hoping for a touch from him.

Holy Ghost power was not limited to leaders, moreover, but was available to all who fasted and prayed. Members shouting, dancing, and testifying during the service were "under the power." Such ecstatic religious practices were linked to the worship styles of the slaves, which many of the members in the early twentieth century could still remember. Unlike their black Baptist cohorts, who shunned ecstatic practices in the hope of attaining respectability, COGIC members embraced the ecstatic worship of the convocation services that gave witness to the outpouring of the Spirit referred to in Joel. The emotionally charged environment of the convocation allowed members who had forgotten the fervor of services in their urban environments to get back in touch with the sacred and to touch the not-so-distant past of slavery.

The ecstatic worship at the convocation, then, allowed the men to experience what COGIC women already were experiencing in their Prayer and Bible Band circles. The intentional connection between COGIC women's practices and the practices of the convocation gave women a place of importance in the modeling of what it meant to be a sanctified person, or Saint. Women's knowledge of the appropriate responses in prayer and in worship helped the men to become open to the "move" of the spirit. In this role, women became a focal point of the convocation. In the 1920s, they acquired their own service, which was called "Women's Day."[33] Mother Robinson led the prayers and conducted a Bible lesson, after which reports of the work done and monies raised by the Women's Department during the year were made.

New missionaries and evangelists to the Women's Department were also appointed on this day. Newly appointed members were expected to uphold the examples of Holiness practices both in and away from the convocation. Serving as "cultural missionaries," evangelists and missionaries, along with the unseen prayer partners and altar workers, helped to remind members how to pray, sing, shout, and dress. If local church members were not following the prescriptions of sanctified life, a COGIC missionary or evangelist might "fire up" the Saints. Their visits were often a necessary reminder of and deterrent against the encroaching modern world. The role of the convocation in appointments and the commissioning of these "cultural missionaries" was crucial in ensuring that practices were reinforced both at home and abroad.

Convocation served an important purpose: it gathered the diasporas of church mothers together in the early days of the women's work. The constant connection to the south via the convocation and constant movement of women back and forth through Memphis assured both a familial and religious connection to the roots of COGIC and the South. Without it, teaching might have morphed into preaching and Saints into "ain'ts," and the close ties between church members might have disintegrated. However, maintaining close relationships was only a part of the sanctified life of COGIC women. Prohibitions were also part of the sanctified life, and they would present a great challenge to the ranks of eager women ready to save the world.

Prohibitions

When I come to church look what I see, real short dresses,
slit skirts and rusty knees . . . change the style!
Lucy Flagg, "Lord, Change the Style"

For all of the freedoms African Americans had in urban centers, there was no escaping the fact that racism was stronger than ever. The racist literature of the late nineteenth and early twentieth centuries, and the rise of social Darwinism, eugenics, and racial classifications all combined to make the black body loathsome and feared and subjugated in the cities and throughout the nation. Black men and women, alongside their religious leaders, took on the task of restructuring the public image of the black physical frame from "bestial" to "Negro." For members of COGIC and other black Pentecostal denominations, that restructuring took place through the construction of a nexus of bodily prohibitions that restricted the freedom of the body and its decorations. Particularly for COGIC women, bodily prohibitions grew out of the idea that one would be better able to meet God in worship unhindered by the trappings of the unsanctified world. COGIC members' bodies were joined to the collective body of the Saints through disciplined dress, sexuality, and worship, and joined to God through the belief that the Holy Spirit lived inside their black bodies.

COGIC women who migrated during the interwar period faced their share of challenges, but none were so daunting as resisting the temptations and avoiding the pollutions of city life. Its rhythms, different from the slower pace of southern cities and the sunup-to-sundown life of the rural South, presented a formidable challenge to the bodies of the Saints. The dress, the sounds, the smells, and the actions of other urban dwellers could not always be counted upon to be in keeping with sanctified living. Numbers runners, prostitutes, spiritualists, and plain old sheep-stealing Christian pastors represented a threat. To counter such temptations, the rules of sanctified living had to be followed to the letter. Those rules, however, both entangled and lifted up the church's members.

The sanctified life weighed down and lifted up both those who lived the sanctified life for years and new converts. Converts to COGIC often felt stifled by the practices of living the sanctified life, and older established members could never stray from the rules without losing their status within the congregation. Rules for sanctified living such as modest dress and fasting could become harsh and unyielding when deployed by church mothers with a hard-edged personality. The ensuing relationships that occurred were oftentimes fraught with tensions and jealousies. Those who questioned the church mothers authority and the purpose of the sanctification rules were labeled troublemakers or unrepentant of past sinful behavior. Those who made the good faith effort to obey the various admonitions at the beginning of their lives as Saints found themselves at the lowest rung of the church hierarchy, having to work their way to trust by proving their allegiance to the purity boundaries. Those faithful to the sanctified life, however, could find themselves lifted to a place of prominence and authority, with the social capital and benefits of the church afforded to them. Of course, maintaining those benefits was a daily challenge and formed the core of the women's work to this point.

Eschewing the world's pleasures was the first step to proving that one allowed the Holy Spirit to work in one's life. Drinking, smoking, snuff dipping, promiscuity, and revealing clothing were the hallmarks of the unsanctified life. The Holy Spirit, according to 1 Corinthians 6, lived in the "temple of the body," and COGIC members believed this fervently. For COGIC women and men prohibition was about more than just abstaining from alcohol; it was about abstaining from anything that would take them away from living a sanctified life. Particularly for women, living the sanctified life meant that one's body and its public presentation was regulated from the tops of one's head to the soles of one's feet.

Perhaps unsurprisingly, the denomination's church mothers were the enforcers of sanctified living. The outward appearance of both COGIC men and women was important, but the women bore the greater burden in keeping their bodies within the confines of sanctification. Those confines, based on Victorian norms and principles, caused COGIC women's bodies to stand in stark contrast to the stylish frames of most urban women. In this way COGIC women served as the models for the sanctified life.

Sanctifying the Body

As discussed in Chapter 3, the dress code developed in the 1920s was designed to combat the vices of the city and to separate the sanctified women from outsiders. COGIC was not alone in promulgating a dress code for its female members; other groups, including the National Baptist Women's Convention, also did so. Evelyn Brooks Higginbotham suggests that black Baptist women developed a politics of respectability in their dress and behavior in order to change the way whites viewed them and to achieve civil rights. The fight for equality and civil rights would be won through proper behavior, they believed, which meant that all blacks had to both *appear* respectable and *be* respectable in order to gain the respect of whites. Christianity gave church members a reason to promote temperance, sexual purity, and cleanliness, but the central purpose of the politics of respectability, Higginbotham argues, was to "bridge the divide between Black and white women, helping them to come together to defeat Jim Crow."[1] Like their COGIC sisters, however, Baptist women did not emphasize their desire to be pleasing to whites but rather their wish to be pleasing to God.[2] While Christian principles of piety and purity could be and were put to use in political ways, for many Baptist and COGIC women alike, devotion to the tenets of the "Bible, Bath, and Broom" seems not to have been primarily about the politics of respectability but largely about serving God.[3]

More often than not, COGIC prohibitions were also used to exert power and control over women and men. The promotion of proper dress and behavior was one way in which church mothers could make sure that women were adhering to the principles of sanctification. In order to present the proper appearance, women in COGIC were expected to be fully covered, showing little or no skin in their everyday dress. Mother Robinson's traveling attire of a heavily starched white blouse, long black skirt, and practical shoes was the template for "holiness dressing." Other church mothers took the admonition to cover the body one step further. Lucinda Bostick, for example, wore a cassock-style garment that covered her entire body from her neck to the ground. No matter that the outfit dragged in the mud—it became Bostick's trademark style of dress for many years, both inside and outside of the church.

In the presence of such extremes of modest dressing, a younger woman entering a storefront COGIC church faced an immediate challenge to her manner of dress, especially if she wore makeup, showed any measure of skin, or sported trousers. Women who came to church wearing flapper-type clothing or trousers were immediately encouraged to change into something more suitable. A church mother might invite a new convert to the Sewing Circle, where she would be encouraged to make use of patterns like "fixing the split," which explained how to convert pants into a skirt. As can be seen from the testimonial of Sister Minnie Carter, whose decision to change her pants into a skirt brought about a spiritual awakening, modifying one's dress was an important step in achieving sanctification:

> I was wretched and undone, and was very sinful. My hair was cut in a boyish bob, and my skirts knee high, most of my blouses were without sleeves, and really, after hearing the gospel preached, I became a penitent. One day I decided to alter a garment so that I would not be ashamed to go to the Altar. But before I finished the garment, time came to prepare dinner, and I went to pick green peas. Oh, what a glorious day for me. While in the pea patch, I believed, and my sins were washed away. Then I began to glorify God. The Holy Ghost came upon me and I fell to the ground. I glorified the name of Jesus, and the spirit took full control of my tongue [and] for a time I spoke with other tongues as the spirit gave me utterance. Oh my, how happy I was for I knew that I was saved, and Baptized with the Holy Ghost and fire, and ever since that glorious day my desire has been to walk with god in the beauty of holiness, and to be of some help, and to assist in some way to improve the character of young women and girls.[4]

A reluctant member of the COGIC church in Belsoni, Mississippi, Sister Carter apparently possessed a rather developed sense of style before her conversion experience. She describes herself as a "sinful" woman with bobbed hair, sleeveless blouses, and short skirts—the very picture of the unsanctified woman. (That too-fashionable dress could pose a problem even for church members in Mississippi suggests both how intractable a problem dress could be and how much more difficult the challenge of making over Saints must have been in the cities.) Her use of the term "boyish" highlights the gendered construction of how a sanctified woman should appear. Everything about her had to speak to her "gendered" identity as a woman; that is, the Spirit could not move into a body that was "confused" about its gender identity. Her decision to "alter a garment" was made because women of the church had been pestering her to wear something more appropriate to the church services. It was the act of being obedient to their recommendations that was the catalyst for the Holy Spirit to take control of her body, and she then spoke in tongues.

Although it is impossible to know if events happened exactly as Carter described them, what is important is that Carter recalled the story in this sequence to make an essential point. The Holy Spirit could not enter an improperly dressed, de-gendered body. Though sanctification itself was inherently an internal affair, the external markers of Holiness dress and behavior served as signs to the community that a convert had submitted to the authority of the Spirit, of scripture, and of the leadership of the church.

That submission, it seems, reaped spiritual rewards for Sister Carter, who after speaking in tongues, discovered a call to "improve the character of young girls," a development that put her squarely on the path to becoming a church mother. Carter's example demonstrates that the acceptance of bodily prohibitions and restrictions was not simply an individual decision but one that had a communal element as well. Self-reformation became world reformation; it turned Carter into, as one sociologist puts it, the "reforming type." Sanctification in COGIC had its own process, and that process mandated that one's lifestyle had to change before one could speak in tongues. It required one to undergo sacrifice, consecration, and cleansing in order to receive spiritual benefits. Modification of dress, part of the process of cleansing, could launch a new COGIC member into a promising future in the church, demonstrating the member's sincere quest for a disciplined spiritual life and moving her one step closer to becoming a Saint—someone in control of herself, someone who had a command of scripture, someone who was a conduit of the Holy Spirit, and someone who, eventually, had control over others.[5]

Reforming the lifestyles of young girls and women proved to be difficult, however. Convincing women that their style of dress was not in keeping with sanctified living was an ongoing process and apparently an uphill battle. Mother Robinson alluded to this challenge in a comment about the style of dress she encountered in the cities:

In Isaiah 20, God told Isaiah to walk naked before the people for three years for a sign and wonder upon Egypt and Ethiopia. He said the Assyrians would come up and take the Ethiopians barefoot and naked, captive with their buttocks showing. Well, this is the time to teach about the buttocks. When the women stoop down you can see their buttocks. We are living in that day right now. So, the women must put their dresses down. The people must be taught. They are getting away from God. Do you not see the women losing their modesty? Don't you see it as a lust breeder?[6]

To Mother Robinson and other church mothers, modernity and its fashions presented a direct challenge to Pentecostal teachings. "Holiness" encompassed the body as well as the Spirit, and the two were clearly linked: women's buttocks, when visible, were sexually enticing, inevitably producing feelings of lust among COGIC men. (It is interesting to note that the scripture Robinson refers to speaks of two biblical kingdoms associated with blackness: Ethiopia and Egypt. Perhaps her allusion was not just an admonition but also an appeal to her fellow church members to keep some sense of racial decorum intact.)[7] In Mother Robinson's view, the sight of the female physical body could only lead to covetousness and sin; in fact, Robinson taught that covetousness itself was a form of spiritual adultery: "The word says, if a man looks on a woman to lust after her he has already committed adultery in his heart. So, a man just looks at a woman, and would like to be with her, he sees her legs and sees how she looks; he has committed adultery without touching her. The women should keep their dresses down."[8] Choosing appropriate clothing, then, was not only about cleansing one's Spirit, it was about cleansing oneself and one's spiritual community of sexual desire. It was COGIC women's responsibility to control men's sexual behavior by controlling their own dress. This role was not unique to COGIC women but had been and continues to be the role of women in many Christian communities.

The role also embodied the expectation that churchwomen could be distinguished from street women by their dress. Many African American women of the 1920s and 1930s favored plain dress in the hope that they would not be mistaken for prostitutes or loose women. Proper dress for women was frequently promoted by churches and Urban League members in places like Detroit and Chicago in order to present a version of the black community more palatable to whites.[9] In COGIC, these early dress codes created a distinctive style that remained in place until the 1950s.[10] (In the 1950s and afterward, COGIC women began to abandon their plain dress and to distinguish themselves instead by trendy, elaborate clothing.)[11] Clothing served multiple purposes: it was a way to test the degree to which new church members had embraced the sanctified life, and it allowed COGIC women in the cities, who risked being shunned by upper-class blacks, to be recognized as "respectable."

The social capital of dress had its origins both inside and outside the COGIC community. Appeals to African Americans in general to project "respectability" by managing their dress and bodily cleanliness influenced the women of COGIC and their work.[12] But it was the denomination's internal belief structure focused around sanctification that really drove sanctified dressing and behavior, turning dress into a form of social capital within the church. As Sister Carter's description of her experience of sanctification makes clear, spiritual power was given only to those who dressed appropriately, and those who ignored the admonitions were marked as outsiders to the sanctified COGIC community. Their clothing labeled them, in Robinson's words, as street women.

Church mothers, who promoted sanctified dress by appealing to scripture, became a potent tool for controlling women's participation in the women's work. Holiness was guaranteed to be taken seriously because the principles and practices were incorporated into the very structure of the Women's Department. Women's Department auxiliaries served to reinforce the standards of dressing as "becometh holiness." The sewing circle, for example, served as a primary means to ensure holy dress. If a woman did not have the financial means to convert her unsanctified clothing into something more suitable, she would be presented with patterns for making modesty cloths (lap cloths to be placed across the lap of a woman with a short skirt) and dickies (to hide the cleavage revealed by low-cut necklines), as well as for closing the split in skirts and converting pants into skirts.[13] In the period from 1912 to 1945, most COGIC pronouncements on sanctification came through the Women's Department and the auxiliaries. The auxiliaries printed most of the material, taught COGIC ideas about sanctification, and disseminated them to the membership through print and the teachings of the church mothers, who embodied sanctification and were important role models for the denomination.

Preached about and sung about, dress became the foremost social marker of COGIC women for decades. During the interwar and prohibition period, however, it was also a source of constant struggle. F. W. McGee, a prominent COGIC preacher who traveled with both Arizona Dranes and Rosetta Tharpe, recorded a sermon on women's dress in 1929 titled "Women's Clothes (You Can't Hide)."[14] Hymns began to appear that were written in part to reinforce the dress code. In a hymnbook used by COGIC from the 1930s to the 1950s, for example, "The Florida Storm" (subtitled "Nahum 1 and 2") incorporated a verse in which dress was a focus:

Evangelist Viola Jackson wearing typical clothing of COGIC women.
Courtesy Glenda Goodson Collection, the Center for African American
Church History and Research, Lancaster, Texas.

Short Skirts and Filthy Dances
Have caused my heart to bleed
And now our country is filled up
With every wicked deed,
But Ah, that's all right,
God's going to visit you one night
And will pour out his judgment upon man[15]

Poems even addressed the issue of women's dress. In a poem titled "Change the Style," Lucy Flagg expressed her feelings about nonsanctified dress:

When I come to church look what I see, real short dresses, slit skirts and rusty knees.
> Change the style,
> Sometimes that skirt's split front, side and back,
> Somebody pass that sister a pin or a tack
When they walk that slit gaps open wide, anyone can see everything inside.
Sometimes that slit is cut up so high, it goes past the knee and you can see the thigh.
Then some dresses are cut so low at the top, all the contents nearly fall out plop.[16]

"Changing the style" meant that one's dress should match up with one's bodily deportment. Even the condition of the body was scrutinized: "rusty knees" indicated not only improper dress but also lack of personal hygiene.[17] Sanctified clothing was not only a sexual deterrent; it also expressed purity and consecration. In some COGIC churches, the church mothers wore white every Sunday. The practice of wearing white began at Women's Day at the general convocation and then spread in the 1950s to the Women's Department's annual convention. White and black both traditionally indicated sanctification or consecration. Colors were virtually never worn in the early days of the Women's Department due to negative associations. Red, for example, was associated with Jezebel, wife of Ahab in the Old Testament story.[18] White attire, on the other hand, represented the surrender of all marks of personal style and distinctiveness in favor of total identification with the worshiping community and God.[19] White attire was also an eschatological symbol, suggesting that the believer was the bride of Christ.

In addition to dress, hair and makeup became forms of demarcation for COGIC women. Makeup was prohibited, and hair was required to be unprocessed and unstraightened. A "Purity Column" titled "Make Up" read:

The purpose of Holy Women is to LURE men into the body of Christ by lifting him up, and not to LURE them to their own bodies by lifting IT up. So, Shun THE VERY APPEARANCE OF EVIL saith the Lord. . . . Oh, you want a nice boy friend or a good husband. Well, I am most certain you would like one who is true to himself, to God and to you. One who will protect your Moral Standing and look into the Future with you and plan that Ideal Christian Home. One who is everything any woman would desire. NOW, that kind is attracted to you through BEAUTY OF CHARACTER AND CONDUCT. Through your pleasing personality and preparation for life. Through your LIFE and Works in the BEAUTY OF HOLINESS. LIPSTICK, ROUGE AND MAKEUP MAY DO HARM TO YOUR COMPLEXION, BUT THEY MEAN DEATH TO YOUR MORAL RATING AS A SAINT.[20]

The column's author, Pearl McCullom, argues that sanctified women's role was to lead men to Christ, not to seduce them with their bodies. She presents the female body as a kind of temple of Christ, able to attract men to Christ if it is properly adorned with holiness, not lipstick and rouge. In a sense, this definition of the body suggests that COGIC women were embracing an African cosmology in which there is no difference between the body, its appearance, and the self. The self is also the body and its appearance; outward and inward appearances are one. The body, therefore, is a marker of the self—the Saint— and if that body does not conform to the self individually and to the corporate COGIC self, it is out of sync.[21] If rouge and lipstick shift the body out of sync, then the normative blessings, that is, a good boyfriend or husband, will not appear.

The appeal to shun makeup, like the rules about modest dress, was an appeal to sanctified life. McCullom's column stated:

Jezebel was a very intolerant woman. (Saints are very patient!) When the time had fully come that Jezebel's power should fail and God's power be shown, she PAINTED HER FACE AND LIPS AND EYES AND HUNG HER HEAD OUT HER WINDOW TO KISS JEHU (the coming ruler) UNDER HER IMMORAL HAMMER. DOES THIS NOT SOUND FAMILIAR TO YOU AS YOU NOTE THE PRACTICES OF QUESTIONABLE WOMEN TODAY? Now HOLY WOMEN, shun the very appearance of these evils. Perhaps there is no wrong intentions harbored, but if it causes the world to stumble and offends our Brothers, God's people will refrain. There must be a difference between Holy and UN-HOLY, between Clean and UNCLEAN, between the Church and the World, saith the Lord.[22]

McCullom makes it very clear that the onus was on women to refrain from appearing to be women of the world. Jezebel, long associated in church circles with disobedient and brazen women, serves as an example of the "unclean woman." McCullom was instructing churchwomen to shun the appearance of evil by cultivating a plain appearance that emphasized holiness and, more importantly, protected men from stumbling. It may seem unfair that women were expected to carry the burden of maintaining COGIC sexual morality, but viewed from another angle, the power women wielded over men commanded respect.

Unfortunately, the reality was a bit more complex, especially for women. Despite all of the admonitions against wearing makeup, advertisements for skin creams, including skin-lightening creams, appeared in the church newspaper *The Whole Truth* beginning in the mid-1930s. Ads for Lucky Heart cosmetic creams and powders, which touted the products' ability to preserve the natural "beauty of holiness" of COGIC women, were also introduced sparingly. Both lines of products left women's faces plain and unadorned, and thus evocative of holiness; they also enhanced beauty but without adding the color condemned as emulative of Jezebel. The same was true for hairstyles. Natural hair, braided or styled appropriately and covered with a plain hat for church, was the norm. Madame C. J. Walker's process for straightening hair may have made her a fortune, but using her product was not an option for COGIC women during the early migration period. Later, when the class structure and public visibility of COGIC women changed in the 1940s and 1950s, the preferred hairstyle became pressed hair, worn long.

These sanctified standards of beauty also affected the men of the denomination and their choices of wives. COGIC founder C. H. Mason's wives, for example were lighter-skinned women, in spite of the fact that a Memphis newspaper referred to him as a "race man."[23] Pictures of COGIC couples in the ministerial ranks from the 1940s and 1950s often showed a darker skinned man with a lighter skinned woman. Though there is nothing in church writings that would prove that there was a "preference" for lighter skinned women, the pictures told a different tale.

The identity of the Women's Department and the identity of COGIC as a Holiness group were defined by the women who conformed their bodies to the sanctified ideal. From 1912 to 1945, this identity required the church's members to be "in the world, but not of it." The sanctified world was a world in which women were most attractive when plain. When the church mothers disciplined their bodies to conform to the image of holiness based on their biblical understanding, they also constructed a self for the Women's Department and for the denomination. This individual and corporate self-construction was codified into doctrinal statements, or beliefs regarding holiness, that worked together to admit those who were willing to accept them—the Saints—and to omit those who would not commit to their embodiment in their person. In COGIC, sanctification was not codified merely because Charles Mason articulated the doctrine in sermons. The doctrines of COGIC became codified also because church mothers emulated, articulated, and embraced sanctification ideas and images in their person. The embodiment in the Women's Department of the practice of sanctification produced a process by which prior experiences of attaining sanctification established correct practices of dress, purity, and behavior for future members. And the structure of the Women's Department ensured that women would be required to embody the sanctification beliefs of COGIC after being exposed to the doctrines in the department's auxiliaries.

Sanctifying Marriage

All of the admonitions regarding holiness and dress, of course, could not keep the sanctified life from becoming problematic on occasion. Rules regarding sexuality and marriage were strictly enforced for COGIC men and women both, but the women invariably ended up paying a higher price for breaking the rules. Those who were unmarried, male or female, were expected to be celibate. The purity class, discussed in Chapter 2, was the primary vehicle for teaching sanctification in sexual matters, although the issue was also addressed in the Prayer and Bible Bands. Biblical admonitions against premarital sex, found in 1 Corinthians 6 and 7, were regular topics of discussion. Men and women in the ministry were given strict rules about traveling together on church activities. One rule specified "that no young [female] missionary [was] to go here and there with any Elder or Brother to for missionary work without the consent of their state mother and pastor." Young women were instead paired off with older women in Women's Department activities. Mother Robinson traveled with her daughter, Ida Baker, to ensure that there would be no whispers about her traveling alone; unmarried women were often suspected of sexual impropriety and were often pressured to marry.[24]

The issue of marriage was a source of both power and pain for the women's work and its leadership. For COGIC women, marriage became an important step to becoming a church mother, but it could also be a hindrance. The issues of who a person married, whether or not the marriage partner was a member of the COGIC church, and whether or not a church member remained married or "put away their husbands" in favor of working for the Lord became central to both affirming and discrediting women's ministerial work. Church leaders preferred for the fictive COGIC family not to become populated with outsiders or spouses not chosen by a revered church mother or elder. When marriages occurred within the ranks without the leaders' seal of approval, trouble often followed. "Arranged" marriages came about in part to ensure that both the husband and the wife in leadership positions understood and practiced sanctification and that they would serve as proper role models for members. They also helped to keep both male and female members under the control of older Saints in leadership positions. Later, arranging marriages became a way to keep prominent COGIC families in leadership positions, but during the period from 1915 through the 1940s, they were primarily a way to make sure that women would submit to both their husbands and the leaders of the women's work. Other COGIC women went to extraordinary lengths to arrange marriages for themselves. A poignant "lonely hearts" letter in the June 1957 *Chicago Defender* is an example: "Dear Mme. Chante: I enjoy reading your lovelorn corner and to know that you are doing such a work for honest people. I am a widow. My age is 50 and I am a missionary in the Church of God in Christ. I have one son 14 years old; I work each day and am considered nice looking. I am 5 feet 2 ½ inches tall, weight 195 lb. . . . I would like to have a man around 55 or 60 because we could still make progress in this life."[25]

Mother Robinson's attitude toward marriage (and the instruction about marriage she provided to COGIC women) can perhaps be best understood by considering her own marriages, the attitude of *Hope* magazine toward matrimony and home life, and the effects of the migratory period on marriage relationships. Robinson, who managed to outlive three husbands, said little about her marriages in writing but was quite outspoken in directing women to find someone to marry of whom she approved. If couples were unable to "hold on" (that is, refrain from premarital sex), then she would arrange their marriages so that there would be "no fornication among her people."[26] For Robinson, the issues surrounding marriage were largely about controlling rampant sexuality and desire.

For COGIC women, marriage presented an opportunity and a hindrance to serving in the capacity of church mother, evangelist, and missionary. Sweetie Salome Lovejoy Williams, who left behind her childhood sweetheart against the wishes of her mother and at the urging of a COGIC elder, is a case in point.

Sweetie came into COGIC through her mother, a Baptist Church member who joined the church following a revival meeting in Washington, North Carolina. Sweetie and her sister converted during the revival meeting as well. During her high school years, Sweetie had a dear friend named Boone who became an evangelist and minister. Her mother approved of Boone, but a COGIC evangelist had other ideas about who Sweetie should marry. In her autobiography, "Back to Pentecost," Sweetie tells the story:

> An old evangelist preacher introduced me to the man who was soon to become my husband. He was very handsome. He was a minister and his name was Elder Adam Little. He was visiting in Little Washington, North Carolina, when his evangelist friend singled me out and declared to Elder Little that this woman was sure to be a good wife. He was determined to mate the two of us together. For a while I struggled within myself and asked: "Is this the man that God has sent for me?" It was certainly a hard decision for any young woman to make. I asked my mother but she was partial toward my friend, Boone, who was on the mission field. The old evangelist must have had a heavy prayer going, because soon Elder Little could think of no one else except me. All I could think of was wedding bells ringing for me. It wasn't long before I was engaged and married to the distinguished Elder Little.[27]

Sweetie's account offers some interesting insights into the process of choosing a mate in COGIC.[28] It is unclear if Boone, her original suitor, belonged to COGIC, but it seems very clear that the "old evangelist preacher," a COGIC elder, strongly influenced the course Sweetie took. Sweetie's internal struggle found her wondering whether God was indeed speaking to her through the elder. Such powerful charismatic authority, linked not only to men but also to women like Mother Robinson, both influenced and alienated women who attempted to choose their own mates. The influence of the elder on Sweetie over and against her mother's desires and her own feelings speaks to the intensity of the fictive family relationships within COGIC's ranks and the pressures that women experienced in attempting to make choices.

Sweetie's choice was in part a spiritual one, but it was also one that mirrored the desire, as she puts it, to "Hear wedding bells ringing for me." Her allusion to being "mated" holds a key to understanding what marriage in COGIC was also thought to be about: sexuality and fertility sanctioned by God. Sweetie would later go on to explicate the role of the woman in marriage. "This union between husband and wife is the physical or sexual part and is very important to the health of the marriage," she explained. "Marriage without love and sex is like an empty Tent."[29] In her words, the role of the woman was to "replenish the earth," and "man could not do this alone. He could not produce without the woman."[30] In COGIC, then, marriage was a space for sexuality sanctioned by God and reproduction of children who would be, in Sweetie's words, "After the manner and likeness of their parents"—in other words, who would be good, sanctified COGIC members.

But marriage was not only about sex and procreation; it was also about one's position in the church. Sweetie's implication that Elder Adam Little was perhaps more "distinguished" than her young evangelist friend Boone speaks to her desire for upward mobility within the church ranks. By marrying an established elder, she would be able to attain a better position. After their marriage, she recalled, her "ministry in the Lord did not slow down, but rather, it accelerated." The opportunities afforded to her by marrying an established elder within the church raised her profile, but not without some personal cost. "Yet, deep down inside," she continued, "I felt that I should have listened to my mother. My married life was full of stormy weather, but now Elder Little and I were one in name, one in spirit, and one in faith. Together we had a mission to accomplish. Should I have waited? There was no time to dwell on that thought. I was swept right off my feet. My new husband carried me away to live with him in Monessa, Pennsylvania. There he pastored a church and worked at a steel mill."[31]

One can only guess at the nature of the challenges and the "stormy weather" that Sweetie experienced in marriage. She wrote later that when the couple moved to New York City, "she had many trials and sufferings, especially in the home." One has to wonder about the pressures that the ministry placed upon the marriage, for she admits that she suffered a nervous breakdown after their arrival in New York City. Of this period, during which she was constantly on the go, she recalled, "My body and my mind were tired, and my nerves were worn to a frazzle."[32] The constant pressures to save souls and to pursue evangelistic opportunities and the strains on her home life together plunged her into depression. For a COGIC woman to admit to feeling depressed in print is unusual, but the effects of the illness lingered in Sweetie's evangelistic messages. In a sermon on the purpose of marriage, for example, she wrote: "It is a common sight to see a work train being pulled by two engineers combining their power to pull the load. It takes the united work of husband and wife to build a home both pulling together. In a good marriage, couples build on love, and constantly confirm this love, they remember to be courteous and thoughtful, they remember to compliment each other. You endanger your marriage when you lose sensitivity as to the needs of each other."[33] Not once did she refer to her own marriage in the sermon as an example, but her words perhaps say more about her experiences than she would have cared to admit to those sitting in the pews. Marriage in COGIC was difficult, in part because the church emphasized creating the perfect "Christian home," in which love, more than sex, sustained the marriage relationship. In Sweetie's reminiscences, she never mentioned feeling love for her husband, and when she recounted her husband's death, she spoke of it in passing, unemotionally. Her silences on this subject perhaps speak more than words could say.

Marriage allowed many COGIC women to raise their profile within the women's work and the denomination, but it was not without its problems: domestic violence, separation during evangelistic trips, and infidelity all made the home lives of many church mothers difficult. Although women were laborers in the mission of spreading the gospel, the traditional, patriarchal African American church worked to trap them in marriages that constricted their opportunities for ministry and personal happiness. Men's position at the head of the home and, if they were pastors, at the head of a church made it at times untenable for women with evangelistic and administrative skills to exercise them outside of the purview of their husbands' control. Women who wished to teach had to set aside their desires in order to serve their husbands. Church mothers reinforced the status quo, often firmly. The only safe release for women who suffered in marriages was to end them altogether.

Being "released" from a marriage was an accepted way to become a woman of independence and freedom in COGIC. A COGIC woman I interviewed described being released as being freed from her general duties as a wife.[34] A woman could be released from her marriage through her husband's death, through divorce, or if her husband abandoned her. She was thus freed from the problems of marriage by the Lord in order to fulfill her spiritual calling without hindrance. All three major women's work leaders—Robinson, Lillian Coffey, and Arenia Mallory—were released from marriage in the 1920s and 1930s. Robinson's husband died, and Coffey and Mallory were divorced. All three of them, then, became "celibate" during their rise to power.[35] Husbands would have been competition for their time and a hindrance to their travel and ministry activities.

In Lillian Brooks Coffey's case, her freedom came when she became estranged from a husband she married in her early twenties while living in Chicago. Samuel Coffey, an interior decorator who was a Pentecostal but not a member of COGIC, was Coffey's husband during the time she served as secretary to Bishop Mason and the denomination. Married only three years before separating, Coffey later expressed regret about her marriage in an interview with *Ebony* magazine:

> There were no quarrels or spats: the vices of life just lured him away from his God and his home. I always think of it as two beautiful lives spoiled. I was very zealous. . . . I often bare that experience to young women, telling them to be more attentive in their homes and not to let their religious work overlap. However, I never neglected our home because I have always liked a nicely-kept, well-ordered home. I really think as I went on, he stood still. Being a man, he waited too long, and when we might have reconciled, I had gone on and become a little more independent. I was daily gaining national and international influence. This may have made the span too wide to bridge.[36]

Coffey's husband's estrangement was, as she makes clear, undoubtedly due to her focus on the women's work and COGIC. Despite her emphasis on the mechanics of keeping house, the real issue lay not with her uxorial abilities but with her inability to remain attentive to her husband when her attentions and affections were focused upon the work of the Women's Department. In her mind, the failure of her marriage was caused in part by the zealousness of her work in the church, but later in the interview she seems to excuse her contribution to their split by explaining that her husband left her, at which point she divorced him. Due to Mason's strict policy on divorce and remarriage, Coffey was unable to remarry. She recounted that Mason "forbade her to remarry, telling her it would 'slap her in the face every time she tried to teach God's pure word.'" She recalled, "This too I often wondered about, but he said do it and remain as I was, so I remained single until this day."[37]

Founder Mason's influence on marriage within COGIC cannot be underestimated. It is likely that his failed first marriage to a woman who do not want him in the ministry set the stage for the denominational politics regarding marriage for years to come.[38] Haunted by rejection, Mason helped to establish strict policies, similar to those of most Pentecostal denominations, about remarriage after divorce. Members could not remarry while the divorced spouse was alive, and, for men at least, marriage was often a prerequisite to ministry. The prohibitions he established, however, did not stop women both inside and outside the leadership of the denomination from marrying men who did not belong to the church.

Besides discouraging marriages to persons outside of COGIC, the church adhered to a variation of what most Pentecostals believed about divorce and remarriage during this time period. The policy of most early Pentecostal denominations was that a divorced member could not remarry until his or her former spouse died and that divorce permanently prohibited a person from ministry. COGIC put a unique twist upon the remarriage policy, focusing as it did not on divorced persons but on those who did not bother to obtain a divorce before remarrying. Mason's teaching on what he called "double marriage" drew from both biblical and pragmatic perspectives:

> Now you women that have other women's husbands or men that are not yours, and husbands that have other men's wives will have to tell the truth when you meet Jesus. It may be at the well, or on your dying bed, but you will have to tell the truth. The Lord says let not the wife depart from her husband and let not the husband put away his wife. (1 Corinthians 7:10–11) . . . Jesus said whosoever shall put away his wife and marry another committeth adultery against her, and [if] a woman shall put away her husband and marry another, she committeth adultery.[39]

The rule regarding double marriage was designed to address bigamy, a relatively common problem among the populations from which COGIC drew its members. It was not uncommon for individuals to simply leave one spouse and take up with another without obtaining a legal divorce.[40] This practice had its roots in slavery. Slave trading, which often divided families, presented problems for the maintenance of cohesive family units. The reconstruction and migration periods both brought an increase in legalized marriages among African Americans, but the fluidity of migration and economic stress put strains upon permanent marriages. For lower-class and impoverished African Americans, common-law marriage and serial relationships were easier to maintain. Migration served to exacerbate the issue, with spouses who left home ostensibly to find work in the North or West remarrying in their new locales. Unless someone could identify and notify the previous spouse, chances were that neither the abandoned nor the new "spouse" would ever learn that he or she was involved with a bigamist. COGIC men and women found to be involved in a double marriage often lost their positions as evangelists, missionaries, and church mothers, and this happened with some frequency during the 1920s, when marriage-related proceedings occupied a major portion of convocation business. The consequences of double marriages were especially harsh for women in COGIC leadership, not only because they were expected to step down from the ministry until the situation was rectified (that is, by leaving the second spouse and returning to the first one), but also because they would lose their spousal support. Two cases of double marriages show how difficult it became for women to retake their positions of leadership, even if the double marriage was not their fault.

Arenia Mallory, future president of Saints School, the COGIC educational arm, followed in Coffey's footsteps and married a man outside of the denomination. Of the marriage, her biographers, Olivia Martin and Dovie Simmonds, wrote:

> There was one mistake made by Arenia Mallory (according to COGIC standards) that astounded most of our church people during the 30's. She married a young man who was not a member of the Church of God in Christ. During those days, if someone married outside the church, you were disfellowshipped: even if you played ball, it was understood that you could not testify until a repentance was made and prayer, asking God's forgiveness, interceded. The young woman already had one strike against her as the head of the Church's only institution of learning—the fact that she was a woman. The Mississippi men felt like another man should have been placed at the head of the school. So she paid a high price for the fault of marrying outside the COGIC. She took a two-year leave from the work that she loved so dearly.[41]

Martin and Simmonds go on to explain that when Mallory, having departed from the school, divorced her husband and wanted to appear in a church to repent of her marriage, some elders closed the doors to her. The real story however, was a bit more complex.

Minutes from the 1928 convocation indicate that Sister Mallory had married a J. Pullum and that the marriage was found unscriptural because she previously had been briefly married to another man, Elder Clemmons. Whether Mallory did indeed divorce Clemmons is unclear, but since her daughter had the last name Clemmons, she must have had some sort of relationship with Elder Clemmons.[42] Consequently, Mallory was stripped of her duties at Saints School for two years. Left with a baby daughter, an absent husband, and debt, she was forced to seek repentance in a COGIC church before being allowed to reassume her position. With the doors of southern COGIC churches closed to her, Mallory traveled to New York City and found a church that allowed her to repent of her "sin" at a Sunday morning service. In her confession of sin before the congregation, Mallory began to sing "Yes, Lord," and the refrain soon became what some called "the anthem of COGIC." The hymnal used by the denomination today is called *Yes Lord*, though the accompanying text obscures the origin of the song. Mallory's case is a fortunate one, since she was able to repent and was reinstated to her position at Saints Industrial School, the fledgling denominational school. For women directly under the authority of Mother Robinson and the Women's Department, the outcome was not so rosy, as in the case of Cora Stevens.

Cora Stevens was a licensed evangelist in the Women's Department. Her marriage to a COGIC elder, R. H. Stevens, was declared invalid when it was discovered that Stevens was still married to his first wife. In the minutes of the 1922 convocation, Stevens was instructed to "put Cora away" in order that he could continue to serve as an elder in the church. Because Cora's marriage was found to be invalid and she was accused of having taken up out of wedlock with another man's wife, she was stripped of her evangelist's license. Cora disagreed with the ruling, and at the 1924 convocation, she brought charges of unlawful removal against Mother Robinson, saying that she had been illegitimately removed from the ministry. Convocation committee members sided with Mother Robinson's decree, however, and the revocation of Cora's license was upheld.

In Elder Stevens's and Sister Cora's case, both parties were in positions of spiritual authority within COGIC. The minutes do not state clearly why Elder Stevens retained his position after returning to his first wife, while Cora was denied her position as an evangelist. Perhaps Mother Robinson's stringent rules regarding missionaries and evangelists came into play, but more likely the case exemplifies the double standard imposed upon the women of COGIC to be chaste and irreproachable sanctified women. Women bore an extraordinary burden both materially and sexually in the case of bigamy. Losing the spousal support they counted upon, they were turned out of their homes, often with "illegitimate" children to support. Many of these women were clearly unaware of their husbands' bigamy, and the revelations and subsequent punishment destroyed their families and disrupted their ministry. Cora Stevens's contestation of her license removal, therefore, was not only about rank but also about livelihood. Without Elder Stevens's support, her evangelist's license would have given her a way to provide for herself. Its removal forced her to take drastic means: Apparently she continued to pass herself off as a COGIC evangelist for a number of years by speaking in churches under the auspices of that revoked license. In 1934, a two-line statement appeared in *The Whole Truth*: "This is to let you know that Sis. Cora Stevens of Texas is not doing mission work in the Church of God in Christ. License revoked by Mother Robinson."[43]

All of the COGIC prohibitions regarding dress, sexuality, and marriage combined to create a closed, closely monitored community that placed the responsibility for upholding, maintaining, and modeling sanctified living squarely on the shoulders of women. This burden took its toll on women's relationships

and caused estrangements from both fictive and biological family life. Prominent COGIC women like Rosetta Tharpe struggled under the onus of sanctified
living.[44] Tharpe, who traveled with her mother, evangelist Katie Nell Nubin,
found herself on the outside of the COGIC fictive family as her fame as a guitar-
ist and singer took her from the storefronts and rural churches to the Cotton
Club in Harlem. Consequently, Tharpe was ostracized and her religious were
convictions questioned in some COGIC circles.[45]

Even more troubling was the role of women in critiquing other women who
did not adhere to the standards of holiness. Mother Robinson's sternness was
often mentioned by other women, both in print and in reminiscences of her
leadership. Women were expected to rein in others who broke the rules of sanctified living, and those who transgressed them were often ostracized and always
limited in their ability to operate as educators, evangelists, or missionaries. The
fact that transgressions occurred, however, meant that there were larger issues
at play, a motivation to reach out and step over the traditional boundaries of
what living sanctified meant. That motivation came in part from two innocu-
ous but soon to be overwhelming factors: women's entrance into the educational and civic worlds of African American and American life.

5

Education

Walk in dignity, Talk with dignity, and Live in dignity.
Arenia Mallory

Pentecostals have not been linked traditionally to educational endeavors. "You don't need an education, you just need the Holy Ghost!" was a common refrain in many early Pentecostal churches. The Church of God in Christ's engagement with education was due in part to many influential members' backgrounds in the Baptist Church. And within the context of the women's work of COGIC, education was advocated because it promoted spiritual robustness and encouraged the practices of sanctification that kept members engaged in the evangelical and spiritual work of COGIC women. The tensions between the Pentecostal viewpoint of education and the practical aspects of COGIC educational endeavors were often mediated through the racial concerns of African Americans in regard to education.

Education in the African American community during the early twentieth century took place either in colleges such as Spellman and Morehouse, which had been endowed in the reconstruction period by wealthy philanthropists and religious organizations, or in rural schools with few or no facilities for students and a shortage of teachers. Agricultural, or land-based, schools concentrated primarily on training for trades and agricultural duties, so schools like Tuskegee Institute were important as places to train African Americans in various skilled labor. Denominational schools such as the one Bishop Mason attended for a time in Arkansas were primarily for the training of pastors, and many times, women who wanted an education would have to have signed on to become a teacher, one of the few openings for women to advance their education during the time period. For persons who could not access these established institutions, the local Sunday school and/or Bible Band presented a way to learn how to read and to become biblically literate.

The Women's Department's Bible Bands were the first systematic educational system in COGIC. Mother Lizzie Robinson set the stage for the educational endeavors of COGIC by training youth and adults in the Prayer and Bible Bands. Much like her mentor Joanna Moore, Robinson believed it was important to incorporate scripture into education in order to establish the proper foundation for knowledge. Bible Bands played a crucial role in teaching the practices and doctrines of sanctification that were at the core of COGIC beliefs. This Bible Band education flowed from a post-Reconstruction conception that education was important for African Americans.

How that education would be attained, and for what purposes was a broader question. For followers of Booker T. Washington, that meant a basic education with and emphasis on training for agricultural endeavors or skilled trades. For leaders like W. E. B. Du Bois, that education was to be on par with that which whites received in order that African Americans be both productive within society as well as classically educated. These debates on what kind of education was appropriate for the African American community would continue until the mid-twentieth century.

For religious institutions, those discussions were important, but of necessity they were located within a context of religious training, in addition to a classical or a trade school education. Many of the clergy of black churches were "called" rather than "trained," and the advantages of being a charismatic preacher versus a learned preacher were debated. Both C. H. Mason and Lizzie Robinson received limited educations. Mason had attended a Baptist school in Arkansas in the early 1890s but dropped out to pastor a church. Mother Robinson, despite being able to read, had a minimal education and most of it came through Bible Band and her time as matron in the Baptist training school in Dermott. Despite these COGIC leaders' backgrounds, both the denomination and the Women's Department would establish a fledgling in-house educational system that would in a number of years become the catalyst for COGIC's ascendancy into the realms of middle-class African American life during and after World

War II. More importantly, education would provide the women's work with connections to the broader world of women's civic engagement, and that trajectory would bring the modern world into the sanctified world.

"The Bible's right": Education through Scriptural Admonitions

What eventually developed in COGIC was a two-tiered educational system: the first level of education took place in the churches, as well as in Bible Bands and Sunday school; the second took place at three separate denominational schools, which eventually were merged to become Saints Industrial and Literary School, later known as Saints Junior College.[1] Both tiers were based on the core principle of sanctified living based on scripture. The training was not about how to move ahead in the outside world; rather, it was designed to prepare young people to serve in the COGIC community, and in some cases, to engage in missionary work for the church. Like most churches of the day, COGIC had Sunday school, but the Sunday school system was organized under the Bible Bands. Sunday school primers would appear in the 1920s and 1930s within the denomination, but at the beginning, the Bible Band and its offshoots, the purity class and the young people's willing workers, taught children of various ages about sanctification and proper moral living.

COGIC education was based on the philosophies of black leaders like Booker T. Washington and Nannie Helen Burroughs, who stressed vocational, agricultural, and homemaking skills. Mother Robinson even appropriated the "Bible, Bath, and Broom" expression from Burroughs for some of the Women's Department training materials. Like Burroughs's training school for girls, COGIC women's education was designed to teach women domestic skills and training for occupations outside of the home. The emphasis for the Women's Department, however, was sanctification and evangelical fervor.[2]

The teachers in this educational system were primarily COGIC church mothers. Education consisted of teachings about sanctification, dress, deportment, and behavior, but teachings dealing with theological themes, such as prayer were always popular. An example of this was the teaching ministry of Mother E. J. Dabney, author of a famous COGIC tome, *What it Means to Pray Through*. In the book, Dabney describes how God started her prayer ministry and highlights the stories of those healed in her prayer ministry. She also provides some insight into what "education" in the sanctified way meant: "I have sixty-nine scholars in my class; they are known as class Number Four. They are a group of refined, well-trained, sober, sensible spiritual girls. These girls are training for different business careers. Above all they are students of the Bible. Many of them spend their week-ends in the church fasting and praying. On Saturday evenings they have a chance to deliver the Word of the Lord. This does not make them preachers, but it is essential for them to express themselves before those with whom they have to deal."[3] The young women in Dabney's school were intent upon pursuing employment outside of the denomination through secretarial or other business type skills; however, their church-based education was primarily for training in the principles of sanctified living. By emphasizing the COGIC practices of fasting and praying, Dabney locates the real importance of a spiritual education by stressing the points that for church mothers would have the most value.

This emphasis on the spiritual practices such as fasting and prayer that were also called "tarrying" was an important part of COGIC education about sanctification. As historian David Daniels frames it, tarrying was the "key symbol that undergirded the COGIC experience of conversion, sanctification and baptism in the Holy Spirit."[4] Dabney's focus on fasting and prayer, practices that were part of tarrying, helped to reinforce women's roles in modeling sanctification and defining it for the church. Tarrying also reinforced COGIC prohibitions against women preaching. Emphasizing outside work but concentrating on the teachings of sanctified life were the initial areas of teaching within the church. The official church school, Saints Industrial, would begin in this manner as well, but the reorientation of Saints educational direction would come from a leadership change and the intervention of the outside world.

Sanctified Schools: Saints Industrial School

Saints Industrial School was founded in 1918 in the basement of the Saint Paul Church of God in Christ in Lexington, Mississippi, by Sister Pinki Duncan. Mason had first preached the message of Holiness in Lexington in an old gin house in 1896, making it the spiritual birthplace of the denomination. Located in the Mississippi Delta region, Lexington was a sharecropping area, and schools were few and far between. The small, modest church school was designed to serve the small community and to act as a refuge for church members' children. It also allowed COGIC to mimic the comparable educational endeavors of its now-distant denominational cousin, the National Baptists. Like other schools catering to African Americans in the early twentieth century, it offered an education that was religiously based, and it provided work training for agricultural or other industrial endeavors.[5] Following in the footsteps of the Tuskegee Institute, established by Booker T. Washington, and Nannie Helen Burroughs's training school for girls, Saints School was designed to train students in homemaking, agriculture, and manual skills.

Under Duncan's leadership, the school was not profitable in its first year, and the following year Duncan was relieved of her post. Professor James E. Courts was appointed principal of the school to replace her, and soon afterward a small building was erected to house the institution.[6] The school's instructors were expected to embrace Holiness teachings—or at least to be willing to serve in a school under the supervision of the sanctified.[7] Minutes of the 1920 denominational convocation state that the school and the two others that were founded at around the same time (Page Normal School in Waco, Texas, and Geridge School in Geridge, Arkansas) were allowed to incorporate at will and to "solicit aid from the outside world"—in other words, to look outside the denomination for additional sources of money and for teachers.[8] For the next few years, however, Saints Industrial School remained impoverished and was used only by local COGIC children.

The founding of these schools was not in keeping with the traditional considerations of Holiness congregations or storefront churches.[9] The impetus for their founding came in part from the Baptist background of COGIC members. The Baptist system of training schools and colleges, established through the ministrations of the American Baptists and other denominational bodies, provided a framework for those African Americans who desired a formal education. Though many of the Pentecostal schools of the early twentieth century were primarily Bible schools, Saints School, which taught reading, writing, and arithmetic, in addition to the Bible, was meant to train children of the denomination more broadly. Unlike their parents, many of whom were ostracized by their families for embracing the practices of a sanctified church, students were taught in a setting in which sanctified behavior was encouraged and rewarded.[10]

For the masses of sharecroppers, learning to read and write was almost an impossibility outside of the church schools or schoolhouses that lucky rural communities possessed. The Bible Bands established by COGIC provided members who were not fortunate enough to be near the three COGIC schools with an education, albeit one that was mostly doctrinal and scripturally based. Far from suggesting that COGIC members were otherworldly ecstatic worshippers, the denomination's established schools and Bible Bands, coupled with their printing of their own denominational newspaper, *The Whole Truth*, suggests persuasively that literacy was just as important to COGIC members as was living holy. That is not to say that the educated and uneducated in the church did not clash: to some, education was seen as a means to get ahead and get a better job but not valuable in spiritual matters. COGIC education would become both a spiritual and material quest, however, under the influence of Arenia Mallory.

Catalyst for Change: Arenia Mallory

Mallory's contribution to the educational endeavors of COGIC began in the humble circumstances of Lexington, Mississippi. Mallory would bring to COGIC not only a willingness to work in the spartan conditions at Saints but also a middle-class background that would prove to be an invaluable resource for the church. In many ways, Mallory was the "connector," a woman whose future alliances with organizations such as the National Council of Negro Women (NCNW) and the Alpha Kappa Alphas (AKAs) and her friendship with Mary McLeod Bethune would indelibly change the orientation of both the Women's Department and the denomination. Mallory's vision for Saints Industrial School, her own colorful background, and her missionary zeal would combine to bring COGIC women and the denomination squarely into twentieth-century modernity and the mainstream of African American life.

Mallory's education was firmly located in a black middle-class upbringing. Educated in local public schools in Jacksonville, Illinois, Mallory took piano lessons at the urging of her mother, who hoped her daughter would become a concert pianist. Her mother's dream did not come to pass, however, for Arenia attended a Pentecostal tent revival, where she was converted to Pentecostalism. But even more troubling to her family than her conversion was her decision to follow in the footsteps of her heroine, Jane Addams, and devote herself to helping the downtrodden.[11]

This independent, missions-minded streak in Mallory would be both a blessing and a curse later in her personal life and future dealings with COGIC leadership. As a young woman, however, her fortitude garnered the attention of Bishop Mason at a meeting in Saint Louis of COGIC ministers and workers of western Missouri and Nebraska. Impressed with her musical ability, Mason hoped that she would eventually replace James Courts, who was ill and unable to continue in his day-to-day leadership of Saints Industrial School, as principal. Mason approached Mallory and asked if she would be interested in coming to

Lexington. Mallory had intentions of going to Africa to become a missionary, but Mason brushed aside her reticence, replying that there was a "little Africa in Mississippi" and that she could be of use there to the school's students.[12] Mallory, who had never been to the South, agreed to travel to Lexington in 1926 at the age of twenty-two. Once again, Mason's shrewdness for finding devoted members who would work hard reaped benefits for the denomination. Nothing in Mallory's upbringing could have prepared her for her experience of going south, and it changed her life's trajectory. Her biographer, Dovie Marie Simmonds, describes her train ride down to Lexington from Missouri:

> A rough hand on her shoulder shook her awake with a startle: All coloreds change cars here! Arenia came alive with shock and anger. She had known what she might have to face if she went south. Even her mother had warned her "They'll hang you if you go down there and meddle around." But now she faced the real thing. She was caught up in a surge of panic and helplessness. She looked at the gold watch chain that spanned the big conductors black vest. Then her eyes swept up to his huge red face. He repeated his command, looking as though this was the most enjoyable task he would have during the long hours of his run. Maybe it was. The conductor's rough voice, rougher than it had been, followed her along the platform, "OOO-Wee! Just look at that good lookin' coon." Embarrassed and shaken Arenia dragged her things up into the colored car.[13]

Mallory found herself in an even less desirable situation upon her arrival in Lexington: the school was in disrepair and extremely impoverished. She found a little frame building erected on brick stilts a mile and a quarter from the heart of the town of Lexington, surrounded by cotton rows, and located on a dark, muddy road. Its equipment included a few homemade benches, two or three lamps, and a few old iron beds. The toilets for the boys and girls were quite a distance from the building; so far that the boys' toilet was called "Memphis" and the girls' toilet "Durant" after the cities in Tennessee and Mississippi. Food was scarce, the classroom where seven grades were taught was poorly equipped, and enrollment was very small.[14] The deplorable condition of the school emphasized that while the denomination had the desire to educate its members, it did not yet have the funds to do so.

Mallory felt the sting of both poverty and prejudice, which shocked her, given her privileged upbringing. Racist white Mississippians, fellow blacks who resented the "northern woman" for her foreign ways and light skin tone and were unhappy that a woman had been appointed to replace Courts, and hostile

Arenia Mallory. Courtesy Mary McLeod Bethune Council House
National Historic Site. Photograph by Fred Harris.

leaders within the denomination who did not appreciate the appointment of an
outsider to the South to the position all combined to make Mallory's first few
years at Saints tenuous and difficult. To make matters worse, during this period
of adjustment, Mallory fell in love and married, but her happiness was short-
lived. Not only had she married a man who was not a member of COGIC. It was
also discovered that she had been previously married and had not divorced her
first husband. As a result, she was asked to leave Saints School for two years.[15]

After making her public repentance, Mallory once again took up the leadership of the school. Her status as both a bigamist and a convert made her something of an outsider in the COGIC fictive family. Her return to Saints School

began in penury.[16] The Great Depression had begun, and the school was in even worse shape than it was when she had left it. The financial situation was dire. Unable to pay the teachers, she and the teachers took a pay cut. Financial pressure and recommendations from the church board to close the school did not stop Mallory, however, but merely strengthened her resolve to keep the school running. Mallory's response was to take to the road in search of funds. She and a singing instructor, Miss Emma Mae Lashley, taught the students spirituals and set out with a girls' quintet, "The Jubilee Harmonizers," to sing for offerings and food.[17] The group at first performed at first only in Mississippi but then branched out, traveling throughout the South and North during the summer, using borrowed cars and obtaining gasoline on credit. They even received attention from the *Chicago Defender*, who described the quintet as "a group of girls singing spirituals and plantation melodies for the benefit of the institution."[18] The Harmonizers also were invited to sing at Abyssinian Baptist Church in New York City, which was headed by the Rev. Adam Clayton Powell Sr. After Mallory twisted his arm a bit to allow the Harmonizers to perform after an early Sunday morning service, Powell convinced the congregation to come back later that day to hear the "little group from Mississippi sing." At two Sunday services and a Monday night service, the Harmonizers raised $8,000—quite an accomplishment in the midst of the Depression.[19] Powell's influence garnered them a singing engagement two weeks later at Riverside Church as well. With the funds from New York, they returned to Mississippi, and the proceeds went into the construction of one of the first brick buildings on campus, Faith Hall.[20] Yet the group's most important singing engagement was not at Abyssinia or Riverside Church but in California, where a prominent African American woman in the sorority movement, Ida L. Jackson, was moved by the Harmonizers performance. Their pivotal friendship would highlight Mallory's gift for connection-making.

Ida L. Jackson was the eighth supreme basileus of the AKA sorority, the oldest black sorority in the United States. Jackson, whose father was a slave, was born into a family in which all eight children were educated. Ida, the youngest, attended the University of California, where she was only one of seventeen African American students on the Berkeley campus. While at Berkeley, Jackson founded the Rho chapter of the AKA's with other African American women. She earned bachelor's and master's degrees from U.C. Berkeley and began teaching in 1926 in the Oakland public school system, becoming the first African American to do so. It was during this time that her path crossed Mallory's. The Jubilee Harmonizers came to the Oakland area on a Christmas singing trip, and Jackson was in attendance. As always, Mallory introduced the group, who explained the students' impoverished situation at Saints and how the young women, many from sharecropping households, were trying to obtain an education in dire circumstances. The story gripped Jackson, so much so that she went to visit Saints School during her Christmas vacation.[21] She recounted her visit for the sorority magazine the *Ivy Leaf*: "The school is very small, situated in the Delta section of Mississippi. It is supported entirely by the free will offerings of interested persons at the lectures given by the supervisor, Mrs. Arenia Mallory, who travels with a girl's quintet. After an investigation made by the writer during the Xmas Vacation, I was more convinced than ever of the needs of the people in that section."[22]

Jackson gave financial assistance to the school and promised Mallory that she would do something more to help. In 1934, soon after being elected supreme basileus of the AKAs, Jackson called for assistance from her sorority sisters to go and help Saints School in Lexington as a summer project. Jackson had observed on her previous visit that the school's teachers had minimal or no training and that the whites who prepared them to teach in the colored schools had little more education. Her idea was to create a normal summer school in which teachers would be trained. The fledgling project was an important turning point for Saints Industrial School, for Mallory, and, eventually, for COGIC church mothers and young women. Up to this time, COGIC members had interacted very little with outsiders. The strict codes of sanctified living discouraged outsiders from having much interaction with COGIC members (except perhaps to ridicule them for their Pentecostal worship practices). Jackson's budding patronage, however, brought the outside world into COGIC in ways that challenged the church's ideas about sanctified life.

In the beginning, her help was welcomed. Excited about the endeavor at the school, Jackson wrote in the *Ivy Leaf* about the summer school project and about how encounters with the Saints changed the "habits" of the sorority sisters as they worked in the Delta during the summer:

Sorors May and Thomas arrived in Plymouth with thrilling tales of adventure, the rumble seat of the car filled with teaching devices, books, radio, tennis rackets, etc. Recalling that they had been told this was a religious institution — Marie or Letteria or both stopped for a while and discarded their scandal[-]provoking shorts for demure dresses, no sleeves for long sleeves, and stockings for socks. For soon they were to learn that cosmetics would be replaced by the maidenly blush of mother nature. Regardless of bewilderment on arrival, heat, dust, mosquitoes, and attendant evils, plus having to wear long sleeves in so hot a climate, there are few teachers who have worked harder or as hard as did these sorors of ours.[23]

This account of how the sorors acquiesced to the sanctified dress and behavior codes of COGIC offers telling insight into the tensions that existed between the sorority sisters, the Saints, and, later, Mallory. AKA members were the epitome of the "new Negro": educated, smartly dressed, intelligent women with a desire to help those who were "downtrodden." The differences between the sanctified world and the world of the upper-class AKA members were obvious in the dress code of the Saints, yet the AKAs, interestingly enough, acceded to the practices of COGIC, perhaps out of respect. The personality clash between the AKA's and Mallory was a source of real tension. The presence at the school of women who were better educated than she was challenged Mallory's position at the school, so much so that she later signed up to complete her college degree at Jackson College in Jackson, Mississippi.

The AKA members' presence also aroused the ire of whites in the community. Jackson's connections at the University of California influenced two white teachers to apply for teaching positions at Saints following their graduation from the university. Mallory welcomed them, and this created problems with the whites of Lexington. Jackson's and Mallory's accounts of what happened differ, but both stressed the racism the teachers and Mallory faced from whites in the community. Jackson described the teachers' short tenure at Saints School succinctly in the *Ivy Leaf*: "They were not permitted to remain and teach because of the feeling of the white residents in the community who unhesitatingly threatened to destroy the buildings if they attempted to teach under the supervision of a Nigger."[24] Mallory's biographer reports a similar story, but one even more frightening. A group of white men showed up one night to confront Mallory on her porch. The men said to Mallory: "Who told you that you could have white teachers out here? You are one of those smart niggers form the North that don't know your place and we came to put you in your place. We came to lynch you tonight." They left after one of them said, "Give her a chance to get them away." Mallory promised to do so.[25]

As this story stresses, education was a dangerous enterprise in the South, especially when it challenged the racial conventions of Jim Crow, and that thought cannot have been far from Mallory's mind. Ironically, the racial tensions strengthened the AKA sisters' resolve to help the school. Mallory requested that sorority members return the following year, and Jackson wrote that although the sisters were "aware of the weaknesses" at the school, she felt that planning would overcome them.[26] Thus, the sorority made preparations to send members the following year. Jackson requested that a health center be added to the normal school program. The unsanitary facilities the sorors had encountered the previous summer had worn on them, and they hoped to take care of both their health needs and those of the community while taking some of the pressure off Mallory, who was also serving as the local midwife.

Jackson decided soon afterward that it was health care, not education, that would make the most difference in Lexington.[27] She asked Dr. Dorothy Boulding Ferebee, a graduate of Tufts University and employee of Howard Medical School in Washington, D.C., to become the director of a health program focusing on children's health. The first summer of the program, twelve volunteers participated, including a doctor, a nurse, and several teachers. The team was to have traveled south by bus, but Jim Crow made this plan untenable, and instead the members drove down in caravans to Lexington from Washington. The original plan was to hold a clinic at Saints School during the day and offer lectures on health for adults in the evening. Attendance was sparse in the beginning, and it soon became clear that this was because white plantation owners were forbidding sharecroppers to attend the clinics held by "outside agitators" (read: northern blacks).[28] The AKA sisters decided that if people could not come to Saints, the Saints would go to them. They made the health clinics mobile, driving cars to the plantations.

Getting locals to participate in the health project was not the only problem the Saints encountered; conflict among the various volunteers proved a challenge as well. Several of the AKA volunteers complained that Mallory was difficult to work with and that she wanted to take credit for the whole project. Jackson had warned Ferebee even before she arrived in Mississippi that Mallory was "sensitive about not belonging." "I think you know what I mean," asserted Jackson, "for we Sorors can make people feel they had no right to be born if we so desire." On Mallory's part, the slight of being mentioned in the *Ivy Leaf* as a soror, only to have a retraction published a month after, may have been embarrassing to her.[29] Problems between Mallory and the volunteers escalated to such an extent that the public health nurse assigned to the project, Mary Williams, described Mallory as "a deceitful, jealous, dangerous person who should be avoided at all costs."[30] The tensions so affected the health project that in 1936 it moved to neighboring Bolivar County, much to Ferebee's relief.[31]

Mallory's difficult relationship with the AKA sorors points to the underlying class conflicts between these different groups of women. Mallory, who was of a higher status than most black women in the Lexington area, may have felt threatened by the AKA volunteers and, perhaps, replaceable. Though she needed the outside assistance offered by the AKAs, Mallory clearly felt that it was her hand that had shaped the school, and she continued to take credit for its existence and successes. In a letter to Claude Barnett, editor and owner of the Associated Negro Press, she wrote:

> We are working in connection with this Victory Corps program; and as chairman of the Rural life committee, of the National Negro Women's council, I am trying to influence the powers that be, to place a Negro citizen both in the Victory Corps Program, and the Red Cross unit for the State. I have done more, perhaps, than any other Negro in this section to bring various types of Health clinics to the rural Negro, and I have made certain important reports from time to time, to Washington, that could not be divulged. The type of service that I render my people in this benighted state must go unsung, and without mention, due to the ignorance and prejudices of the other group.[32]

Even in 1942 Mallory was taking credit for the AKA health program. The tensions between Mallory and the AKA highlighted Mallory's need for recognition, her own insecurities, and the culture clash between the upper crust AKAs and the school. The result was that the experience of the AKAs at Saints would indelibly change the curriculum, focus, and orientation of the education for the students of Saints, and begin to perceptibly affect the Women's Department as well.

After the AKAs left Lexington, the ensuing years saw a tremendous change in the manner of education at Saints. The school had been primarily a training school that focused on the basics, as well as technical and farming related skills, but in the late 1930s and into the 1940s the school began oratory programs, musical performances, and "social events" designed to prepare the students for society events. "May Day" parades were held at the school, and, according to the *Tri-State Defender*, they drew the entire town of Lexington and the surrounding county. Social activities for the students, of course, conformed to the standards of sanctification, and social events for young men and women consisted of, as one school attendee put it, "longing looks across the room while marching in a circle to Mallory's piano playing."[33] The student body population would also begin to change as well. Mallory solicited students from the upper echelons of COGIC, establishing a boarding school for the COGIC elites' children. In terms of promoting the "fictive family" this was an astute move, as it ensured the "right" children would meet and marry.

For all the changes, however, Mallory did not lose sight of her initial goals. In an article in the COGIC missions periodical, the *International Outlook*, Mallory wrote of her ideals about church based schools: "The church's schools inculcate those lessons which most vitally concern the well-being of the nation; that is, respect for law, honor for authority, and a deep sense of civic duty. They impress upon the child that authority is from God and that all laws derive their binding force from Him. Your church's schools teach the child the civic virtues upon a basis of religion. They inject the matter of religious duty in habits of personal honor, self-restraint, respect for one's fellows and the dignity and blessedness of labor."[34]

Mallory's ideas about education were not far from the ideas of Washington and Burroughs in terms of orientation, except that her focus on civic engagement would prove to be a very fortuitous for the future success of the school. The emphasis on being a good citizen in spite of the realities of Jim Crow points to a belief in the American dreams of progress, social uplift, and prosperity. These principles were beginning to take hold alongside the emphasis on the sanctified life. Contrary to Robinson's admonitions to stay away from political action, the focus on being good citizens as part of sanctified beliefs would carry Mallory and the school into a broader realm than that intended by the founders of the school. Mallory's alliance with the foremost black educator of the time, Mary McLeod Bethune, would prove pivotal to the school's expanded purpose.

A Sanctified Friendship: Mary McLeod Bethune and Arenia Mallory

Mary McLeod's Bethune's life as an educator is well known, but what is less discussed is her relationship to the Holiness movement and her training at Moody Bible Institute. Bethune, like Mallory, always wanted to be a missionary, expressing a "missionary spirit—the spirit of doing things for others."[35] In an interview with Charles S. Johnson, president of Fisk University in 1940, Bethune spoke of how religion and her religious experiences influenced her life's work. "I heard Dr. Bowen's Address on Africa's need of people . . . need of missionaries to carry them the light. . . . As I heard him tell about the African People and the need of missionaries, there grew in my soul the determination to go and it has never ceased, and I sent up a prayer to God to give me the light, to show me the way that I, in turn, might show others. And for years, I just had a yearning to go to Africa and thought that when I was through with my education I could be sent, but instead, I found my way into the deep south."[36] Trained at the Moody Bible Institute in Chicago, Bethune applied to become a missionary upon her graduation but was declined a position because she was black.[37]

Moody Bible Institute, led by Dwight L. Moody, was one of the leading educational centers of the nineteenth-century Holiness movement, and the reforming outlook of those who embraced Holiness shaped Bethune's missionary desires.[38] In Bethune's reminiscences of her time at Moody Bible Institute, she remarked on how she became dedicated to a life of service. Bethune described her experience of receiving the baptism of the Holy Spirit: "One evening Mr. Moody called us all in to the great assembly room just before returning to Scotland and asked all who felt the need of baptism for the Holy Spirit to meet. I was so happy, I was there and could kneel in that great presence with open heart and mind awaiting the realization within my own life and the baptism of the Holy spirit of the service. I realized a quickening and awakening that I had not words to express from that day to the present. During all the years in my dealings with many I have drawn up this source for effective service."[39] Like COGIC women, Bethune found her strength for service within the sanctification experience. Also like COGIC women, by linking her experience of receiving the Holy Spirit to being endowed with power for service, Bethune put herself into the Holiness, rather than the Pentecostal camp of belief.[40]

Bethune's impulse to convert and reform the world was solidified not only by her experience at Moody Institute but also by a chance encounter with the Holiness evangelist Amanda Berry Smith. Smith felt that Bethune was the woman to carry her mantle forward. Bethune reminisces: "I remember when dear Amanda Smith came to me one day and said: 'Mary McLeod Bethune, I have been to Africa three times; I have traveled around the world; I have been looking for someone upon whom to throw my mantle. As I talk with you, Mary Bethune, I believe you are the one to wear my mantle. Get down here child, and let us pray.' We were in the middle of the grounds, but we dropped to our knees. This consecration that I received as a young woman and the inspiration I received from Dr. Dwight L. Moody carried me though the years."[41]

Bethune's and Mallory's shared belief that sanctification empowered them spiritually for service perhaps provided a basis for their friendship. Their desire to educate the race did not flow simply from their realization that education would improve black women's condition. Both also felt it was a higher calling, a calling from God, that required them to put aside self, to consecrate their lives

Mary McLeod Bethune.
Courtesy Mary McLeod Bethune Council House National Historic Site.

to the larger work of God. Bethune believed she could no more escape Amanda Berry Smith's consecration of her than she could escape being a black woman. Bethune and Mallory may have differed in their views about in worship styles, but they found a shared calling and commitment to pursue the sanctified life through service. The importance they assigned to education and their missionary focus based on their shared Holiness backgrounds provided a firm foundation for friendship.

It is unclear how and when Mallory and Bethune first met. Mallory is described as a protégé of Bethune's and probably came into contact with her during her travels with the Harmonizers in the 1930s on fund-raising tours; perhaps they were introduced by Ida Jackson. Bethune visited Saints School sometime in the 1930s, riding in a horse-drawn cart that was met by the students of the school. Her friendly outreach to Mallory and Saints School was initially related to her own work as an educator. When she was raising funds for the Bethune Training School for Girls, which subsequently became Bethune Cookman College, she experienced many of the same trials and tribulations as Mallory did at Saints School.[42] Unlike Mallory, however, Bethune had an entrée to the middle- and upper-class black women involved with the National Association of Colored Women (NACW) and other organizations. That she was a dark-skinned, African-featured woman who came from humble sharecropping beginnings did not hamper her climb to prominence within the African American community and the hallways of governmental power. Bethune was somewhat of an anomaly in Mallory's world as well. When Mallory took Bethune with her for several appearances at COGIC churches to raise money for Saints Industrial School, Bethune caused a bit of consternation in COGIC circles with her fashionable dress. In an interview, one COGIC member remarked that she could still remember Mallory and Bethune's visit to their local church very clearly, because Bethune came to the service in a bright red dress. The member recalled one of the mothers of the church remarking, "Not only is that dress too red, she is too black to wear it."[43]

The relationship between Mallory and Bethune became a close one over the years, and Bethune's educational work—combined with Mallory's relentless fund-raising efforts—paid off. By the mid-1930s, Mallory had turned Saints School into a viable operation, with 350 acres of land, $50,000 worth of buildings, 15 teachers, and 400 students. The school eventually taught grades 1 through 12, becoming the first high school for blacks in Holmes County, Mississippi. Students boarded at Saints, as well as traveled each day to the school, and for those who could not pay cash, sweet potatoes, cotton, pigs, and the like were taken as payment. Mallory repeated her U.S. tour with the Harmonizers, this time to gather clothing for the students and the impoverished in the Holmes County area. She managed to collect over 25,000 garments.[44]

Mallory's friendship with Bethune also helped her gain visibility in circles previously closed to COGIC. *The Crisis*, the official organ of the NAACP founded by W. E. B. Du Bois, for example, featured Mallory's picture on the May 1936 cover with an accompanying article titled "Mississippi Mud." "Residents of the famous and infamous Mississippi Delta," the article read, "look almost with reverence on the woman who, coming on the scene a total stranger a scant eleven years ago, has wrought the miracle of feeding clothing and educating children without the aid of financial appropriations or endowments from any source. Hundreds of them call her 'Mother,' and thousands pray for her life to be perpetuated. She gave them hope when they had done hoping; she gave them opportunity when all other doors were kept shut, and so they would look upon her almost as they would a god."[45] Chronicling Mallory's work with Saints Industrial School and the conditions of its early days, the article placed Mallory prominently among the black women educators of the day: "Florida has its Mary McLeod Bethune, North Carolina its Charlotte Hawkins Brown, and Mississippi Arenia Cornelia Mallory, who, out of Mississippi mud, has made it possible for children born, or yet unborn to have a better heritage than chopping cotton."[46] While the article also mentioned the AKAs' Mississippi health project, it made one glaring omission: not one mention was made of Saints School's affiliation with the Church of God in Christ, nor was any mention made of how Mallory came to be associated with the school in the first place. It seemed that she had just appeared out of thin air as savior of the school.

This could not simply have been an oversight. On one hand, *The Crisis* was very concerned with education within the black community. On the other, Pentecostal church schools were not the type of schools that would have earned enough clout to be featured on the cover of *The Crisis*. Historically black colleges and universities like Morehouse, Spellman, and Hampton, established for African Americans with donations from white philanthropists and denominational bodies after the Civil War were the types of schools featured in the magazine up to this point. So how might the public become interested in the story? For one thing, the school's AKA affiliation might have made it worthy of the extensive coverage it received. It also helped that Mallory's story was overhauled for the piece. According the article, Mallory was "the daughter of affluent, accomplished concertists" and her employment at Saints originated not from Bishop Mason's request but from a trip "down South for a vacation on a motor trip, where she saw the conditions in Lexington." The article placed Mallory into an entirely different social class than those she was educating.[47] It would seem, then, that someone was taking liberties with the story of Mallory's work at Saints School. It is hard to determine whether the spin came from Mallory herself or one of her benefactors. Given Mallory's attempts to take total credit for the health project, some embellishments could have come from her. Whether or not this is the case, Mallory was depicted in the article not as a faithful Saint who happened to run Saints Industrial School but rather as a race woman who was at the forefront of educating the downtrodden masses in

Mississippi. It was this Mallory, the race woman, whose Jubilee Harmonizers were invited to sing in 1937 for the president and Eleanor Roosevelt at the White House and who attended events there several times with Mary McLeod Bethune.[48]

In spite of all such accolades, there were still hurdles for Mallory and Saints School to jump that were put in place by the male leadership of COGIC. The church structure had solidified by the early 1930s to include a new board of education. The board was critical of the school for being a drain on COGIC finances, and Mallory had to account for her spending and the lack of funds at the school at many annual convocations. *The Whole Truth* reported on the school's difficulties and the reaction of the board in 1931:

> The school has passed through a great crisis this year, due to the failure of the farm crop this year and the low price of cotton. The destitution in Mississippi this year has been very acute. The leading white colleges and schools have had to eliminate one to two months from their usual nine-month's schedules. The tuberculosis sanitariums, insane asylums and other institutions have contemplated closing their doors due to lack of funds. . . . In the midst of these great tribulations it did not seem possible to operate our little school, which had no possible way to receive help other than God's grace. The board of education suggested closing the school, but Sis. Mallory felt that the work was too important and that too many sacrifices had already been made to give up so easily. She and the faithful faculty offered their services at a minimum salary and without probable chance of receiving that in the future.[49]

The denomination was eager to mention Saints School in *The Whole Truth* during the 1930s, primarily because of the singing and fund-raising tours that Mallory took the students on. Her integral work with outsiders and the relationships that Mallory was forming were not mentioned, however, nor were the tensions between Mallory and the board highlighted. The articles kept to a testimonial-style format, focusing on the religious aspects of Mallory's work rather than the educational ones. They alluded to but obscured the fact that Saints School was run by a woman who, in the view of the bishops and the executive branch of COGIC, had transgressed in her marriage and was an outsider to boot.

This view may have caused Mallory some problems, but she could be sure of support from the church mothers in the women's work. Mother Robinson, the stalwart first overseer of the women's work, was in her seventies during the 1930s and was not able to travel as often as she would liked to survey the work of the local, district, and state mothers. Having a sick husband also slowed her down. Yet, despite her advanced age and limited mobility, Robinson kept her fingers on the pulse of activities in the Women's Department, especially those that caused trouble. Robinson's support of the school, although not explicit, was evident in her lending Lillian Coffey to assist Mallory with fund-raising for Saints. In the meantime, Robinson's efforts were more focused on the educational endeavors in which COGIC women participated outside of the United States.

The women's work had gained an auxiliary—the Home and Foreign Missions Band—in 1926, and with women missionaries being sent out to such far-flung places as Haiti and Liberia, COGIC women were in charge of more than they had ever been within the denomination. Minutes from the General Assembly meetings show that Robinson defended the women's auxiliaries against interference from some ministers.[50] Articles in *The Whole Truth* record her admonishments.[51] The work of the Foreign Missions Band and the Bible Bands, which continued to provide education to the masses of COGIC members who were unable to attend Saints Industrial School, ensured the perpetuation of COGIC beliefs and practices. By the 1930s, COGIC was using its own publishing house to produce Sunday school materials and had started its own publication, *Christian Hope*, modeled after *Hope* magazine. Much like Mother Robinson's leadership, this educational system was still caught in the nineteenth century, with a focus on home and family. While other black churches struggled with issues of modernity, encroaching gospel music, and other social concerns, Robinson's education for the masses consisted of the tried and true "Bible, Bath, and Broom" taught in the Bible Bands. She trusted her second-in-command, Lillian Brooks Coffey, to assert her continued focus on home, family, and the sanctified life. Trusting Mother Coffey, however, was an interesting proposition for Mother Robinson. Coffey's close relationship to Bishop Mason and her budding friendship with Mallory pointed to signs that Coffey was moving away from Robinson's heavy-handed emphasis on obedience and sanctification. Coffey's freedom and prominence within the denomination and her connections did not make her overtly opposed to Robinson's leadership, but the simple fact was that Robinson, with her advancing age, would not be able to be as active as Coffey was in Women's Department affairs. When she was appointed as assistant general mother in 1935, Coffey's new position elevated her church profile and changed the types of endeavors she engaged in. In addition, with her appointment to the newly established COGIC Board of Education to help with facilities and supplies for Saints School, Coffey would begin to raise funds for Saints School, and in the meantime develop a strong friendship with Arenia Mallory.[52] The implications of their friendship would change the face of the COGIC women's work.

Education changed both the impetus and the meaning of sanctified living for COGIC women. Sanctified living, as both Mallory and Bethune showed, required not only proper behavior and deportment but also serving and educating others. The focus outward on education proved to be the entrée for the outside world to confront, complicate, and validate sanctified life. By preparing COGIC members to be active members of African American society, the church was acquiring a middle-class profile within urban communities and becoming a force within rural communities for organization. Mallory, through her friendship with Bethune and fund-raising efforts for the school, was soon to become a powerful voice within the denomination and the black women's club movement. Slowly, mainstream life was beginning to encroach upon the women of COGIC. It was no longer enough to simply allow Holiness to change one's life: Holiness needed to change other lives as well. What was becoming increasingly clear was the civically based church education of Saints would redefine church mothers' teachings on sanctification. The new teachings would rely on civic engagement to sanctify the world.

6

Civics

Avail yourselves of the necessary preparation to fight the Battle for Democracy.
Lillian Brooks Coffey, in *Chicago Defender*

The COGIC convocation was in session on December 7, 1941, the day that the Japanese attacked Pearl Harbor. The normal rhythm and flow of prayers and church business was disrupted for several days while COGIC members fretted about the country's entrance into war. Convocation minutes show the concern of those in attendance: "Upon receiving a report that the shores of our country were in imminent danger of being bombed, the council offered a prayer to God for the safety of the people. Upon the recommendation of the chair, it was moved by Bishop E. R. Driver and seconded by Overseer Bostick that a telegram be sent to our President, expressing our spiritual and moral support to him in this perilous hour."[1] The *Chicago Defender* noted in its coverage of the convocation that Mother Lillian Coffey made "the most emphatic statement with political references" in an address at the early session of the convocation.[2]

It was a definite departure for the COGIC leadership to express its support for a war: during World War I, the church took a pacifist position, and its constitution forbade the "shedding of blood." The articles of faith of COGIC read: "We believe that the civil magistrates are ordained for the peace, safety and good of the people. That it is our duty to pray for them and obey them in all things which is not contrary to the word of God, and that does not take authority over, or force the conscience in matters of bearing arms or going to war."[3] In 1917, Bishop Mason had been arrested for preaching pacifism, and the fledgling FBI compiled dossiers on both Mason and Mother Robinson as a result of the church's pacifist stance.[4] And just two years prior to Pearl Harbor, the COGIC convocation sent a telegram to President Roosevelt, praising his administration and thanking him for keeping America out of war.[5]

While the attack on Pearl Harbor was monumental for the entire nation, it was also a defining moment for the Saints. During the Depression era, groups like the Alpha Kappa Alpha sorority had brought attention to the denomination and, importantly, had exposed some COGIC women to a new realm of civic activity and engagement. Arenia Mallory's membership in the National Council of Negro Women (NCNW), fighting for both educational and civil rights for African Americans, and Coffey's introduction to the NCNW and invitations to activities such as tea with 700 other blacks with Eleanor Roosevelt were perceptible shifts in focus from domestic duties to civic life.[6] Mallory and Coffey's work for Saints Industrial had placed both women at the forefront of civic engagement in COGIC. COGIC women's interactions with "new Negro" women, who were educated and socially and financially well connected would begin to change how the church interacted with the world. The entrance of the United States into World War II blew away the walls separating the Saints from the modern world. In their place the church—and COGIC women in particular—built bridges to the rest of world through their educational endeavors, the women's work, and civic engagement.

Reframing Sanctified Life

Saints Industrial School and Arenia Mallory's fund-raising activities provided the initial impetus to the turn toward intentional civic engagement and bridge building. The relationships that developed between Arenia Mallory, Mary McLeod Bethune, and the AKA sorority on behalf of Saints Industrial School opened doors of extraordinary access to the civic and social worlds for COGIC women. Soon after meeting both Ida Jackson and Mary McLeod Bethune, Mallory was invited to the White House and to events sponsored by a range of civic organizations that would connect her and other prominent COGIC women to a broader world of African American civic life. These bridge-building endeavors had largely gone unnoticed by the majority of COGIC church mothers and women, and their import was only hinted at in *The Whole Truth*, which described them solely as fund-raising activities. Yet these activities enabled the men of COGIC to feel confident in interacting with the outside world. The fact that Mallory had already been to the White House with the Jubilee Harmonizers no doubt emboldened COGIC leaders to write their letter to Franklin Delano Roosevelt showing their support for the war. COGIC men's engagement with civic culture and life was yoked to the agency of church mothers who had gone before them.

The 1940s and early 1950s, then, were a pivotal time in terms of how COGIC members and the denominational leadership defined the church's relationship to the world. Instead of trying to draw the world into the realm of the sanctified, COGIC turned its attention to sanctifying the world. This shift in emphasis was the result of increasing civic engagement and community involvement. The manner in which this civic life would be engaged was couched in the language of sanctification, making it both palatable and recognizable to the women's work. It would also connect COGIC members to broad-based community work and organizing.

When those who chronicle African American religious life speak of community involvement, the role of the church in the civil rights movement is often at the forefront of their discussions. Historically, religion has played an important role in African Americans' ongoing quest for equality. Many times, the story of that quest is cast through a patriarchal lens, but some scholars realize that the bulk of community work in the African American community was done by women. In her works on community and church motherhood, for example, sociologist Cheryl Townsend Gilkes has explicated the roles of women in the civic and religious realms who have worked for the advancement of the race. She argues that COGIC women's community motherhood was filtered through denominational restrictions on ordination and the sharing of power with men in the denomination.[7] COGIC women's participation goes deeper than Gilkes's arguments regarding community motherhood. Beliefs grounded in sanctification were of the utmost importance to COGIC women, so the very alliances they formed were based both on a fictive family relationship and on a shared understanding of what it would mean to transform the world through sanctified living. It was COGIC women themselves who shaped the denomination's engagement with the community, political figures, and the social world through their alliances outside the denomination. Their integration of the sanctified life with civic engagement was an important step in the denomination as it emerged from its storefront, marginalized space into an expanded realm in the 1940s and 1950s.

This new civic engagement, however, was not the engagement of Mother Robinson, who believed it was important for the Saints to keep away from the types of organizations that were most readily available to middle- and lower-class blacks during this period: social clubs and lodges. One of Robinson's more oft-quoted statements is her 1945 admonition "to continue in the faith, to stay out of lodges, and to not engage in politics." Her belief was based in part upon her nineteenth-century focus on racial uplift through respectable homemaking. But perhaps it also originated in her experiences of being followed by the FBI during World War I. Whatever the case, Robinson's policy was to avoid positions and places that reeked of "the world," because she felt "the world" was not a place for a woman to be. The very things she did treasure, however—families, education, and home life—in time became the avenues of COGIC women's civic engagement.

What Robinson could not have foreseen was that it was in home mission work that women she thought were being groomed to be wives, mothers, and sanctified women were finding their broadest power. By the 1941 convocation, the Women's Department had female Saints working within the larger cities of the nation, as well in Haiti and Africa. The work of these women abroad was largely seen as missions work, while the work closer to home, including the running of Saints Industrial, was seen as part of COGIC women's work to spread the message of sanctified living to everyone. But women like Mallory and Coffey were also involved in missions work—a home mission work of education. Their home mission involved not only migrants and poor rural African Americans but also the middle- and upper-class African Americans who participated in sorority life, philanthropic endeavors, and social events. With the onset of World War II, COGIC women leaders also took on the role of "rallying" the denomination for increased participation in a war that was seen not only to support the country but also to bring democracy to the world, for all people. It is in this context that Coffey could say, "I firmly believe that the church should take an active part in the affairs of the government."[8] A desire to work for democratic ideals, and the "prospects" for evangelistic gains, harnessed the attention of the budding COGIC women's hierarchy.

The new relationship to the outside world that formed as a result of Bethune's budding friendship with Mallory went beyond the scope of the educational endeavor. The NCNW, which Bethune founded in 1935, provided another arena in which Mallory and other women that Bethune had befriended could participate. Bethune's foundation of the NCNW grew in part out of her desire to redistribute the power of the black women's club movement away from the elites. The National Association of Colored Women (NACW), for example, had welcomed Bethune as a member, but she feared that the colorism and class barriers within the group would prevent many other black women from joining. For women who were not in the social strata of elite black female philanthropists, including educators and the members of sororities, secret societies, and religious and professional organizations, the NCNW became an umbrella organization.[9] It also provided a venue in which lower-class and upper-class civically active women could participate together in one organization. Bethune noted this in her remarks at the organizational meeting of the NCNW in 1935: "Six years ago I visited a National Baptist convention. There was a large group of reports from crude places, but it showed that they were blazing away for better things. No organization has done a greater job for womanhood than the National Association of Colored Women. The Business and Professional women have made an enviable record, also the Sororities with the high ideals. But for the past seven years I have thought seriously of all National organizations as well as individuals forming a council of Colored Women so that we can make a stronger appeal for putting over big projects."[10]

Bethune saw the NCNW as a coordinating and planning body that would help in the economic, social, educational and cultural welfare of Negro women on local, national, and international levels. Bethune hoped to link black women together, for, as she put it, there was "wasted strength" in "failing to harness the great power of nearly a million women into a force for constructive action."[11] Bethune's emergence as an educator and a point person for African American issues could only help the NCNW to succeed. Bethune's appointment by President Franklin D. Roosevelt as director of the Division of Negro Affairs of the National Youth Administration, a position she occupied from 1936 to 1943, helped to solidify her clout. Moreover, Bethune's friendship with Eleanor Roosevelt would give her tremendous access to and influence with the administration.

Bethune then set about soliciting as many women as possible for NCNW membership. Mallory was a charter member of the organization, and other women's religious leaders such as Nannie Helen Burroughs and Sarah Willie Layten, president of the National Baptist Women's Convention, were also participating in the NCNW. What would also stand out about the NCNW was Bethune's insistence on interracial cooperation. By moving away from the elitist and "colored" moniker to embrace a more encompassing vision of race relations, Bethune, with her White House connections, could ask and expect more from the New Deal administration. The emphasis on interracial cooperation was also attractive to COGIC women, who were used to Mason's appeal to interracial cooperation, despite the racial separateness that was de rigueur in many southern Pentecostal denominations of the day.

The real benefit to Mallory's participation in the NCNW, however, was to pursue social equality, while becoming part of a network of resources that could benefit Saints Industrial School. Because some NCNW concerns (for example, political action) clashed with the sanctified beliefs of Mother Robinson, the COGIC women's involvement in the organization initially remained separate from their duties as church mothers. For instance, Mallory attended a meeting in 1938 of the NCNW in Washington and Mrs. Roosevelt regarding participation of women and children in federal welfare programs, but *The Whole Truth* mentioned only in passing that Mallory traveled to Washington, D.C., to participate in a meeting. What the denominational officials did not realize, however, was that the die had already been cast in terms of Mallory's participation and leadership role in the NCNW because of her commitment to promoting "civic education."

As a charter member of the NCNW, Mallory followed Bethune's lead into another organization that held beliefs compatible to COGIC's: the Moral Re-Armament (MRA) movement, founded by Frank Nathan Daniel Buchman in 1938. Moral Re-Armament was Buchman's response to what he believed to be the corruption of mankind: he wished to use the power of God to change mankind and make a hate-free, fear-free, and greed-free world.[12] Buchman's decision to found Moral Re-Armament was influenced by his time in the Oxford Group, first known as the First Century Christian Fellowship, which focused on triumphing over sin through scripture and Bible studies. Buchman first introduced the concept of Moral Re-Armament in London in May 1938, and by the time it was officially introduced in the United States at Constitution Hall, the movement had gained ground through the MRA's vision of using moral force to win wars and to build a just peace. Buchman's movement attracted the support of prominent political figures and labor leaders, including Mary McLeod Bethune. It was Bethune's connection to MRA that brought in Arenia Mallory, who expressed her support of Moral Re-Armament in a broadcast program on Moral Re-Armament weekend in December 1939. During the broadcast, highlighted in the *New York Times*, Mallory spoke about how Moral Re-Armament helped her in her daily duties.[13]

Mallory's intersection with the MRA highlights a trend that affected the work of COGIC women leaders first and then of the ranks more generally: the relationships to which Bethune introduced Mallory and others in the leadership echelon of COGIC mothers began to affect the Women's Department and the denomination as a whole. Mallory's position in COGIC, though often fraught with controversy, was one in which she acted as the connecter, the liaison between outsiders and COGIC. And the first and most important person to whom she connected in the outside world was Lillian Brooks Coffey.

Though Mallory was making a splash through participation in Bethune's endeavors, she did not leave behind someone who had been of support to her within COGIC: Lillian Coffey. Coffey and Mallory's friendship came about in part because of their shared fund-raising endeavors for the school, but what also bound them together was their status as divorcées within the denomination. Both women had an equal amount of power in some respects: Mallory was the president of Saints, and in 1935 Coffey had been appointed assistant general mother (or supervisor, as the position came to be known) in 1935. For all intents and purposes, Coffey was leading the women for Robinson as she advanced in age, while Mallory was leading the educational endeavors. It was from that platform then, that Mallory's introduction of Coffey to Bethune anticipated the day that Coffey would become the national supervisor of the Women's Department. This was a shrewd move on Mallory's part. Coffey had been resourceful throughout the 1930s in lobbying for more money for Saints Industrial School as a member of the board and as treasurer for the denomination. Bethune took note of Coffey's fund-raising prowess and appointed her to the NCNW's Committee of the Department of Religion. In the letter Bethune wrote to Coffey extending her the invitation, she wrote: "We want you and your women to actively participate in the work of the Council. I hope you will send in your membership for your organization. I need your help. You and your women can do a great deal to help the cause of Negro Womanhood, if you will. . . . Mrs. Coffey, I need your service very much, and I am asking you to bring your women into the National council."[14] Coffey's response was equally gracious: "I was never so happy as when I received the letter from you, stating that you were thinking of me and my women. I read carefully each letter, for I am intensely interested in the work of the council. I admire you as a leader, I think you are grand in your setting, a God given jewel to your people and to all people, rightfully deserving the title Queen of the Negro race. . . . As to my organization I shall put forth strenuous efforts and do all I can to interest them in the work of the council."[15]

These two letters represent the official beginning of the link between the NCNW and the COGIC Women's Department. Bethune was wise in her pursuit of Coffey and the women of COGIC, knowing that a woman whose leadership had been proven in church circles would prove useful in fund-raising and other endeavors of the NCNW regarding race relations, education, and civic service.

Almost immediately, Coffey began fund-raising for the council. In the letter thanking Bethune for the invitation to join the Religion Committee, she noted that she had not given a tea, as Bethune had previously requested, but used "another method" that in a few days "would remit a nice sum for the cause."[16] Coffey quickly rose through the ranks of the NCNW, becoming chairman of the Office Supply Committee and then chairman of finance by 1944. Around this same time, Mallory was appointed director of the NCNW's Region IV, which encompassed Mississippi, Louisiana, Arkansas, and Tennessee; she held this position for eight years. Within the space of a few years, two prominent COGIC women had become lynchpin members of the NCNW. Bethune had come to rely on both Mallory and Coffey for their fund-raising abilities.

Yet Bethune provided much more to both women. The new access to women's work and other alliances outside of COGIC began to affect the ways in which Mallory and Coffey pursued a broader profile from within and without the denomination. Mallory, accustomed to canvassing the country for money for the school, began corresponding with Claude Barnett, founder and editor of the Associated Negro Press, and placing promotional materials about Saints Industrial School in newspapers.[17] Coverage of her NCNW activities and her work at Saints Industrial appeared in black newspapers such as the *Chicago Defender* and the *Memphis World*. Her promotional work paid off, as she was selected twice, once in 1940 and again in 1945, as one of the outstanding women in America by the NCNW.[18] Her friendship with Coffey also afforded her some measure of clout within the denomination. Fewer questions were being asked during this time about the school's finances, and Mallory managed to raise funds through Ida Jackson for a library to be built on campus to house the minutes of the denominational meetings.

Coffey was equally busy, but her energies were focused upon the Women's Department's affairs, namely, foreign missions work and particularly the care of aged missionaries. Perhaps it was Mother Robinson's advanced age and limited mobility that spurred Coffey to begin to think of the aged women of the denomination and other churches. Coffey's vision, as she described it, was to find a home for COGIC missionaries and superannuated Christian workers. Mother Robinson was not one of these women, since, after he husband died in the 1930s, her daughter, Ida Baker, was able to care for her. But many women were not so lucky. Migration continued to disconnect families, and aged woman could not continue to count on the traditional networks of care. Furthermore,

Lillian Brooks Coffey, supervisor of the Women's Department.
Courtesy Glenda Goodson Collection, the Center for African American
Church History and Research, Lancaster, Texas.

the missionaries of COGIC and other churches were not awarded retirement
funds, and many had to enter public or governmental charitable institutions.
Coffey may also have considered creating the home due to her own compro-
mised health. After suffering a serious heart problem in 1939, her infirmities had
hampered her normally busy schedule, and she regained her strength only very
slowly. What better way, then, to both insure the care of the women of the denomination and create a place worthy of her position in which she might reside
in her old age?

In 1943, Coffey obtained permission from the COGIC Board of Bishops to
find a suitable home to use as a rest home for Christian missionaries inside and
outside of COGIC.[19] Not content to use just any house, in 1944 Coffey purchased a house in the exclusive Arden Park section of Detroit for $30,000. The
opulence of Arden Park attracted other religious types during this time: the
flamboyant Pentecostal preacher Prophet Jones also purchased a house in the

Arden Park area, now listed in the National Register of Historic Places.[20] Coffey's dream for the home was to make it available to "women who have made an outstanding contribution to humanity and religion regardless of race color and creed."[21] Coffey's foresight in purchasing the house was evidence not only of her generosity of spirit but also of her reaching out to form alliances with different people and organizations for the betterment of the Women's Department and the condition of women as a whole.

The house itself was a showpiece for COGIC. Containing three floors of living space, plus a basement housing the kitchen and offices, the home was equipped with every modern convenience. It was described in *The Whole Truth* in May of 1945 in glowing, flowery terms: "Just a step and you are in the dining room with all of its finery and admiration. The built in Library just across the hall, with its antique fireplace and imported bookcases, was the educators dream. The drawing room with its mahogany space interior place with its fleur-de-lis angle irons, was a room of quietness for the aristocracy who once lived in the house."[22]

The house spoke to a new determination of COGIC women's leadership, and later its members, to take their place among African Americans of the middle and upper classes. COGIC women on the East Coast had several retirement homes for mothers, such as the Susie Cypress Home for the Aged, but the opulence of the Arden Park home suggested that the residence would serve as a symbol of the growing status of the Women's Department.[23] Coffey could have purchased a less lavish house to serve the needs of the missionaries, but Arden Park was to be the showplace residence for Coffey's leadership as second-in-command to Mother Robinson, and it could be used for entertaining visitors, who were becoming more prominent with each passing year. The purchase of the Arden Park home also signaled a new commitment on the part of the Women's Department to have a building to complement the new Mason Temple in Memphis, which was going up during this same period.

Perhaps, then, the beginning of World War II was the final catalyst in cementing the role of civic engagement for COGIC women. Up to this point, civic engagement had come about through educational endeavors. The war presented new challenges for women and men in COGIC leadership. Old beliefs about pacifism were challenged by the threat from both the Japanese and the Germans. The promises of the benefits of wartime participation for African Americans despite the racist conditions of the armed forces drew both men and women to the ranks. The claim of Hitler and the Nazi Party that Aryans were the master race was another catalyst in African Americans' quest for civil rights. Those who signed up for the war went not only to support the nation but in the hope that their service would stand as a testament to their love of country and their right to be treated as equals.

For COGIC members, the stakes were even higher, affecting their identities both as Americans and as sanctified people. Letters from soldiers and COGIC leaders written during the war highlight the tensions between COGIC beliefs regarding war and killing and the desire of church members to be a part of defending the American way and democracy. One, written from "Somewhere in France," spoke of the temptations and trials of the war: "When I went in to the army, I did anything my superiors asked me to that would help my country, and did not compromise what I believe. I thank God for bringing me out. Army life has not been a flowery bed of ease." Samuel Crouch, a COGIC bishop in Los Angeles, corresponded frequently with the COGIC magazine *Christian Hope*. In December 1943, he wrote: "So many are blinded and deceived with jealousy and hatred. Crooked politicians, in the world and in the church, and other things too numerous to mention here, are the factors that have brought on this global conflict. Let there be no strife between thee and me, because we are brethren. There is no supreme race!!" Other COGIC soldiers were very clear about their role in supporting democratic principles. One soldier wrote, for example, "Our victory must bring in its train the liberation of all peoples. Discrimination between peoples because of their race creed or color must be abolished. The age of imperialism has ended."[24]

For some in COGIC, the war was a decisive battle in which the very definition of their humanity was threatened. Perhaps this is why COGIC members began to change their ideas about living the sanctified life and about the identity of sanctified women and men. The war provided a prime opportunity for church members to prove their patriotism and to assert the humanity of African Americans, who were still being treated as second-class citizens, particularly in the South.

While men wrote about their struggles with the war, the women of COGIC rallied to assist the war effort, showing their allegiance to the nation and the cause. Mallory and Coffey both joined the Women's Army for National Defense (WANDS). Founded, with the assistance of Bethune, in November 1942 by Lavonia Brown of Chicago, WANDS was designed for women to assist in war activities, such as providing basic personal supplies to African American servicemen and servicewomen and mounting a civil defense.[25] The WANDS promotional brochures explained that the group's purpose was to call attention to the great need for women's participation in the war effort. Phrases like "maintaining the freedom of the nation and working for a decisive victory" were in much of the WANDS promotional literature, and women were required upon signing up to say the Pledge of Allegiance and to sing the national anthem. These simple acts inculcated a sense of patriotism and of civic duty in the women.

The organizational structure of WANDS was modeled on the armed services, with Bethune serving as general alongside captains, first lieutenants, second lieutenants, chaplains, sergeants, and corporals. Participation was based on traditional principles of democracy and service. And, much like the NCNW, WANDS was organized by black women but open to women of all races. The constitution and the by-laws of the WANDS stressed the importance of fostering democracy home and abroad, preparing women for war work, promoting educational programs about defense preparation, "engender[ing] a united effort toward American victory, and [maintaining] the democratic freedom of the nation."[26] Mallory served as a colonel in the WANDS, traveling throughout the country and opening new chapters for Bethune, as this passage from the *Michigan Chronicle* reported: "Colonel Arenia C. Mallory of the Women's Army for National Defense was in Detroit Sunday Jan 13, and organized a chapter of the WANDS in this city. The chapter was named after Col Mallory who is one of the outstanding leading Negro women. Col. Mallory is President of the Saint's industrial School in Lexington, Miss. . . . All the activities and duties of the organization are voluntary by officers and cadets."[27]

While Mallory organized and served with the WANDS units, Coffey traveled to bases and training centers to speak on behalf of the Women's Department and COGIC. WANDS chapters in various cities were named after famous African American women, such as Lena Horne and Harriet Tubman, and uniforms were commissioned and sold at the price of $20.00 each from David Chapman's Ladies Clothing in Chicago. The uniforms were designed to draw attention to the WANDS. In a letter to Coffey, Bethune remarked on this briefly: "We have commissioned you as a Major so that you can get the right emphasis, both in appearance and representation."[28] The uniforms were an important way to remind outsiders of the war effort and of the authority of these women who had devoted themselves to supporting the armed forces. Organizational meetings raised money for the war effort, provided canteen materials to black soldiers, and assisted with housing for soldiers' families.

The Second World War proved to be a powerful motivator for Coffey and Mallory, as well as the women who saw them dressed as colonels and majors, to participate in civic affairs. The uniforms may have been feminized, but the authoritarian demeanor of the women who wore them signaled the birth of a different kind of COGIC woman: strong and assertive, not simply "motherly." Their participation in all-women's meetings structured around procuring materials for soldiers and discussing national defense, wartime protocol, and civic duty began to shift the Women's Department's emphasis away from the home and the church as the locus of women's engagement.

COGIC women's involvement with the NCNW, Moral Re-Armament, and the WANDS challenged the very core of what sanctification meant in COGIC. No more could COGIC women or men stand apart from the world's events, simply praying for leaders without taking an active stance. Coffey and Mallory's participation outside of the denomination was beginning to restructure COGIC members' self-definition and identity. Assisting the war effort was a far cry from Mason's protest against the First World War, but the stakes for African Americans had been raised. After the war, Samuel Crouch published his assessment of the war effort in the November 1945 issue of the *Christian Hope*: "The world is war-torn, many dead and many will die, because of deprivation and lack of food. War is sin, and the wages of sin is death. Billions of dollars spent for the prosecution of war, millions of homes lay in ruin, cities devastated, lives sacrificed, some things can never be replaced. The world has been effected socially, spiritually and morally. . . . The only hope is to pray for a world's revival, the whole nation needs a new birth."[29] Crouch may have considered the war a sin, but one principle true to sanctification remained in his comments: the world needed a revival. In this way, the evangelistic thrust of sanctification was redirected in the postwar Church of God in Christ for both men and women: now was not the time to detach from the world, the Saints began to argue, but rather the time to engage it. Investing in the war and the democratic process through evangelism proved that COGIC's future was inextricably tied to the freedoms of peoples around the world. The earlier emphasis on sanctification solely for the purpose of cleansing oneself before God and belonging to the COGIC community was beginning to shift into a broader focus, a focus that would alter COGIC women's goals from promoting self-sanctification to taking the message of sanctification into the world. The platform from which that message would be launched was the newly built Mason Temple.

The 1945 Convocation

During the war, COGIC launched a large building campaign to complete a new meeting place, to be named Mason Temple. A fire in 1937 had consumed the previous building, and the yearly convocation was growing so rapidly that convocation services had to be scheduled in shifts to accommodate all the Saints. Bishop Mason wanted the denomination to have a place that would be its centerpiece. Steel was difficult to come by and expensive during the war, but through the ministrations and lobbying of several COGIC members, including a prominent white member, Reverend Delk, the church managed to acquire enough materials to build the temple. The Women's Department also helped by encouraging its mothers and daughters to raise funds for the construction. The building was completed in time for the 1945 convocation, which marked the jubilee anniversary of Bishop Mason's first year in ministry.

The opening of the convocation in November 1945 was a festive occasion. The new temple was practically complete, and even the white newspaper in Memphis, the *Commercial Appeal*, featured an article about its opening: "Described by Elder C. Range of Boston, Mass. as 'the largest convention hall owned by any Negro church group in America,' a massive brick, stone, concrete and steel structure at 958 South Fifth Street has been dedicated as international headquarters of the Church of God in Christ. Named Mason Temple in honor of the founder, Bishop C. H. Mason, the dedicatory service was a feature of the 38th National convocation of the denomination. It coincided with bishop Mason's 50th anniversary in the ministry."[30]

The article perhaps did not do justice to the impressive structure or to that fact that it had been built through the sacrifices of the women and men of COGIC. Built at a cost of $275,679 and funded by member donations, it measured 29,672 square feet. Gone were the days when Mother Robinson would have to call for bedding and blankets to be brought from home to the convocation. A new dormitory, office, and hospital, as well as a cafeteria for the Saints, had been built into the temple to accommodate the convocation and other meetings throughout the year. All parts of the building were connected with a public address system, so that at any time, anywhere in the building, a person could hear the convocation proceedings.[31]

For Mother Robinson, it was a glimpse into a future that she would not share with the denomination. Robinson came to Memphis ill. She had battled several ailments through the years, and at eighty-five, it was difficult for her to get around. Having suffered several strokes she spoke slowly. The distance via train from Omaha, Nebraska, to Memphis was long and had taken its toll on her. She arrived at the convocation tired but satisfied. Out in front of the temple burned a neon sign reading, "Church of God in Christ, National Headquarters."[32] It was literally a sign of her hard work in raising funds, for her daughter had set up a fund specifically for the purchase of a sign for the new temple. The mothers did not raise enough to pay for the $1,600 neon sign, so Mother Robinson provided the remainder herself.[33]

A document recording the history of the Women's Department described her arrival at the temple in poignant terms:

> She was greatly interested in the building of our National Headquarters, and with her very efficient daughter as her secretary, She kept her national drives functioning until she knew the building was ready for dedication. She journeyed southward to the 1945 Convocation; she felt that her days were numbered and that she would not return home. After reaching Memphis, she took new strength, walked through the building, looked at the work of her hands, sat in the assembly hall, which bears her name, held conference with her State mothers, revised her constitution, examined every phase of it for soundness, sat by her windows, saw the large electrical sign, allocated the balance of the funds needed to make possible its purchase.[34]

The account, written after Mother Robinson's death, has a breathless quality about it, as though in her advanced age she could still move with the adroitness of her youth. The temple must have seemed to Mother Robinson proof of God's favor of the sanctified life she had helped both men and women to lead. At the same time, it symbolized a future that she would not share and that would change with her passing.

The history of the Women's Department recalls Robinson's last message to the women at the 1945 convention: "Mother Robinson ably admonished her daughters on the Women's Day of the Convocation to continue in the faith, to stay out of lodges, and to not engage in politics. She turned to her daughter, Lillian Brooks Coffey, who she had trained from girlhood and who later became assistant, to courageously lead the women in the fear of the Lord, to stick to the Bible, not to depart from the Law of the Lord."[35] Robinson's definition of Holiness called for the faithful to remove themselves from worldly pursuits such as politics. Sanctified men and women had no place in the temporal affairs of the day, she felt, but should keep their minds fixed on spiritual matters. This perspective was Mother Robinson's reality, and she saw it as a means of protecting those in the church from straying from Holiness. Robinson's admoni-

Lizzie Robinson. Courtesy Glenda Goodson Collection, the Center for African American Church History and Research, Lancaster, Texas.

tions were consistent with the nineteenth-century definition of Holiness and the twentieth-century Pentecostal conception of how to live a sanctified life. Her stance had not changed because of the times. She expected her daughters to do as she had done.

After the evening service on December 12, 1945, Mother Robinson went to bed in her suite in the dormitory named after her. At 2:20 A.M., she died of sudden cardiac failure at the age of eighty-five.[36] Years of service, travel, and sacrifice had finally caught up to her. Her death, though it was not unexpected, was a blow to her daughter and the convocation. In the two days left before the convocation's close, the church needed to hold a "home going service" for Mother Robinson and to install Coffey as the new general mother and national supervisor of the women's work. Preparations were made quickly, and on the last day of the convocation, the service was held for Mother Robinson. The Associated Negro Press carried an article about Mother Robinson's passing:

Mother Lizzie Woods Robinson, national supervisor of the Woman's Department, Church of God in Christ Inc., who ranked with Elder Mason, senior bishop[,] in the esteem in which she was held by thousands of followers throughout the country, died Wednesday morning just two days before the official closing of the 1945 Holy convocation. . . . Through her ability to organize inspire and direct, Mother Robinson left to the church a rich heritage of 20,000 missionaries, 100,000 laymen, and numerous divisions to the women's department. She remained clear minded throughout her 80 years of service.[37]

Mother Robinson's legacy of service to the Women's Department was evident at her memorial service at the temple. Her funeral, the ending service of the convocation, was packed, and the mourners included Mary McLeod Bethune. With Coffey presiding over the service, the eulogy was delivered by an ailing Bishop Mason. To close, Coffey was installed as the second general mother of COGIC. She wore a white habit and a full-length pleated gown with a cross around her neck that was placed there by two state mothers and two bishops.[38] The transfer of power complete, Mother Robinson's body was shipped via train back to Omaha, Nebraska, for final rites and burial.

Robinson's death was, perhaps, the capstone of the inauguration of the new Mason Temple. Robinson embodied the legacy of nineteenth-century women's work, Holiness, and the move to Pentecostalism. She had remained true in her teachings to what Joanna Moore, who had long since passed away, had taught her, and, more importantly, she had set the tone of what sanctification meant for COGIC, including the resistance of modernity. By blending the principles of motherhood, homemaking, and cleanliness into a doctrine of sanctification, Robinson had influenced the temporal and spiritual lives of black women who were at the margins of American society and COGIC, organizing them through the office most revered by the black community: motherhood. By placing church mothers in a position of authority, she was able at once to influence and direct the course of the denomination as it was transformed from merely a sanctified church to a large woman's organization that conveyed and embodied the message of Holiness. In her thirty-three years of service, she managed to accomplish an amazing feat of organization with little formal education, funds, or assistance. She was a pioneer in every sense of the word. Even if she died trying to hold on to a world that was rapidly passing by, she had laid the foundation for those women who had never been in slavery to move COGIC forward. Her death signaled a fundamental change in the post-Reconstruction leadership roles of black women.

Now, at Robinson's bier, the transfer of COGIC's foundations to a younger generation was complete. Rapid changes in American life and in African American life in particular were encroaching upon the women of COGIC in profound ways. Coffey, as the new, modern church mother, would lead her women into the 1950s. The cover of the Women's Department newsletter, *Lifted Banners*, from 1949 suggested what direction she would take. Depicting the American flag and the Christian flag entwined together, it suggested that religion, nation, and civic engagement would combine for COGIC women in the 1950s, so that their identities as sanctified women became firmly entrenched not just in self-sanctification but in the sanctification of the entire world. Coffey would be the catalyst for that change, but it would have far-reaching effects on the lives of other COGIC women as well.

The turn to greater civic engagement for COGIC women is linked to their beliefs about what sanctified life meant and the influences from the organizations with which they had relationships or interactions, namely the NCNW. The ideas about democracy and civic life encompassed both social reforms and a religious orientation that ascribed an equality for all racial groups. The stress on interracial cooperation was tantamount to COGIC ideals, and it framed the manner in which the Woman's Department worked for civil rights in the 1950s and 1960s. The work of the women of COGIC, then, would reach its zenith both in promoting home, family, and country and in increasing their social and economic status by taking the church to a new level of prominence both in African American circles and on the worldwide stage.

Conventions

Folks are beginning to take the "Saints" more seriously.
D'Natural, in *Memphis Tri-State Defender*

Mother Robinson's death continued to reverberate throughout the COGIC community as Mother Coffey took over as the national supervisor. COGIC newspapers *The Whole Truth* and *Lifted Banners* printed many accolades and remembrances of Robinson, but they signaled an uneasy awareness of the uncertainty about the changes that were about to come to COGIC women. "Under her direction as the spiritual leader, under her guidance and inspiration as a molder of women, local missionaries have risen to every opportunity and shared with her in the extraordinary growth of the church," lauded one *Whole Truth* article. Individuals shared their own observations: "How are the mighty fallen in the midst of battle! Mother Lizzie Robinson life and teaching shall ever live in my memory, and be a source of inspiration to higher saintly ideals," chimed Mother Anne Bailey, national finance secretary of the women's work.[1] It was as though her memory would be looked upon as the arbiter still of all things sanctified, holy, and true. Robinson was the benchmark of a sanctified woman.

Yet another vision of sanctified womanhood was visible outside of the denomination. For a number of years, news of COGIC women like Arenia Mallory and Lillian Coffey had been appearing on a regular basis in newspapers such as the *Chicago Defender*, the *California Eagle*, and on wire services from the Associated Negro Press. Most of the articles were about their work with the National Council of Negro Women (NCNW), or the events such as teas or socials for fund-raising at Saints School. In the 1940s, however, their work with the WANDS, the start of the Lillian Brooks Coffey rest home, and social events had begun to garner the notice of the society pages in black newspapers. By the time that the D'Natural column in the *Memphis Tri-State Defender* declared in 1951 that "folks were starting to take the 'Saints' more seriously," a quiet transformation had taken place that would redefine the meaning of living the sanctified life for the majority of COGIC women.[2]

The transformation of the women's work came through an intersection of alliances and civic engagement that first occurred among COGIC women leaders. Mallory's and Coffey's participation in the NCNW had opened up the doors of women's civic engagement to COGIC women who had previously been involved only in COGIC activities. The wives of prominent bishops and pastors within the denomination had become NCNW members through Coffey's instigation, and the change in women's work leadership also signaled an important change in how sanctified living would be regarded. To help to bring about change, it was important that not just the prominent women in COGIC embraced these ideals and changes; local church mothers would prove to be an invaluable resource in negotiating this engagement. In order to bring COGIC women into this "new world," the social and political realities of class, coupled with a quest for civil rights, would have to be articulated through a language that women could understand: sanctification. Being a sanctified woman then, would have to be reconfigured from a woman who was dressed as becometh holiness, with little interest in political activity, to a smartly dressed, well coiffed and well versed church mother with a vocabulary steeped in scripture yet attuned to social realities on earth, rather than heaven. Instead of standing on the street corners to find converts, the new converts to COGIC would come through the engagement of the church mothers with the world in social and civic arenas. The first order of business for COGIC leadership was to take on the spotlight; sometimes this occurred intentionally, and other times, it happened accidentally.

Class, Status, and the Media

The changes that would occur after Mother Robinson's death came from Mallory's and Coffey's years of cultivating relationships both inside and outside of COGIC. Mallory's relationship with Mary McLeod Bethune was the most obvious and influential, but Mallory would have other avenues to advertise her work in the denomination. One such opportunity involved her brother. As noted previously, Mallory came from a prominent vaudeville family, and in the 1930s, Mallory's brothers Eddie and Frank would provide notoriety for Mallory and COGIC.

Frank Mallory had just received his commercial pilot's license. On July 17, 1936, he, his sister Arenia, and William Roberts, son of COGIC elder W. M. Roberts, were at the Harlem airstrip in Oaklawn, Illinois, to enjoy a ride on the plane of a noted young black physician, Dr. Earl Renfroe. Mallory, deciding to wait her turn, allowed Roberts to fly first in the small biplane. Mallory watched in horror as the plane rose then suddenly plummet to the ground. Both her brother and Roberts were taken to the hospital, but they died shortly thereafter. The news of the crash was on the front page of the *Chicago Defender* on July 18, 1936, featuring a photograph of Mallory's brother and a large picture of Mallory, with the headline "Sees Crash." In its coverage of both the crash and the funeral for the two men the *Defender*, did not mention Mallory's position at Saints Industrial School but instead keyed in on her brother Eddie, who at the time was a successful musician who happened to be married to the famous singer and actress Ethel Waters. The funeral was held at Roberts Temple COGIC, and William Roberts preached his son's funeral. Coverage in the *Defender* included a poignant picture of the two coffins being carried out of Roberts Temple and condolences extended to Mallory's family.

On one hand, the story of the crash is newsworthy. The downing of a plane piloted by a black man in 1935 is certainly unusual. Mallory's class status afforded to her by her brother and famous sister-in-law set her in a different category than the church mothers of the storefronts. Mallory's and her brothers access to black middle- and upper-class society afforded them a place that most of the COGIC Saints could not hope to hold in 1935. Because of this, Mallory owned a house on Martha's Vineyard in the late 1930s and was able to call upon Ethel Waters to help with for fund-raising for Saints Industrial School. These familial connections not only opened doors for her, but also marked the decade of the 1930s as the beginning of a shift in COGIC from otherworldliness to the embrace of modernity and media. It also highlighted the presence of an elite group of COGIC members who either by birth or by social position had attained status in the broader African American society. For a Pentecostal church like COGIC, it would be these members and their pursuit of social and public recognition that would help to eventually transform COGIC from a poor storefront church into a middle- and upper-middle-class, upwardly mobile, and educated church.

COGIC members would begin to seek out the black news outlets to promote church social events and the yearly denominational convocation. Mallory's influence as an educator, and her ability to bring Coffey and other women to events that were covered in the black newspapers, began to pull like-minded progressives into a COGIC elite. A group of important male and female leaders comprised the inner circle of COGIC leadership. Bishops William Roberts and Elder Louis Ford, in Chicago, Mallory at Saints School, and Bishop Samuel Crouch in Los Angeles all were friends of Coffey and had contacts outside the church in the political and social worlds of both African Americans and whites.[3] Coffey, having served as treasurer of the denomination and moved up the women's work ranks, had made contacts with many of the male COGIC leaders across the country and had garnered their respect. Mallory's familial and educational connections coupled with Coffey's denominational status made for a formidable team of women whose ambition in fund-raising and promotion could not be matched. Both women's reach into the religious and social circles was deep and firm.

Coffey had a strong relationship to the COGIC churches in Chicago in part because of her pioneering church planting work there. Roberts, a friend of both Mallory and Coffey, had made it his business to court the elite African American population in Chicago and the Midwest. Another Chicago pastor, Louis Ford, who would be elevated to bishop, was an avid golfer and hobnobbed with the likes of Joe Louis and other black celebrities. Photos of these "connectors" and coverage of their fund-raising events and socials began to appear in black newspapers in Chicago, Detroit, Philadelphia, and Los Angeles. The new visibility highlighted the denomination's growth and began to paint a picture of COGIC that differed dramatically from the one of Mother Robinson's era.

The radio was another means in which COGIC ethos flowed out into the city. COGIC songs and preaching were promoted on record labels like Okeh Records, and COGIC musical artists such as Rosetta Tharpe, F. W. McGee, and Arizona Dranes attracted listeners and worshipers alike to the COGIC sanctified sound.[4] Both radio and increased newspaper coverage were raising COGIC's profile, and the time was ripe for Coffey to use these means of exposure to expand the Women's Department, and even Bethune began to pay more attention to COGIC as a formidable force in shaping African American public policy.

Bethune, realizing the value of the COGIC women to the NCNW, offered Coffey the position of chairman of associates and annual membership soon after her appointment to head the women's work. Coffey was torn between her work for the NCNW and her responsibilities to lead 150,000 COGIC women. That number in and of itself pointed to the tremendous power and authority she wielded over the denomination. Accurate membership figures for the denomination are not readily available, but even if Coffey oversaw 20 percent fewer women, she would have still led more women than belonged to the NCNW, which placed her among the top women leaders the United States.

With the death of Mother Robinson, Coffey had swiftly become a woman to be reckoned with. Coffey knew, however, that she would need all of her energies to deal with the Women's Department. Coffey expressed her concerns about taking further responsibilities within the NCNW to Bethune: "We lost our General supervisor of the Women's Work during this meeting, the one to whom I have been assistant. We had her funeral on the last day of the convocation. The officials then felt to confer the honor of General Supervisor upon me, thus, I now have one hundred and fifty thousand women in organized groups under my supervision. It is with that responsibility in mind that the thought occurs to me that I am unable to take the position you have offered me in spite of my willingness to do so."[5] With her decline to take the NCNW, Coffey extended an invitation to Bethune to speak at the fall 1946 convocation, which Bethune accepted. With the letter acknowledging that Bethune had accepted her invitation, Coffey also sent dues and a list of women purchasing lifetime memberships in the NCNW, including prominent COGIC women such as Carrie Cantrell and J. V. Hearne.[6] With Coffey's ascension to national supervisor, Bethune could tap into the women of COGIC to fill her rolls. Meanwhile, Coffey could tap into Bethune's power to bolster her position in COGIC. What Bethune had provided Coffey was the inspiration to marry sanctification and modernity into a new phase of growth for COGIC women. Coffey even took members of the COGIC women's work to the 1948 NCNW convention, stopping to pose for pictures in front of the White house.

Coffey's NCNW connection was in large part the catalyst for change. The link between the women of COGIC and the clubwomen was one that would fundamentally bring the class structures of the middle- and upper-class African Americans into COGIC. Coffey, at one time a struggling hotel worker, now had homes not only in Chicago and Arden Park but also on Martha's Vineyard.[7] This upscale style of living and her fund-raising for the NCNW had put Coffey into a totally different social stratum. Her sanctified connections, however, did not disappear with all of the upward mobility, and Coffey would eventually bring the socialite life of the NCNW to COGIC women.

NCNW women in front of the White House. Left to right: Ruth Scott, Bertie Demk, Ellen Dailey, Arenia Mallory, Mrs. Perry, Lillian Brooks Coffey, and Elsie Mason. Courtesy Mary McLeod Bethune Council House National Historic Site.

Shifting demographics of the Women's Department also brought change. A larger contingent of younger women in COGIC due to marriage and converts were populating the urban areas. Many were still engaged in domestic work, but many were also working out of the home as beauticians, educators, office workers, and the like. The entire denomination as a result was undergoing a class overhaul; the composition of membership roles ranged from rural farmers and migrants to urban dwellers, many of whom were educated and held jobs that were not only in the domestic sphere or restricted to manual labor. All of the changes signaled a new era in COGIC, an era in which the world was to be embraced and evangelized.

In order to accommodate the changes happening within and without the women's work, Coffey decided to do what she did best: organize. To increase participation in the women's work, Coffey added auxiliaries that would give women more opportunities for leadership and visibility. Church mothers, traditionally older women over the age of fifty, did not represent the larger population of COGIC women. It was crucial, then, that the women's work embrace the younger generation of women within the denomination. By organizing women already in the COGIC ranks into groups, such as ministers wives, hospitality groups, missionaries, and ushers, Coffey ingeniously figured out a way both to increase participation and to raise the status of women in the denomination. By the early 1950s the following groups had been added to the women's work: Young Women's Christian Council, Huldah Club, Volunteer Counselors, Missionaries, Hospitality Group, Ushers Unit, Editor's and Publisher's unit, Religious Education Club, Ministers' Wives Circle, Bishops' Wives Circle, Stewardess Board, Church Mothers' Unit, National Evangelists Unit, and Secretaries Unit.

These new auxiliaries, modeled after those in the NCNW, would allow all women, no matter their age, to take part. Rather than relying on the advanced age of church mothers, Coffey shifted the focus to the potential for leadership at all age levels. The auxiliaries brought the women's work into the 1950s by focusing on the broader concerns of women in the postwar era: professionalization, education, and civic engagement. But they also continued to focus on women's traditional concerns: homemaking, child rearing, and hospitality. This dual focus enabled COGIC women of all ages and classes to participate in the new structure. The fact that the women's work took on the name the Women's Department during this period also indicates that the women of COGIC were not just engaging in work that was ancillary to the leadership of the men; they actually stood apart and on their own.

The auxiliaries were grouped into four different areas of responsibility that reflected both the traditional core of women's work the concerns of the modern world and urban space: service, hospitality, administration, and clerical spousal auxiliary organizations such as the Bishops' Wives Circle. Women were able to gain leadership positions, but at the same time, another layer of hierarchy was being created. As a result of the increased number of auxiliaries, women had more opportunities for leadership—but the additional layers of bureaucracy within the new auxiliaries meant that there were more midlevel leadership positions and a longer trajectory to rise through the ranks of the Women's Department. The additional layers of leadership also began to establish a different style of modeling sanctification through dress for COGIC women. Clothing suggesting leadership status, like smartly tailored suits rather than the plain dress of holiness in Robinson's day, became an important way to set oneself apart from the women in the pews. With this change in dress, suggestions of status and wealth beyond women's normal reach also began to creep into the discourse of women's publications.

With all of the new auxiliary activity, it was important to promote COGIC women's events. Mallory was already working with Claude Barnett of the Associated Negro Press to promote the Saints School, so Coffey used that connection to promote Women's Department events as well. In addition, Coffey established an auxiliary to handle both the publicity for and the publications of the Women's Department. In this way, she could control the way in which COGIC women were portrayed. At times, however, it seemed that the push for publicity taxed the resources of the Women's Department. Now and again, letters from Claude Barnett about a bill in arrears would appear addressed to Coffey, and she would always hastily send in the funds, along with a profuse apology.[8]

In spite of these problems, the editor's and publisher's unit for the women was an important link to the outside world. Internal issues of the denomination regarding who would run the publishing house and print the denominational newspaper, *The Whole Truth*, threatened to stymie the women's work, due to lack of coverage. Since no formal publishing board existed from the denomination, various individuals of the church published *The Whole Truth*, as well as COGIC Sunday school materials, independently. With the rapid grown of the church, it became clear that in order to ensure that COGIC beliefs and news were properly represented, and that revenues from the published works would be reinvested into the church, a formal publishing board would need to be established. In November 1948, resolutions were put forth outlining that need and suggesting that the printing be done in Memphis, rather than at the printing house in Kansas City under the supervision of an Elder H. C. Young. While the discussions took place, the Women's Department began printing a newsletter called *Lifted Banners*. Published in New Orleans by one of the Women's Department members, it provided Bible studies, helpful homemaking tips, and messages from the general mother. In addition, the newspaper *The Evangelist Speaks* was established to chronicle COGIC women's missionary activity at home and abroad. Both papers soon began to highlight the Women's Department's shift in direction. *Lifted Banners* perhaps was the best gauge of the department's evangelistic service coupled with civic duty. The cover of a 1949 issue of, for example, featured both the Christian flag and the American flag. Inside, Lillian Coffey's letter to the women focused on the home in Arden Park that was purchased by the Women's Department. "It is wonderful," she wrote, "to sit here and look out on the beautiful surrounding buildings, on the well-kept lawns, the beautiful shrubbery and flowers . . . then the thought comes to me that God in His goodness has granted us the Home that was built for the richest of the rich. It is a confirmation of His word that some should build houses and others should occupy them. Thank God that we, the women of God were the OTHERS to occupy this beautiful mansion at 154 Arden Park."9

Coffey's emphasis on how "some build houses and other should occupy them" is an interesting theological shift for Coffey. Perhaps remembering the privation she experienced when she first moved to Chicago and Detroit, the rise from rural Tennessee to a mansion in Arden Park must have seemed surreal. One cannot make the claim that Coffey understood "otherness" as it is understood today, but it is clear that a house of this magnitude was not the norm for most COGIC women. In the same issue of *Lifted Banners*, the Four Corners column, which was a listing of the Women's Department social events around the country, mentioned the fact that Mother McGlothen from California met Coffey on a trip out to California in "her brand new 1949 Fleetwood Cadillac." Both Coffey's remarks about her Arden Park home and this detail about the car point to how COGIC women's concerns were shifting toward God's material blessings. Material possessions were important not in and of themselves but because they were symbols of God's favor and of sanctified living. The mention of these types of details concerning cars and homes denotes the very perceptible shifting markers and priorities of what "sanctified life" was beginning to mean in the post–World War II era for COGIC women. One large marker of sanctified life, dress, was undergoing a change under Coffey's direction.

In addition to the move toward acquiring markers of wealth, Coffey slowly began to change how COGIC women dressed, by incrementally changing the ways in which COGIC women thought about their roles within and outside of the church. The new auxiliaries provided more opportunities for formal dress, and this began to translate into a different self-presentation for COGIC women. Under Mother Robinson, women were required to dress based on traditional Victorian values and the holiness ethos of moderation and piety. When Coffey assumed leadership of the Women's Department, COGIC women were still following this code. Coffey and Mallory, meanwhile, had both "church clothes" and street clothes. NCNW events, in particular, required proper attire: form-fitting suits, short skirts, and fashionable shoes. Plain dress was not the symbol of holiness anymore, but the symbol of backward living. Coffey set out to model what a "modern" sanctified woman looked like.

At Mother Robinson's funeral, Coffey wore a long white gown, with a simple cross around her neck. Soon after her installment, however, Coffey inaugurated her changes. She contracted with a woman's foundation maker to sell bras, girdles, and slips to the Women's Department members, hoping to help the women "smooth themselves out."[10] Hosiery was sold as well, in white and skin-tone colors. Coffey also straightened her hair, which was another direct violation of Mother Robinson's unwritten rules about appearance, and she even managed to convince Bishop Mason to allow her to wear a slightly opened–toe shoe because of her corn problems.[11] Pictures of Coffey smartly dressed in suits appeared in the denominational news on a regular basis, and she began to set the style trend because of her high-ranking position and visibility. The new revealing of the body for COGIC women could also be interpreted as a restatement of sexual boundaries. The new attire that Coffey encouraged clearly showed more of the shapeliness of a woman, and the binding effects of the girdles and undergarments called attention to the feminine form. Women in COGIC were able to accentuate themselves and appear more attractive without violating the denominational standards. This also allowed for those women who chafed against the dress code to move closer to the new standard of holiness being set by Coffey.

Traditional COGIC concerns were not totally abandoned, however. One of the major areas of Coffey's attention was the missionary activities of COGIC women. In Robinson's day, the focus was primarily on missions and evangelistic work in rural and urban areas of the United States. Coffey, however, was keenly interested in missions work in Africa and Haiti. One such mission was the Light Burners of Africa, a fund-raising organization established to provide electricity for the missions station and schools. The Home and Foreign Missions Board was under the Women's Department purview as well, providing materials for educating and housing those in need. Coffey's emphasis on fundraising for COGIC missionaries stationed in Liberia at Tugbake Station was particularly satisfying: "I have begun the effort of supplying refrigerators for our Foreign Fields and she (Sister E. Collins) so gladly took up this task for me," Coffey wrote. "On August 1 the contract was completed for the shipment of two refrigerators (operated by kerosene) to be shipped to Africa. . . . Mother Collins is now in the field soliciting for two dynamos (missionaries) that we might light up the jungles. . . . Oh, what a happy day when the light will be so bright on our various stations campuses that the wild animals will not dare approach or harm our missionaries."[12]

The 1951 Women's Convention

With both class-based and hierarchical relationships entering into the women's work through the creation of new auxiliaries and women marrying clergy members, COGIC women needed a space not only to plan and discuss evangelistic and church activities but also to address issues specific to the Women's Department. Women had always had a place at the convocation since the 1920s with Women's Day, in which women who led the Prayer and Bible Bands and evangelists were allowed to teach. Yet Coffey wanted something more, where the women's work could take prominence, and perhaps where she could bring some of what she had experienced in the NCNW annual meetings to COGIC women. Coffey wanted a forum in which COGIC women could both be recognized for the work that they did throughout the year on behalf of the Women's Department and reach outside of their denomination to form broader partnerships with other like-minded groups. That forum would be the Women's Convention.

According to COGIC hagiography, it was at the 1950 convocation during the women's Leadership Day that the idea for the convention was born: "On Monday morning, between 9:30 and 10:30, it was begotten by the Holy Ghost by Mother Lillian Brooks Coffey. It did not go the full nine month period, but came forth 5 months later, a Mighty Baby convention."[13] The real story was that Coffey long desired a way to have the women meet together to support the mission activities of the denomination, and in order to do that, it needed to be away from the convocation. Coffey also desired a platform for the work that she felt most committed to, missionary work. She had already traveled to Haiti to visit missions there, raised funds to purchase a refrigerator for the school station in Liberia, and was an ardent supporter of both home and foreign missionaries. The fact was that, Coffey, based on her lifelong relationship with Mason, also could ask for what she wished and would get it from Mason. Thus, at the November 1950 convocation, Mason drew up and signed an agreement authorizing the Women's Convention. Coffey was invited to hold the convention in Los Angeles, California, by Bishop Samuel Crouch, head of the COGIC Missions Board. Crouch, an avid supporter of missionary work, felt that Los Angeles would be the perfect setting for the first Women's Convention. Soon after, Coffey began the organizing work that would be crucial to making the convention a success.

Setting up steering committees similar to those of the NCNW, Coffey enlisted capable women to carry out specific tasks in anticipation of the convention. In a letter to COGIC evangelist Reatha Herndron, inviting her to participate in the planning, she outlined her goals for the convention: "There is something special I would like you to do. I would like you to serve as chairman for the committee that will serve as part of the steering committee. . . . Someday sometime during the convention we would like to have an international hour or day where would like to get as many missionaries from various foreign fields as possible."[14] Reatha agreed to work on the committee for Coffey. Modeling her plans for an elaborate but elegant welcome for the COGIC women on the NCNW annual conventions, Coffey set up various committees to handle details and recruit women for the trip to Los Angeles. She also came up with the idea to take a train from Chicago's Union Station to Los Angeles, picking up COGIC women along the way. Choosing Chicago was a wise choice because of the strong COGIC presence in the area, and it would ensure that the trip would be covered by the Associated Negro Press, headquartered in Chicago, and the *Chicago Defender*. State mothers were urged to encourage women to take the trip to the first convention, and attendance was mandatory for Women's Department state mothers. Coffey worked tirelessly on the plans for the convention and, in the latter part of April 1951, a train, dubbed the Lillian Brooks Coffey Special set out from Union Station to Los Angeles, California.

The cost for COGIC women to take the train from various cities along the way to Los Angeles was $100, and it covered their room and board, sightseeing, and the registration fee. Those who purchased the packages were called Red Card delegates, a term still in use at COGIC women's conventions today. During the train ride, Coffey collected money from the delegates for the missions offering, which she planned to present to Bishop Crouch in Los Angeles. When they arrived into Union Station at Los Angeles, a large entourage awaited them, and Coffey stepped off the train. Behind her was a porter holding a large sign that read: "The Lillian Brooks Coffey Special." Dressed in a smart suit, hat, and fur wrap, she led the women off the train. Lucille J. Cornelius, an early COGIC historian, described the scene: "It was a most exhilarating sight to see the train come in bringing women from various parts of the world as they landed in L.A. There was a big welcoming committee to greet them. It made history as all the news media and advertisement went into action. The delegates were led by Mother Coffey, singing, 'We have come this far by faith, leaning on the Lord.' It seemed to me that women would never stop getting off that train, it was such a huge number of them."[15]

The event exceeded Coffey's expectations. Coverage of the festivities by both the white and the black press, including the *Los Angeles Sentinel*, the Associated

Lillian Brooks Coffey at 1951 convention. Courtesy Glenda Goodson Collection, the Center for African American Church History and Research, Lancaster, Texas.

Negro Press, and the radio secured a high profile for the COGIC women in attendance. The mayor of Los Angeles and his wife greeted the delegates at the train station, inaugurating the annual tradition of government officials (especially Democrats) hitching their stars on the COGIC Women's Convention. Coffey was photographed with California governor Earl Warren, the future Supreme Court justice, and his wife. The convention opened on April 24, 1951, just months after its approval.[16] Daily meetings were held at the Emmanuel Temple Church of God in Christ, hosted by Bishop Samuel Crouch and his wife. The convention program for the week consisted of discussion of various issues of concern to the Women's Department: Christian education and edu-

Lillian Brooks Coffey with California governor Earl Warren and his wife.
Courtesy Glenda Goodson Collection, the Center for African American Church
History and Research, Lancaster, Texas.

cation at large, racial issues, and missionary activity. The keynote address was given by Dr. Bethune, whose picture, along with Coffey's was featured prominently in the society pages of the *Sentinel*.[17] Later that week, Coffey had the state mothers and missionaries march in carrying banners representing the various states and countries that COGIC women's missionaries served in, to accentuate the focus on missionary activity. And in the midst of all the excitement, Coffey presented to Bishop Crouch the sum of $10,000 in cash in a paper bag as a donation from the Women's Department for the missions work of COGIC.

This certainly was not the Women's Department of Mother Robinson day. The plainly dressed women who rigorously studied the Bible, and rejected the trappings of the world had been replaced by fashionable, educated, and civically oriented women. Bishop Mason attended the Women's Convention, staying apart from the proceedings but participating in the nightly events.

The weeklong convention was a resounding success. That success, however, took its toll on Coffey, who, soon after the convention ended, suffered a stroke that left her partially immobilized. She announced that she would be taking a break in a letter to the state mothers (who were now called supervisors):

Attention Supervisors:

I am in much need of rest after a serious illness, and I am turning the work into the hands of Mother Annie Lee Bailey. Any of you who wish help at your state Meetings write to Mother Bailey, immediately. She is sound in faith and doctrine, and she can help you to have an effectual program. Work in peace with the Brethren. You may not be able to do all you desire to do, but be mother-wise and God-fearing and He will bring you through. If it is His will, it won't be long before I will be back on the fighting front. — Lillian B. Coffey[18]

The letter alludes to some internal tensions between the women and the male-led episcopate. Her "work in peace with the brethren" comment suggests that the men were having some problems with asserting their supposed "authority" over the church mothers in leadership positions. The admonition to be "mother-wise and God-fearing" suggests that Coffey wanted the women not to lose the ground they had gained through her reorganization and the convention. In an interview in *Ebony* magazine some years later, Coffey alluded to the fact that perhaps the men were feeling threatened by the new power that the women were gaining. "The men haven't given me the status," she explained. "They haven't given me the figures on women membership. I'm supposed to reach every woman and to organize them in one or another of our groups, but this had never been accomplished. The men don't want the women to have too much influence. The big thing is the church and they have that all but it's hard to make them see it."[19] By creating a separate space for their concerns, independent of but connected to the national convocation, the Women's Department could organize like other women's groups, away from male oversight. In addition, their generous donation to the Home and Foreign Missions Board demonstrated their financial independence from the denomination. And no matter what the men might attempt, despite Coffey's illness, the Women's Department's place in the COGIC was firmly established.

Coffey would soon begin the long road to recuperation, even managing to attend the November 1951 convocation, flying to Memphis from Detroit with Arenia Mallory and Birdie Whitehead, leader of the Purity class. Coffey was unable to resume her normal duties as general supervisor, so Mother Anne Bailey took her place at the Women's Day part of the convocation, as well as in the parade honoring Bishop Mason. Coffey watched the parade from the window of her quarters at the Lelia Mason home, near Mason Temple.[20] For Coffey it was a moment of pride and of frustration. Her body, used to hard work, had given out on her. The question that perhaps lingered in many women's minds was whether she would resume her leadership position, despite her health. That question would be answered with the subsequent Women's Conventions.

The 1950s and the Women's Conventions

As Coffey's health began to improve after her stroke, the Women's Conventions moved forward in the work of uniting and educating women and expanding the women's work of COGIC. The conventions took place in cities throughout the country such as New York City, Miami, Boston, Detroit, Chicago, Seattle, and Kansas City. The format of the conventions was more organized a than the first, and in addition to highlighting missionary activity, the conventions focused on topics like establishing leadership conferences that women could attend during the convention to prepare them to improve their homes, schools, and communities through Christian service. The phrase "better homes, schools, communities, and world" became a slogan during the 1950s conventions and it continues to guide the thinking and advocacy of COGIC church mothers and women's leadership today. The leadership conferences, focusing on both the mission of the saints to the world and maintaining the proper Christian home, were designed to both evangelize and teach COGIC doctrines. Using titles such as Christian Stewardship, Community relations, Social welfare, and Financial Development, the message of the sanctified life was transmitted in an updated language that women inside and outside of COGIC could understand. Concentrating on race relations, civic affairs, law enforcement, church and economic life, COGIC women began to use the teachings of the Bible, and sanctification, to articulate sanctified ideals for family life and social conduct in the modern world. Each annual leadership conference focused on issues important to the community, and a published group of resolutions were presented to the Women's Convention delegates for their approval.

The nine resolutions of the 1953 convention held in Miami, Florida, provide an excellent example of the scope of the concerns of the Women's Convention. Put forth by the state mothers/supervisors, the resolutions, covering issues such as race relations, economics, education, and social action, provide an important insight into how much the role of the church mother had changed.

Resolutions and Recommendations presented to the women's international convention of the Churches of God in Christ in session at the Church of God in Christ 1747 N. W. 3rd Ave, Miami, Florida, May 5–10, 1953.

In order to create, maintain and extend to peoples whom we serve a means by which more amicable relationships in various phases of human life may be brought into being, we purpose and submit the following Recommendations:

I. That we shall persistently deny the horrors of bloody warfare and violence in human relationship while at the same time we shall give moral, spiritual and material assistance to those agencies which are seeking in spite of the present crisis to bring peace.

II. That we shall endeavor to spread through prayer, unity of purpose and spirit, cooperative intellectual, economic and spiritual enterprise, the rich benefits of the Christian religion to peoples in our nation and throughout the world. In this connection we further recommend that training be given to the unmarried whom we serve, to fit them to become responsible partners in daily living.

III. We recommend that efforts be made to encourage academic training that is not contradictory to the principles of the Christian faith and to discourage that training that puts the student at conflict with these Christian principles. That we seek to increase through united efforts our educational facilities. That our educational program include training to strengthen the principles of democracy as against communism.

IV. As Christian women who believe in the word of God as a foundation for democracy, we recommend that our vigilance will never cease until the blight of discrimination be eradicated from our fair land. To this end we will cooperate with any and all organizations within the framework of our American government who are seeking justice, equality and integration of all Americans into the democratic way of life.

V. That we shall see to foster more wholesome culture and inter-cultural relationship by calling upon those persons who are captioned Christian to put into action those principles of the Christian faith which emphasize the brotherhood of man.

VI. That we shall emphasize, by practical example, the prime significance of religious life in the home, and seek to make our world better by making our homes better.[21]

The resolutions resemble the teachings of Mother Robinson's era in clarity and scope, but they differ significantly in substance. COGIC was still in principle antiwar, but it supported the military during World War II because of its new emphasis on civic engagement. Resolutions I, III, and IV confirm a very democratic and patriotic stance that continued the departure from Robinson's original restrictions on women's involvement in politics. The statement noting that democracy was founded on the "word of God" links COGIC women to larger

Christian democratic endeavors. Like most Christian groups of the 1950s, communism was seen as a definite threat to democracy, so the mention of communism is not surprising. It is clear that patriotism for these women was inextricably linked to the struggle for civil rights. Far from being political rabble rousers, the women of COGIC were adamant for their equal rights, but they were mindful of the partnerships that needed to be created in order to achieve their goals for racial equality. The old ideal of holiness that was coupled with social concern for not just the Saint but for the world at large became a capstone of the resolutions that helped to connect COGIC women to those outside of their church communities.

The resolutions also addressed the importance of family life in creating a better world. Resolution II specifically recommends that those who are unmarried be trained to become "responsible partners in family living." The preparation of both young men and women for family life was a primary goal of the Women's Department, and maintaining a Christian home remained at the core of COGIC doctrine. The resolution helped to make clear both to the women of COGIC and to outsiders that despite the increased numbers of women in the workplace, the Christian home was the foundation for making the world better. No matter that Amana refrigerators were streamlining the homemaker's duties, the "practical examples of COGIC women making religious life the center of the home was the best example of 'Sainthood'" that a young woman or mother in COGIC could aspire to.

The resolutions, along with the leadership conferences, gave new visibility to the redefined role that Coffey had created for the church mother. She was no longer the staid Saint with unprocessed hair and plain clothes. She was part of a dynamic group as important as the National Baptist Women's Convention or the NCNW. Reports of the weeklong conventions held in the nations' metropolitan areas appeared in both the society and church columns of black newspapers. The press coverage provided COGIC women a vehicle in which to share their social and political platform throughout the 1950s and to carry forth their religious agenda. Democratic politicians, from aldermen, to mayors, to governors, made sure that their letters of welcome graced the pages of the convention programs. Pictures of politicians with Mallory and Coffey were featured prominently at the Women's Conventions. Both Coffey and Mallory participated in other events as well, such as the World Council of Churches meeting in Evanston, Illinois, in 1954, and the International Women's Council in Helsinki, Finland. The women's convention had achieved the success and visibility

Coffey desired. That did not mean, however, that all was rosy for the women's leadership.

Disappointments and Decisions

Despite all of the frenetic activity and the rise of the social and civic profile of COGIC women, there were still barriers both within and outside of the Saints' world that combined to make life difficult for them. Mallory, despite her rising profile and being chosen as one of America's top educators for 1949 in *Ebony*, would suffer the sting of defeat after a contentious election process in the NCNW. Touted as one of the front-runners for Mary McLeod Bethune's post of president of the NCNW at her retirement in 1950, Mallory at the last minute withdrew from the race for unknown reasons, making way for Dorothy Boulding Ferebee to win as the sole candidate for the presidency of the NCNW. It must have been rather upsetting in a way to give way to Ferebee, given the history of the heath project at Saints Industrial School, but Mallory strove to be diplomatic, helpful, and open as Ferebee took office. Mallory would be up again for president in 1955, but, once again, she would withdraw from the race to allow Vivian Carter Mason to run so that she could "finish the task that she says that Bethune asked her to do before her death."[22] Despite the accolades that Mallory had received, and the work she had done for the NCNW, she would never ascend to the presidency of the group.

A larger, more looming issue that faced the women and the denomination was Bishop Mason's advanced age and ill health. In order for him to be more comfortable, the Women's Department, under Coffey's direction, purchased a ranch-style home for him in a Glenview, a white neighborhood in Memphis, Tennessee. When Mason moved into the home in 1957, a cross was burned on his front lawn, and the following year, Mason's son's home in the same neighborhood burned under suspicious circumstances.[23] White protesters had held a protest to discourage blacks from moving into the neighborhood and to appeal to whites not to put their homes up for sale. In addition, the burning of Mason's church to the ground under suspicious circumstances during this period put a tremendous strain upon the denomination at a time that its profile was increasing, and the civic gains all the more important. Perhaps the most troubling, however, was the ability of Mason to address these issues because of his failing health.

Despite his ill health, Mason was still able to spend time between Memphis and Detroit, and by this time had a full-time dietitian to regulate his food intake. Always one for protracted prayer and fasting regimens, Mason's advancing age meant that he could not travel as much. Because of his status within COGIC, no provision had been made for his successor. It was as if no one expected him to ever die. So when he finally did die during a visit to Detroit to see his other two daughters it was quite a shock. Called to his bedside, Coffey described her vigil:

> I stood by in those hours when he was slowly leaving us and prayed out of my broken heart for God to leave this great man with us. One whom I had seen prophesy and his prophecies came to pass. . . . Few of his sons left the church under his administration. I have seen him go where there was great confusion, and pray for hours and hours. When he would get up the trouble would all be over. He always kept some of his daughters near him, and would let the women of God work in the Church and make use of our God-Given talents. He loved his sons and daughters![24]

Mason's death on November 17, 1961, marked the end of an era for COGIC. The charismatic leader, believed to be 100 years old at the time of his death, had been a shepherd to the denomination, and had provided Mother Coffey and the women a COGIC a position of leadership within the carefully contrived gender constructs of the times. With his demise, the future was uncertain, especially for the Women's Department. Coffey had even alluded to this uncertainty during a conversation with Mason some years back: "I don't want to be here after you are gone. If I go first, I will linger in the corridor of heaven till I hear you coming."[25] Coffey's grief, personal as well as public, seemed to even cause her to lose direction for a time. "I have missed the sweet communion (with Mason) and Oh, this has been a year of years for me!" she lamented. "It was from HIS Mouth that I got my order of the day. As I consider his advice—his instructions—his great love—his humility—his peaceable disposition. . . . Will we have another Brother Mason?"[26]

However deep her sorrow, Coffey could not afford to dwell on it. Within six months after Mason's death, the twelfth annual Women's Convention was held in Oakland, California. Amid the shaky leadership of bishops in the wake of Mason's demise, Coffey was looked to as the last in the legacy of leadership within the denomination. How that legacy would continue would become an important question in the last years of Coffey's life.

The decade of the 1950s brought tremendous changes to the Women's Department, transforming it from a nineteenth-century women's work into a twentieth-century women's organization that could take its place among the premier black women's organizations of the times like the NCNW and the National Baptist Women's Convention. By reorganizing and expanding the women's work through additional auxiliaries, Coffey was able to expand the visible and material definitions of sanctification to a more modern expression of sanctified womanhood to include civic engagement and black prosperity, helping to shed the image of sanctified church members as poor and otherworldly. Reframing the deployment of the belief in sanctification from the plainly dressed church mother to the smart, civically engaged older church mother, Coffey had managed to bring the women's work and its concerns into the twentieth century. With all of the gains, however, questions remained: How would the women fare in the rapidly changing landscape of the 1960s and the civil rights movement? And would this restructuring prove to be beneficial to the women's work, or would it prove detrimental to both their stature within the denomination and their power?

Epilogue

When I die and you set my funeral for a certain hour, If you're not on time; if there's any way possible, I'll rap on my coffin and ask, "What are you keeping me out for?"
Lillian Brooks Coffey, in *Ebony*

With Mason's death, the denomination was thrown into turmoil. Without a clear-cut charismatic leader to take Mason's place, some of the membership looked to Coffey as the last in the legacy of leadership within the denomination. There were even those who, despite the prohibitions of women in the episcopate, supported giving Coffey interim leadership of the church until a permanent head of the church could be chosen. She backed away from the endorsement, claiming that the church would not function well under a woman.[1] Fortunately for Coffey, she was able to avoid the issue after Bishop Orzo T. Jones was elected bishop at the November convocation in 1962, presumably by the presiding board of bishops. It became clear later, however, that the appointment did not sit well with other bishops, since Mason had not expressly named a successor, and, consequently, the 1960s were filled with struggles concerning the eventual leadership of the denomination.[2] For the meantime, though, the issue had been settled.

The specter of the Cold War, the escalations in the civil rights movement, and the changing morals of society made the impetus to sanctify the world more important than ever for the COGIC mothers. And the most effective way to get the message across was an interview with *Ebony* magazine. The May 1963 issue featured an interview with Coffey, titled "Woman on the Go for God." The article is a neat encapsulation of Coffey's work in the Women's Department and her opinions on leadership within the church. Its publication coincided with the Women's International Convention being held that year in Chicago, Illinois, the home of the Johnson Publishing Company and of Coffey. Perhaps it was her long-standing relationship with the city of Chicago, or her leadership of the women's convention, but whatever prompted the article, it served as a showcase for her talents and the entourage at her beck and call. The writer, Lillian S. Calhoun, described Coffey this way: "Women church leaders in most denominations are generally strong-minded enough to deal with God and a male hierarchy, but few can hold a candle to Lillian Brooks Coffey, indomitable General Supervisor of the Church of God in Christ's Women's Department. Partially blind and paralyzed after a massive stoke in 1951, she made speeches the following year by sniffing oxygen every ten minutes, and the only time she failed to speak from the dias, held conferences under an oxygen tent during her churches convention."[3] Coffey's tenacity despite her illness set the stage for an article in which she reminisced about her conversion into Holiness, the subsequent problems in relation to her conversion, and her work in the church. Remarkably candid and forthright, she discussed diverse issues, such as the failure of her marriage, her loyalty and devotion to Bishop Mason, and her goals for the Women's Department. In her interview, she doesn't refer to scripture overtly but is clear about holiness and what it means. Her comment about unmarried women bearing children is representative of this theme: "She is concerned about the charges of immorality made by welfare officials about young Negro women who bear illegitimate children," the article reported, quoting Coffey: "I believe no race can rise above the moral standards of its women. At the same time I must exercise mercy as a Christian, But the real me, the authoritative leader abhorring weakness asserts, has very little patience with a young woman who will fall again and again in this rut."[4]

This particular comment also reflected the post-Reconstruction ideals surrounding African American women's roles. The manner in which holiness was portrayed to the outside world had changed through Coffey's repositioning on doctrinal rule regarding clothing, and the fundamentals of sexual abstinence for unmarried women remained a strong thrust of COGIC teachings. She went on to mention that the Young Women's Christian Council, the auxiliary designed to teach young women how to become wives and homemakers, helped to provide for unwed mothers. Though the focus of the COGIC women had changed with the times, the core of the church was the home, and from the home all other activities flowed. The underlying point to her comments was that if the home is a Christian, sanctified home, problems like unwed pregnancy would not occur.

Calhoun described Coffey as at times stern, authoritative, vigorous, and forceful during the interview, except when Coffey was speaking of the regrets of her personal life. One wonders how the strain of ill health and leadership responsibilities may have changed her fundamental demeanor. The responsibility of leading over 150,000 women, plus dealing with a male hierarchy in increasing turmoil after Bishop Mason's death, perhaps required her demeanor to toughen. Referring to her struggles with receiving a proper census of women's membership in COGIC, she voiced frustration with the male leadership: "The men haven't given me the status. They haven't given me the figures on women membership. I'm supposed to reach every woman and to organize them in one or another of our groups, but this had never been accomplished. The men don't want the women to have too much influence. The big thing is the church and they have that all but it's hard to make them see it."[5] The male leaders may have feared that if Coffey knew the actual number of women members, she would wrest power from them. However, Coffey had not earned power in the sense of taking it from the men but rather in sharing it with them. Now, with Mason gone, the men had the right to be fearful of the one leader left who could garner the support of the overwhelming constituency of COGIC women, and a good deal of the men as well. Her implicit power through her relationship to Mason had become explicit with his death. For Coffey, however, that power and authority came from her knowledge of COGIC beliefs: "Having been raised and tutored by the Senior Bishop and founder," she commented, "I knew thoroughly the doctrine, rules and regulations. He never left me out of the leadership . . . he never left me out of the knowledge of leadership. I was his personal secretary for years, and 21 years financial secretary of the church."[6] In Coffey's estimation, she did not earn her qualifications from the fact that she was a woman but that she was a person who knew the doctrine that qualified her to lead.

It is unclear how COGIC leaders responded to the *Ebony* article, and it is perhaps even more difficult to gage how the perceptions of the public toward COGIC women may have changed, but the pictures included with the article of her well-appointed home and the retinue of seven men and women at her beck and call, along with the article's friendly tone suggests that the piece could only help to change the perception of COGIC. After all, appearing in *Ebony* magazine was a sign of the denomination's importance, affirming its climb out of the storefronts into the mainstream of African American society. Coffey referred to COGIC in the article as "not being a treasured church," perhaps in reference to being overshadowed by the National Baptist or the African Methodist Episcopal churches. It was the work of Coffey, Mallory, and countless church mothers, however, that brought COGIC into the mainstream of African American life.

The End of the Line

The *Ebony* article was to be the last major public piece on Coffey. Her heart, enlarged, caused her to have to reduce her traveling schedule to make sure she got adequate rest. She made it through the Convocation of November 1963, at the time of President John F. Kennedy's assassination, and she oversaw the preparations for the Women's Convention of May 5–10, 1964. The convention met in Albany, New York. In the convention program, along with the usual pictures of church mothers and auxiliary leadership, a brief history of the Women's Department was included. At the end of one of the programs, a tribute to Coffey's leadership was included:

> We boast of a group of women, sound, steadfast in faith, teachers of good things. Our women do not smoke, drink, or chew tobacco. But as the scripture says: We believe in temperance. Whenever you see the Church of God in Christ, moving onward and upward; there is an organized group of women. The supervisors range in years from the late 20's to beyond ages. Some are past 80 years and are still active. It is ours as a convention of women to know how earnestly Lillian Coffey has labored in this work, along with the tasks of supervision of the Women's Department in the General Church, which has meant long days, sleepless nights—problems that have caused her body to weaken, her heart to lose its beat at times, yet through it all we hear her saying. "Fight on my soul, 'til death shall bring me my reward."[7]

Soon after the Women's Convention was over, Coffey's health deteriorated. She was able to make the postconvention trip to the World's Fair in New York, and then she returned home to Chicago. Two weeks later, she suffered a heart attack and was admitted into Jackson Park Hospital. She died soon after, on June 9, 1964. The woman who had seemed so indefatigable had finally succumbed to the inevitability of death. Immediately, notices appeared in both black and white papers across the country, with headlines such as "Lillian B.

Coffey dies; World Church Leader." Her funeral on Saturday, June 13, 1964, was attended by over 4,000 church members, family, and friends. Eulogized by the presiding bishop, O. T. Jones, with Arenia Mallory holding forth as mistress of ceremonies, the funeral featured a combination of Coffey's favorite hymns, scriptures, resolutions, and acknowledgment of cards and telegrams. The COGIC magazine, *The Evangelist Speaks*, recounted her passing in a rather interesting use of language for a woman considered to be the mother of all the women in the denomination: "We sincerely regret the loss of Dr. Coffey as she was an outstanding patriarch, who was a faithful soldier of the cross from her pioneer days until her death."[8] Long a leader of women, Coffey at the end, was viewed as the patriarch, not the matriarch, of the denomination.

—⚭—

A picture of Mallory and Coffey standing in front of the gates of the White House has been over my desk as I have toiled to complete this book. When I look at that photograph, I often wonder two very distinct things: What was going through their minds at the time the picture was taken, and what would they think if they attended a COGIC Women's Convention of the twenty-first century. I may not be able to discern what was on their minds that day, but I think I can guess what they might think of today's Women's Department, and where their story has taken the women of COGIC.

After Coffey's death, Mother Anne Bailey, Coffey's second-in-command, took on the role of national supervisor and, as COGIC men put it, "held the work together and in harness" while the men argued their way into a split in the denomination and eventually reconciled under a new presiding bishop, J. O. Patterson, in 1969. Patterson brought COGIC out of the turbulent 1960s into the 1970s with a new sense of purpose, but Coffey's diligent work to restructure the Women's Department would prove to be a major reason why COGIC women's power would be reconfigured. Throughout the 1970s the roles of the women underwent a small but noticeable shift. Because of the proliferation of bishop's wives and first ladies who were now able to participate in denominational and women's activities with the same amount of fervor as the church mothers, church mothers and state supervisors experienced a shift in status. Other women's roles that were more status-oriented began to influence women's roles in the church. Outside forces like the women's movement threatened to undermine years of careful work and teaching about sanctified womanhood. As a result, the very space that Coffey had created to enable a broader base of participation would soon become restrictive. Women who were

Arenia Mallory and Lillian Brooks Coffey in front of the White House.
Courtesy Mary McLeod Bethune Council House National Historic Site.

involved in the Women's Department not only needed to be called; they also needed to be connected to power. Power did not come simply from being an enterprising sanctified women but now could come through ones' husband, position, or connection to Patterson's leadership. Power brokers like Mallory who were still revered by many found themselves on the outside of this new configuration of women's leadership. Even more crucial to this shift in power was the restructuring of the women's works and its concerns.

The 1970s and the ensuing decades were the beginning of a major shift in

COGIC women's concerns and outside influence, although the women of COGIC would not perceive it to be as such. While Coffey's and Mallory's work within the denomination had been enhanced by their connections to the women's club movement and the like, the new COGIC women of the 1970s and beyond began to retreat in certain ways. COGIC women did not join organizations like the National Council of Negro Women (NCNW) as much, nor did they know how to reach out to a younger generation of professional women. COGIC women's former alliances gave way to an internalized, hierarchical system. The tension women felt between their roles of sanctifying the world and of living the sanctified life prompted many women to try to retreat back to the old sanctified life, albeit with a twist. COGIC women became more feminized, and less confrontational with society. They would also take on the role in a much more flamboyant way. The growing prosperity of COGIC members in the 1970s led to a major change in both style and functions for COGIC members, especially women. The *Memphis Commercial Appeal* began to report on how much money the Saints spent in Memphis on cars and clothing. The mothers led the way to the changes in the style of dress, and the restructuring of sanctified life would continue at a brisk pace, moving from civic concerns to individual prestige and position. What would this do, then, to the trajectory of COGIC women's preoccupation with first sanctifying themselves, then reaching out to sanctifying the world? The women leaders who followed Coffey, Anne Bailey, Mattie McGlothen, Emma Crouch, and current international supervisor Willie Mae Rivers, would each find themselves challenged by the male episcopate, which had always grudgingly accepted women's power because of Mason. Without Mason on their side, women were expected to model submissiveness rather than simply teach it, in part because of the feminization of the church mother's role. Being a church mother now meant being well-dressed and dignified, not civically engaged.

The project of sanctifying the world through civic engagement was lost in the 1970s and beyond, I believe, because of COGIC's preoccupation with internal issues and a refocusing on its interior life. The struggles to maintain the Saints' difference over and against the world helped to close the ranks not only to outsiders who did not believe in sanctification but also to those allies to the educational and social pursuits that the women's work had always supported. With Mallory's death in 1977, it seemed that COGIC's connection to the world outside became tenuous, and the women's work turned inward. The project of sanctifying the world was turned away from slowly, until the concerns of the women were focused on maintaining their work and authority against the changing presiding bishops, and to unfortunately, become the fashionable older women with sequins, hats, and furs, all articles of clothing that Mother Robinson would have been vehemently against, and would have actively denounced.

In short, a formidable women's organization, born of the humble women's work of COGIC, was undermined, I believe, by the very prosperity and engagement in the world that was designed to bring unbelievers into a sanctified life. The transformation of the meaning of sanctification through the addition of auxiliaries, decreased engagement with broader African American social and educational organizations like the NCNW and the NAACP, and the increase in both membership and economic power of COGIC members all combined to turn sanctification inward. The very impetus to live a sanctified life that had been central under the diligence of Robinson and Coffey and their church mothers was lost as COGIC women sought to become the most distinctive looking women with denominational prestige. Dress went from a way to model what it meant to live the sanctified life to a marker of social status and material blessings among COGIC members, men and women alike. Younger, educated women who were less likely to adhere to the fine lines between teaching and preaching, and even less likely to emulate the elaborate dress of their elders, were leaving the COGIC ranks to find welcome in other Pentecostal and charismatic churches open to women's preaching and leadership.

Although this is not the end of the story for church mothers in COGIC, it would be a troubling situation if this trajectory of aging, overt feminization, and disengagement from the civic realm led to the demise of the women's work. Rumblings within the denomination about proposed constitutional changes in 2004 and 2005 suggested that the general board might like to subsume the women's work into the episcopal structure, effectively canceling out the women's autonomy. It would allow the Women's Department to dissolve like other women's groups. All of the emphasis on feminization of the women and on emulating models of women's engagement such as that of white evangelical women threatens to dilute the power and authority that COGIC women gained in the past, both charismatically and through the teaching office. Additionally, the gains that COGIC women made both within and without the denomination through engagement with the NCNW and other women's organizations all began to dissipate in the post–Mallory and Coffey era. The shift in focus from civically engaging the world through sanctified living to internal COGIC squabbles and internal status has eroded the power of the women. With outside alliances, the Women's Department could assert to the male leadership both its institutional and its financial clout. As of this writing, that has not been the case. As a consequence, there have been rumblings from the recent constitutional convention about attempts to limit the Women's Department's power by reorganizing the department within the Episcopal structure, with bishops rather than the national supervisor nominating candidates to women's leadership positions. Should this happen, COGIC women will certainly no longer be powerful mothers, teachers, and leaders but rather become beautifully dressed foils to the bishops and pastors of the denomination.

But what of the bigger picture? Why should anyone who is a student or scholar in African American religious history, or American Religious history, for that matter, care about the story of COGIC women? They should care because the issues COGIC women faced mirror broader issues for women in America in general. The advent of the feminist and womanist movements promised greater equality for women, and although women have made advances, particularly in the workplace, there has been a backlash, as Susan Faludi terms it, for women's rights within society. The rise of Evangelical Christianity and the Christian Right has largely reframed the discussion about what women should do for their families and children, and affluence now means that women can stay home to take care of their children if they choose to, an option even Mother Robinson did not have as a washerwoman at the turn of the twentieth century. Women are less apt to join organizations like the NCNW, in part because very specialized organizations have taken their place. They cater to women who want to better themselves but do not encourage partnerships in order to change women's situations. Like many American religious organizations, women's groups that survived the 1960s and 1970s are more focused on individual piety rather than corporate strategies for social and spiritual advancement. The turn to the individual in American religiosity has created the megachurch ministries of the T. D. Jakes, Juanita Bynums, and others who use principles of holiness and sanctification for "spiritual improvement programs" rather than for community-based improvement and social concerns. In short, living the sanctified life has become a personal preoccupation rather than a church-related one. For COGIC women, this turn may prove to be the end of a once powerful and formidable women's organization. The broader implications of this turn for African American religious bodies, however, may prove to destroy the core values of community and self-determination, principles that made "the black church" representative of the moral compass for civil and human rights in the twentieth century.

Notes

Abbreviations

ADBC   Anthea D. Butler Private Collection, Rochester, N.Y.

BHL   Bentley Historical Library, University of Michigan Library, Ann Arbor, Mich.

CHS   Chicago Historical Society, Chicago, Ill.

MBC   Mary McLeod Bethune Council House, National Park Service, Washington, D.C.

MML   Mattie McGlothen Library and Museum, Oakland, Calif.

SSDC   Sherry Sherrod DuPree Collection (African American Pentecostal and Holiness Collection), Schomburg Center for Research in Black Culture, New York Public Library, Harlem Branch, New York, N.Y.

SSDP   Sherry Sherrod DuPree Private Collection, Gainsville, Fla.

Introduction

1. Marie Griffith, *God's Daughters*, does an excellent job of chronicling women's negotiation of male headship with women's leadership.

2. Lincoln and Mamiya, *Black Church*, 275. See also Gilkes, *If It Wasn't for the Women*, 66–73. I believe that Gilkes does a good job with the definition of "church mother," but the historical antecedents of the term are fuzzy at best. For an early history of church mothers, see Baldwin, "Black Women."

3. Cayton and Drake, *Black Metropolis*; Fauset, *Black Gods of the Metropolis*; Powdermaker, Williams, and Woodson, *After Freedom*. This genre of sociological research tells us much about the community life of "sanctified outsiders" but does not sufficiently explore belief as the motive behind the practices and ethos of sanctified churches. For a better explication of the dichotomies between description and practice, see Butler, "Observing the Lives of the Saints." Wallace Best (*Passionately Human*, 25–34) also does

a fine job in deconstructing the Chicago School of Sociologists responsible for much of the "negative depictions of belief especially in Pentecostal and storefront churches."

4. Here I am thinking of Gayraud Wilmore's book *Black Religion and Black Radicalism*, although there is myriad scholarship on deprivation theory that has labeled those within the sanctified church or Pentecostal traditions as simply otherworldly, compensatory, and disengaged. A good rebuttal to this is Miller, "Pentecostalism as Social Movement."

5. For an interesting take on this assumption, see Best, *Passionately Human*, 25–32. Best counters that sociologists' "rigid binarism" between southern religion as primitive and urban religion as progressive distorts the discussions about modernity and the black church.

6. In this regard I look to Robert Orsi, who is very eloquent on this subject of subjectivity in the introduction to the second edition of his work, *The Maddona of 115th Street*. Although I am not a member of the COGIC, it has been very helpful to be present for many COGIC events to understand the historical trajectory of both beliefs and persons within the denomination.

7. I cannot claim creativity for using a single word for chapter titles. Grant Wacker's book, *Heaven Below*, uses this convention cleverly, and I tip my church hat in his direction.

Chapter One

1. During this time period it was common to name daughters after their mothers.

2. "Voice of Mother Robinson," 3. Robinson apparently wrote a biography, *A Slave Became an Organizer*, but I have been unable to locate this book despite its being cited in Tinney, *Black Pentecostalism*, and in Jones, *Guide to the Study of the Pentecostal Movement*.

3. "Voice of Mother Robinson."

4. Johnson, *God Struck Me Dead*, 58–60.

5. "Voice of Mother Robinson."

6. Scholars are apt to focus on traditional Victorian notions of motherhood as the fountain of spirituality, so less has been written about the impact of slave and rural women's spirituality on their children.

7. See Gaines, *Uplifting the Race*, 6; Wolcott, *Remaking Respectability*; Higginbotham, *Righteous Discontent*; Paisley Harris, "Gatekeeping and Remaking," 213; and Litwack, *Trouble in Mind*, 348.

8. See Wolcott, *Remaking Respectability*. See also Paisley Harris, "Gatekeeping and Remaking," 214.

9. Gaines, *Uplifting the Race*, 173; Higginbotham, *Righteous Discontent*, 96–97.

10. See Moore, *In Christ's Stead*, 221.

11. Ibid., 23.

12. Ibid., 25.

13. Ibid., 170.

14. Joanna Moore to the postmaster of Plaquemine, 1885, Moore files, Joanna P. Moore Collection, American Baptist Historical Society, Valley Forge, Pa.

15. Moore, *In Christ's Stead*, 219.

16. Eaton, *Heroine of the Cross*, 64.

17. Stewart, *Later Baptist Missionaries*, 115.

18. "Peep of the Day" was actually a title by Mrs. Favel Lee Mortimer designed to teach very young children bible verses. Moore's "Peep of the Day" was modeled after Mrs. Mortimer's book.

19. See Dayton, *Theological Roots*, and Stanley, *Holy Boldness*. Women involved in the Holiness movement included such figures as Phoebe Palmer, Elizabeth Mix, and Joanna P. Moore, and the movement was fueled by Holiness camp meetings attended by Christians in many different denominations.

20. Jacobsen, *Thinking in the Spirit*, 69–73.

21. Daniels, "Cultural Renewal," 15. Daniels asserts that the Holiness movement should be viewed as a reform movement within African American life in the post-Reconstruction period. I agree with his assessment.

22. Moore, *In Christ's Stead*, 227–28. This camp meeting was perhaps part of a Holiness camp meeting, and attendance at subsequent meetings would have introduced her to a network of ministers.

23. Ibid., 229–31.

24. Moore, *Power and Work*, 26–27.

25. The scripture reads in the King James version: "What? Know ye not that your body is the temple of the Holy Ghost which is in you, which ye have of God, and ye are not your own? For ye are bought with a price: therefore glorify God in your body, and in your spirit, which are God's."

26. Moore went on to say, "Our bodies must be kept pure and clean, for they are the holiest thing on earth, in fact, the only holy thing on earth" (*Power and Work*, 26).

27. Ibid.

28. Lizzie Woods to Joanna Moore, *Hope* 17, no. 192 (January 1902): 499.

29. Stephens, "Who Healeth All Thy Diseases," 22–29.

30. *Hope* 18, no. 204 (December 1902): 726.

31. *Hope* 18, no. 211 (August 1903): 884.

32. On race mixing and other prohibitions, see Moore, *In Christ's Stead*, 217.

33. Giggie and Winston, *Faith in the Market*.

34. *Hope* 22, no. 7 (September 1906): 23.

35. *Hope* 23, no. 3 (November 1907): 63.

36. *Hope* 24, no. 3 (November 1908).

37. Ibid.

38. "Voice of Mother Robinson."

39. Weisenfeld, *African American Women*.

40. I am using "black church" in quotation marks primarily out of a sense of frus-

tration that this term cannot be used for the myriad religious expressions of African Americans during this period. When I use "black church" in the context of this text, think Protestant, formalized, and patriarchal.

41. In Houchins, *Spiritual Narratives*, 37.

42. Higginbotham, *Righteous Discontent*, 73.

43. Daniels, "Cultural Renewal," 166.

44. Ibid., 31.

45. Robert Anderson, *Vision of the Disinherited*, 104–5. Anderson's claim that many Pentecostal notables suffered from illness before recognizing they were "called" is an astute observation.

46. Jacobsen, *Thinking in the Spirit*, 19–56. This is the best and most balanced explication of Parham's somewhat convoluted theological formulations.

47. For a good treatment of the Azusa Street revival, see Robeck, *Azusa Street Mission*, 60–69.

48. Ibid., 3.

49. Pleas, *Fifty Years Achievement*, 9. Pleas's account indicates that Robinson had been mentioned to Mason and that he inquired after her, subsequently forming an acquaintance. Other reports, however, including Robinson's, tend to be more spiritually oriented and hagiographical. Subsequent stories refer to Mason and Robinson's meeting as "providencial" or "God ordained."

50. Gilkes, "Role of Women," 52. Mason's first wife died in 1904 or 1905, clearing the way for Mason to marry Lelia Washington, mother of his eight children, sometime in 1905. She died in 1936 after thirty-one years of marriage. Mason then married Elsie Washington in 1943.

51. "Voice of Mother Robinson."

52. Most Baptists of the day were cessationists, meaning that they believed the charisma, or gifts, given to the early church by God had ceased after the apostles' death and were not available to believers in the modern era.

53. "Voice of Mother Robinson."

54. Ibid.

Chapter Two

1. See Brekus, *Strangers and Pilgrims*, 125–26; Stanley, *Holy Boldness*, 5–17; and Chaves, *Ordaining Women*, 64–66.

2. Pentecostals are not fundamentalists, despite their belief in a literal interpretation of the Bible. Pentecostals also believe in "extra" biblical revelation from the Holy Spirit, which early-twentieth-century Fundamentalists would have condemned. See Jacobsen, *Thinking in the Spirit*, 355–59.

3. Gaines, *Uplifting the Race*, 126.

4. Ibid., 137.

5. For these biblical admonitions, see Eph. 6:22 and 1 Tim. 2:12.

6. Higginbotham, "African-American Women's History."

7. Pleas, *Fifty Years Achievement*, 8.

8. "Voice of Mother Robinson."

9. Ibid.

10. See Brekus, *Strangers and Pilgrims*, 273, and Goldsmith, "Women's Place Is in the Church," 68 n. 45.

11. James Anderson, *Education of Blacks*, 111; Gilkes, *If It Wasn't for the Women*, 105.

12. "Voice of Mother Robinson."

13. Wacker, *Heaven Below*, 166. See also Blumhofer, *Restoring the Faith*, 121. Women were able to become licensed missionaries or evangelists but not elders.

14. Roebuck, "Limiting Liberty," 146–48.

15. Burgess, McGee, and Alexander, *Dictionary*, 1115. See also Mendiola, "Hand of a Woman," 315.

16. Trulear, "Ida B. Robinson," 313. See also Burgess, McGee, and Alexander, *Dictionary*, 1029.

17. Wacker, *Heaven Below*, 175.

18. Chaves, *Ordaining Women*, 80–81. Chaves links Pentecostalism's loose coupling between "rule and practice to account for Pentecostal women's access to leadership positions." But the reality was that Pentecostals were just as concerned about regulating women's right to ordination as other denominations.

19. "Voice of Mother Robinson."

20. This tactical practice would replay itself in COGIC history. For more about the notion of practice as tactic, see Butler, "Observing the Lives of the Saints," 160, and Certeau, *Practice of Everyday Life*, 39–42. See also Chesler, *Woman's Inhumanity to Woman*, 127.

21. Bean, *This Is the Church*, 47.

22. The convocation is now usually the first week of November. It continues to be held in Memphis, Tennessee, although presiding bishops since Mason have threatened to move it. See Aubrey Ballard, "World Headquarters of Church Opens Here," *Commercial Appeal*, December 12, 1945.

23. Some accounts argue that Lillian Coffey, who became the second supervisor of the Women's Department, was his initial choice. See Bean, *This Is the Church*, 148.

24. The term "overseer" is defined in the COGIC manual as follows: "bishops (episkopi). Overseers. Overseer emphasizes what the elder or presbyter does." See Range, ed., *Official Manual*, 139.

25. Holt, *Brief Historical and Doctrinal Statement*, 9, War Department, FBI records, DuPree Private Collection.

26. Pleas, *Fifty Years Achievement*, 12.

27. Griffith, *God's Daughters*, 152. In Aglow, a "network of caring women," men provide legitimacy by accepting honorary titles at the local, state, and national levels. They hold no real power, however; women allow them access to the space to legitimize their own authority and to pay respect to their belief in biblical headship roles.

28. Lincoln and Mamyia, *Black Church*, 275. See also Baldwin, "Black Women and African Union Methodism."

29. Gilkes, *If It Wasn't for the Women*, 103.

30. Lillian Brooks Coffey, comp., *Yearbook of the Church of God in Christ for the Year 1926* (Memphis: privately printed, 1926), 103, Assemblies of God Archives, Flower Pentecostal Heritage Center, Assemblies of God, Springfield, Mo.

31. "Voice of Mother Robinson."

32. Lelia Mason Byas, interview by author, ADBC.

33. McCullom, *Historical Sketches*, 40.

34. In Joppa, there was a disciple named Tabitha (Dorcas) who was always doing good deeds and helping the poor. She became sick and died, and her body was washed and placed in an upstairs room. Lydda was near Joppa, and when the disciples heard that Peter was in Lydda, they sent two men to him and urged him, "Please come at once." Peter went with them, and when he arrived he was taken upstairs to the room. All the widows stood around him, crying and showing him the robes and other clothing that Dorcas had made when she was still with them. Peter sent them all out of the room. Then he got down on his knees and prayed. Turning toward the dead woman, he said, "Tabitha, get up." She opened her eyes and, seeing Peter, she sat up.

35. Minutes of the National Convocation of the COGIC, 1916, in Cornelius, *Pioneer History*, 52, 56.

36. Moore, *In Christ's Stead*, 185–87.

37. Ibid.

38. Unlike the Sunshine Band, which was the jurisdiction of the women's work, the Sunday school was under the jurisdiction of the denomination's central organization.

39. McGlothen, *Women's Department*, 27, MML.

40. Hardesty, Dayton, and Dayton, "Women in the Holiness Movement."

41. Program for the Women's International Convention, COGIC, 1956, ADBC.

42. *Yes Lord: Church of God in Christ Hymnal*.

43. Ruether and Keller, *Women and Religion*, 2:110.

44. Quoted in DuPree, *African-American Holiness Pentecostal Movement*, 184.

45. Pleas, *Fifty Years Achievement*, 42.

46. Johnson, *Life and Labors*, 9, BHL.

47. Cornelius, *Pioneer History*, 52.

48. See Gilman, "Surplus Negro Women," 182–92. Gilman posits that because of migration, black women outnumbered available, single black men in the North. Therefore, marriage was not available for many women, subjecting them to the perils of prostitution, spinsterhood, and low economic status. In this context, many women turned to the haven of the church.

49. Minutes of the 1924 COGIC Convocation, 38, SSDP.

50. *Hope* article, 1937, in Program of the Church of God in Christ's Thirty-Seventh Annual Women's Convention, 1988, ADBC.

51. Ibid.

Chapter Three

1. Wolcott, *Remaking Respectability*, 116.

2. Milton Sernett makes the important observation that women's roles in the transfer of southern religious practices to the urban North deserve more attention. See Sernett, *Bound for the Promised Land*, 195.

3. "Dr. Lillian Brooks Coffey Dies," *Evangelist Speaks*, July 1964, 4.

4. Cornelius, *Pioneer History*, 26.

5. Ibid.

6. Ibid.

7. Baer and Singer, *African-American Religion*, 156, 159. Baer and Singer discuss intersecting sets of personal relationships in the African American church, and COGIC is no exception. Within COGIC, it is interesting to note how many bishops, pastors, and women's leaders historically have had either familial relations through marriage or other loosely bound family connections within the denomination.

8. Cornelius, *Pioneer History*, 26. Apparently, Coffey's husband left her after a time, and she divorced him. Due to Mason's strict policy on divorce and remarriage, which dictated that a divorced spouse could not remarry until his or her ex-spouse died, Coffey was unable to remarry. She recounted that Mason "forbade her to remarry, telling her it would 'slap her in the face every time she tried to teach God's pure word.'" She questioned the policy but nevertheless accepted it: "This too I often wondered about, but he said do it and remain as I was, so I remained single until this day" (ibid.).

9. Johnson, *Life and Labors*, 11, BHL.

10. Wolcott, *Remaking Respectability*, 59. The Urban League tried to close up the bear trap on Eliot.

11. DuPree, *African-American Holiness Pentecostal Movement*, 191–92.

12. Duff, *Saint's Home Church*, 20.

13. "Biography of Elder McKinley McCardell," 1944, reprinted in *Twenty-Fifth Silver Anniversary, Women's Department of California Northwest Jurisdiction, COGIC, May 1982* (n.p.: [1982]), 11, MML.

14. Pleas, *Fifty Years Achievement*, 15; Minutes of the COGIC, 1917, in Cornelius, *Pioneer History*, 51–55.

15. "Mother Cotton Sounds Bugle," *Foursquare Crusader* 2, no. 46 (May 13, 1936): 3.

16. *California Eagle*, February 2, 1935.

17. Ibid., February 8, 1935.

18. Johnson, *Life and Labors*, 12–13, BHL.

19. Wolcott, *Remaking Respectability*, 115.

20. Gilman, "Surplus Negro Women."

21. See Hurston, *Sanctified Church*, 103, and Sanders, *Saints in Exile*, 3.

22. Gilkes, *If It Wasn't for the Women*, 47.

23. Brown, *Sewing Circle Artistic Fingers*, 15, SSDC.

24. Rooks, *Hair Raising*, 65–69.

25. Lillian Brooks Coffey, comp., *Yearbook of the Church of God in Christ for the Year 1926* (Memphis: privately printed, 1926), 148, Assemblies of God Archives, Flower Pentecostal Heritage Center, Assemblies of God, Springfield, Mo.

26. Williams and George Walker had a vaudeville act called "The Two Coons." See Chude-Sokei, *Last "Darky,"* 28.

27. Simmonds and Martin, *Down Behind the Sun,* 5.

28. Minutes of the National Convocation of the COGIC, 1916, in Cornelius, *Pioneer History,* 52.

29. Byas and Hunt, *From Priors Farm,* 72.

30. Bean, *This Is the Church,* 48. In 1925, the "Tabernacle" was built so that the saints had a place to worship and eat together.

31. Brown, *Sewing Circle Artistic Fingers,* 15, SSDC. Other scriptures referred to are Joel 2:15, Exod. 34:38, Lev. 23:27, Deut. 9:9, and 1 Sam. 7:6.

32. Byas and Hunt, *From Priors Farm,* 70.

33. I have been unable to ascertain if this idea was borrowed from Nannie Helen Burroughs's initiation of women's day in the Baptist tradition, but it certainly might have been. See Higginbotham, *Righteous Discontent,* 165.

Chapter Four

1. Higginbotham, *Righteous Discontent,* 189–204.

2. See, for example, the statements of Virginia Broughton, who experienced sanctification through the Bible Band ministry of Joanna P. Moore. See Broughton, *Twenty Years' Experience of a Missionary,* 9–12.

3. Nannie Helen Burroughs coined the expression "Bible, Bath, and Broom" to describe the type of training young women would receive at her training school in Washington D.C.: Bible knowledge, purity (bath) skills, and housekeeping. See Easter, *Nannie Helen Burroughs,* 63.

4. Swan, *Brief History,* 27, ADBC.

5. Sanders, *Saints in Exile,* 65.

6. "Voice of Mother Robinson."

7. Perhaps this is a bit of a stretch, but given that COGIC women were also required not to process their hair, the appeal to "natural dressing" suggests something more than an accommodationist or "wishing to be white" tendency.

8. "Voice of Mother Robinson."

9. See the discussion of the role of dress and respectability in Wolcott, *Remaking Respectability,* 56–58.

10. See Bourdieu, *Distinction,* 106–8.

11. COGIC women began to redefine their manner of dress and their attitudes about Holiness in the post–World War II era. For a discussion on Rosetta Thorpe and dress, see Jackson, *Singing in My Soul,* 95–96.

12. Early literature of the Women's Department cribbed Nannie Helen Burroughs's motto of "Bible, Bath, and Broom" prominently.

13. Brown, *Sewing Circle Artistic Fingers*, 34, SSDC. The term "to fix the split" meant to close the split in skirts that were open to allow movement. Hems were also measured at times in the congregation to ensure skirts were of a "modest length."

14. See the *Complete Recorded Works of Rev. F. W. McGee, 1929–1930*, vol. 2 (Reissue, Eden Records, 1991).

15. *Sing unto the Lord a New Song*, ADBC.

16. Lucy Flagg, "Lord, Change the Style," date unknown, ADBC. Other interesting lines include, "We used to be too modest to show under the arm / but now we expose our pits and call it charm."

17. These admonitions have persisted in the church. Even I was subjected to scrutiny while interviewing Bishop Mason's daughter in 1996. Wearing an ankle-length sundress to the interview of Lelia Byas, I thought that my dress would pass muster. Unfortunately, the dress was short-sleeved. I was politely but firmly told by Sister Byas that in "her day" women would always wear sleeves that covered "even the bone at the end of their wrists" out of fear of being thought wanton. The interview went forward, but I often wonder what I might have discovered had I worn sleeves of the proper length!

18. Pearl McCullom, "Make Up," Purity Column, *Evangelist Speaks*, November–December 1954, 2–3. "Jezebel's main weapon of prey was her Red painted cheeks and lips . . . the test of ages has proved that Lustful debased advances from the opposite sex is from Red on the Face!!"

19. Sanders, *Saints in Exile*, 68–69.

20. McCullom, "Make Up," 2–3.

21. O'Neal, "African American Church," 129–30.

22. McCullom, "Make Up," 2.

23. D'natural, "Dark Shadows," *Tri-State Defender*, December 8, 1951.

24. Pleas, *Fifty Years Achievement*, 14. When Robinson first started out as a church mother, she traveled with several women before making them state mothers, and she took her daughter, Ida, along on mission trips.

25. *Chicago Defender*, Lovelorn Corner, June 1, 1957.

26. Lelia Mason Byas, interview by author, ADBC. See also DuPree, *African-American Holiness Pentecostal Movement*, 473. In an interview, Estella Cobb recounts that Mother Robinson choose a husband for her but that both partners were saved and not offended by this nuptial arrangement.

27. Little, *Back to Pentecost*, 5, ADBC.

28. Sweetie's use of the term "mated" might suggest that there was more going on here than meets the eye. Perhaps the elder thought that the children produced from this marriage would be better in some way than other children.

29. Little, *Back to Pentecost*, 31, ADBC.

30. Ibid.

31. Ibid., 5.

32. Ibid., 7.

33. Ibid., 32.

34. Phyllis Barnett, pastor's wife, interview by author, New Canaan, Los Angeles, Calif., COGIC, May 31, 2000.

35. At the time of Robinson's appointment to overseer of the women's work, she was a widow.

36. Lillian S. Calhoun, "Woman on the Go for God: Church of God in Christ's Woman Leader has Overcome Illness, Adversity to Work for Faith," *Ebony*, May 1963, 81, 84.

37. Ibid., 84.

38. Mason, *History and Life Work*, 21–23.

39. Minutes of the 1926 COGIC Convocation, reprinted in *The Whole Truth*, 149, 1990.

40. Powdermaker, Williams, and Woodson, *After Freedom*, 156–57. This study notes that legal divorce in the town of Bronzeville was something "more than a luxury, it savor[ed] of pretensions and extravagance."

41. Simmonds and Martin, *Down Behind the Sun*, 39–41.

42. The ensuing story was much more complicated in the convocation minutes for the matter. The minutes seem to indicate that Mallory had first married J. Pullum and then later married Elder H. C. Clemmons without having first divorced Pullum. The minutes also note that Clemmons annulled his marriage to Mallory in California and there married Sister Emma Lee Harper, leaving Sister Mallory alone with a baby. Upon further investigation, the COGIC committee determined that Clemmons had not legally annulled his marriage to Mallory in the California courts, since he filed the papers under false pretenses. The committee's first decision in the matter was to require Clemmons to leave Sister Harper and return to Mallory. Mallory's responses are not noted in the record (although I suspect that she may have had much to say on the matter). For his part, Clemmons came back to the convocation to contest its decision that he return to Mallory. He claimed to have received encouragement from Bishop Mason to marry Sister Emma Lee Harper. The committee decided after hearing from Clemmons the second time that he should be disfellowshipped from the brotherhood until he repented and made restitution. It is unclear if Clemmons ever reconciled with the denomination, but in any case he did not return to Mallory. See Minutes of the 1928 COGIC Convocation, 88–90, SSDP.

43. *The Whole Truth* 10, no. 1 (March 1934).

44. Jerma Jackson's *Singing in My Soul* is an excellent accounting of Tharpe's life and the struggles of sanctified music with the secular market.

45. Ibid., 112–13.

Chapter Five

1. Texas, Arkansas, and Mississippi all had COGIC schools. See Pleas, *Fifty Years Achievement*, 41.

2. Daniels, "Live So You Can Use Me," 296.

3. Dabney, *What It Means to Pray Through*, 127.

4. Daniels, "Live So You Can Use Me," 296.

5. Pleas, *Fifty Years Achievement*, 47.

6. COGIC, *From the Beginning*, 66. There had been several struggles in COGIC between male and female leadership. Robinson advocated for the traditional roles for women. The leadership conflicts between men and women dominated the decade because of the rapid growth of the Women's Department. See Butler, "Peculiar Synergy," 45.

7. Pleas, *Fifty Years Achievement*, 74.

8. Minutes of the 1920 COGIC Convocation, SSDC.

9. Deprivation theorists often maintain that Holiness adherents and Pentecostals are not overly concerned with education. See Miller, "Pentecostalism as Social Movement," and Clark, "Sanctification," 545.

10. Lillian Coffey, future general supervisor/mother in COGIC, was put out of her home when she spoke in tongues. See Butler, "Peculiar Synergy," 57.

11. Simmonds and Martin, *Down Behind the Sun*, 6.

12. COGIC, *From the Beginning*, 66. Mallory met Jane Addams of Hull House as a young woman, and this inspired her to want to go to Africa.

13. Ibid., 10.

14. Mayme Osby Brown, "Mississippi Mud," 142. This article was apparently one in a series of articles on Mallory in the black press during the 1940s and 1950s. It was included in the papers of Claude Barnett, the founder of the Associated Negro Press wire service for African American newspapers, which are housed in the Chicago Historical Society.

15. Simmonds and Martin, *Down Behind the Sun*, 39. See Chapter 4 for a fuller explanation of Mallory's marriage.

16. This was in part due to her leadership position at Saints School. See Church, "Accommodation and Liberation."

17. They modeled the group, of course, after the Fisk Jubilee Singers.

18. "Dayton," *Chicago Defender*, July 2, 1938.

19. People put wedding rings and watches into the baskets, according to Mallory's biographers. See Simmonds and Martin, *Down Behind the Sun*, 20.

20. Ibid.; COGIC, *From the Beginning*, 67.

21. Smith, *Sick and Tired*, 152–53. Thanks to Smith for illuminating this story, which is glossed over in COGIC accounts of the AKA's presence at the school.

22. *The Ivy Leaf* 12, no. 3 (September 1934): 6.

23. Ibid., 10.

24. Ibid., 9; *The Whole Truth* 7, no. 10 (October 1931).

25. Simmonds and Martin, *Down Behind the Sun*, 18.

26. *The Ivy Leaf* 13, no. 3 (September 1936): 3.

27. Smith, *Sick and Tired*, 152.

28. Ibid., 155.

29. Ibid., 156.

30. Ibid., 156.

31. Ibid., 156.

32. Arenia Mallory to Claude Barnett, November 13, 1942, Claude Barnett Papers, CHS.

33. Juanita Faulkner, interview by author, April 2002, ADBC.

34. "Why We Have Church Schools," *The International Outlook*, October 12, 1964, ADBC.

35. Mary McLeod Bethune, "Self Revelations," in McCluskey and Smith, eds., *Mary McLeod Bethune*, 42.

36. Ibid.

37. Giddings, *When and Where I Enter*, 199.

38. The Holiness movement has been thought of as having promoted reformist or revolutionary outlooks that questioned the status quo. See Hardesty, Dayton, and Dayton, "Women in the Holiness Movement," 241–48.

39. Mary McLeod Bethune, "A Yearning Long Appeased," in McCluskey and Smith, eds., *Mary McLeod Bethune*, 5.

40. The difference between Holiness and Holiness Pentecostalism is best chronicled in Jacobsen, *Thinking in the Spirit*, 366 n. 5.

41. Minutes of the Special Called Meeting of the Board of Trustees, Bethune-Cookman College, 1942, in McCluskey and Smith, eds., *Mary McLeod Bethune*, 125. For more about Moody, see Evenson, *God's Man for the Gilded Age*.

42. Ruether and Keller, *Women and Religion*, 97.

43. Juanita Faulkner, interview by author, New Jersey, 2001, ADBC.

44. Mallory, Arenia Cornelia, in *Encyclopedia of African American Religion*, 480.

45. Brown, "Mississippi Mud," 142.

46. Ibid.

47. Ibid.

48. Smith, *Sick and Tired*, 165. Mallory attended a conference in Washington, D.C., in 1938 organized by Bethune titled "The Participation of Negro Women and Children in Federal Programs."

49. *The Whole Truth* 7, no. 10 (October 1931): 2.

50. COGIC, *Minutes of the General Assembly*, December 6, 1938.

51. See, for example, *The Whole Truth* 20 (September 1931): 1.

52. Ibid., 49.

Chapter Six

1. COGIC, *Minutes of the General Assembly*, December 9, 1941.

2. "God in Christ Churches End 20 Day Confab," *Chicago Defender*, December 20, 1941.

3. Articles of Faith, Church of God in Christ, N.p., n.d., 2.

4. DuPree and DuPree, *Exposed!*.

5. "God in Christ Convocation Greets F.D.R.," *Chicago Defender*, December 23, 1939, 6.

6. *Chicago Defender*, December 10, 1941.

7. Gilkes, *If It Wasn't for the Women*, 66–72. Gilkes argues for putting the community mothers (women who worked socially both in the church and in the African American community) into a place of shared power with men but also being hindered by the fact that they could not be ordained. I think that rather than being hindered, women created alternative alliances that enabled them to gain the power outside of ordination.

8. *Chicago Defender*, December 13, 1941, 10.

9. White, *Too Heavy a Load*, 148–50; Seller, *Women Educators*, 50.

10. "Minutes of the Organizational Meeting of the National Council of Negro Women," in McCluskey and Smith, eds., *Mary McLeod Bethune*, 171.

11. National Council of Negro Women Inc., *Women United*, 7.

12. See religious movements homepage on Moral Re-Armament at <http://religiousmovements.lib.virginia.edu/nrms/moralrearm.html>.

13. *New York Times*, December 3, 1939, 59. Wilson and Smith went on to start Alcoholics Anonymous, based on the Oxford Group's principles of truth telling.

14. Letter dated April 21, 1943, NCNW Files, series 5, box 6, folder 9, MBC.

15. Letter dated June 12, 1943, ibid.

16. Ibid.

17. Claude Barnett founded the Associated Negro Press, a wire service for black newspapers, in 1919. For more on Barnett's life, see Hogan, *Black National News Service*.

18. Smith, ed., *Notable Black American Women*, s.v. "Mallory, Arenia C.," 722–24.

19. "Press Release, Lillian Brooks Coffey Home, Inc.," 1944a, n.p., n.d., Claude Barnett Papers, microfilm, series J, reel 5, CHS.

20. See "Prophet Jones Lands in Jail: Nab Cult Leader on Morals Charge," *Chicago Daily Defender*, February 21, 1956, 1.

21. Ibid.

22. *The Whole Truth* 15, no. 6 (May 1945): 2.

23. *Lifted Banners* 6, no. 2 (1949): 9. A picture of the modest home is included in the article, along with a portrait of the Elder Charles S. Cypress and his wife, Mrs. Susie A. Cypress.

24. *The Whole Truth*, no. 3 (September 1944); *Christian Hope*, December 1943, 11.

25. NCNW Files, series 18, box 9, folder 2, MBC.

26. Constitution and By-laws, WANDS, NCNW Files, series 18, box 9, folder 2, MBC.

27. "Wands Organized in Detroit Unit," *Michigan Chronicle*, February 26, 1944, 5.

28. Letter dated February 22, 1944, NCNW Files, series 5, box 6, folder 10, MBC.

29. *The Christian Hope Magazine*, November 1945, 3.

30. "World Headquarters of Church Opens Here," *Commercial Appeal*, December 12, 1945.

31. Ibid., col. 1.

32. The signs still stands today, although I do not know whether it can still be lighted.

33. *Commercial Appeal*, December 11, 1945. See also Program for the Women's International Convention, COGIC, 1956, ADBC.

34. Program for the Women's International Convention, COGIC, 1956, ADBC.

35. Ibid.

36. Lizzie Robinson, December 13, 1945, Soundex record, State of Tennessee, reel 152, Tennessee State Library and Archives, Nashville.

37. Associated Negro Press, "Mother Robinson, Church of God Leader, Passes," December 26, 1945.

38. This dress is described in detail in the Women's Department handbook, as well as the COGIC official manual. See McGlothen, ed., *Women's Department*, and Range, ed. *Official Manual*.

Chapter Seven

1. *The Whole Truth* (January 1946): 2, 5.

2. D'natural, "Dark Shadows," *Tri-State Defender*, December 8, 1951. This column is a very interesting discussion about Bishop Mason and the parade honoring him by the denomination. Mason is lauded as a "race man" despite the fact that he married a light-skinned woman.

3. Mason, *Saints in the Land of Lincoln*, 32–35.

4. See ibid., 88–104, and Jackson, *Singing in My Soul*, 46–49.

5. Letter from Coffey to Bethune, February 1946, NCNW Files, series 5, box 6, folder 18, MBC.

6. Letter to Bethune from Coffey, August 22, 1946, NCNW Files, series 5, box 6, folder 18, MBC.

7. Lillian S. Calhoun, "Woman on the Go for God: Church of God in Christ's Woman Leader has Overcome Illness, Adversity to Work for Faith," *Ebony*, May 1963, 84. Coffey often lent the house out to NCNW members.

8. Claude Barnett to Lillian Brooks Coffey, Claude Barnett Papers, microfilm, series J, reel 5, CHS.

9. *Lifted Banners* 6, no. 2 (1949): 2, Omaha, Nebraska, Raynard Smith Private Collection, Edison, N.J.

10. Sherry Sherrod DuPree, interview by author, June 1996, ADBC.

11. Ibid.

12. *Lifted Banners* 6, no. 2 (1949): 11.

13. Leadership Conference, San Francisco, California, May 1975, Women's International Convention book, Silver Anniversary edition, 3.

14. Letter to Reatha Herndron from Lillian Brooks Coffey, January 6, 1951, Glenda Goodson Private Collection.

15. Cornelius, *Pioneer History*, 23–24.

16. Ibid., 23.

17. "Well Merited Praise," *Los Angeles Sentinel*, May 3, 1951, B2.

18. Dr. Cora Berry, Director. "Women's International Convention, Church of God in Christ," paper delivered at the Leadership Conference, San Francisco, California, May 1975, in Women's International Convention book, Silver Anniversary edition.

19. Calhoun, "Woman on the Go for God," 86.

20. "Noted St. Mother Sees Parade," *Tri-State Defender*, December 8, 1951, 2.

21. "Women's International Convention 1953," paper delivered at the Women's International Convention, Church of God in Christ, Chicago, Ill., 1953, 54.

22. "Tantrums and Agreement," *Chicago Defender*, November 12, 1955, 2. The article describes a rather heated private meeting of the women in a hotel room in which Mallory stepped aside for Mason to run.

23. *Commercial Appeal*, March 4, 1958; *Chicago Defender*, February 1958.

24. Cornelius, *Pioneer History*, 26.

25. Calhoun, "Woman on the Go for God," 75.

26. Cornelius, *Pioneer History*, 26.

Epilogue

1. Lillian S. Calhoun, "Woman on the Go for God: Church of God in Christ's Woman Leader has Overcome Illness, Adversity to Work for Faith," *Ebony*, May 1963, 78.

2. The ensuing battles in the 1960s led to lawsuits, counterlawsuits, and even fistfights on the convocation floor. The denomination experienced a small split in factions in 1969 as a result of the turmoil. For an overview of the crisis and its eventual resolution, see Blake, *Church of God in Christ*, and Owens, "Dark Years."

3. Calhoun, "Woman on the Go for God," 78.

4. Ibid., 88.

5. Ibid., 86.

6. Ibid., 82.

7. 14th Annual Women's Convention Booklet, Church of God in Christ, 17, ADBC.

8. "Dr. Lillian Brooks Coffey Dies," *Evangelist Speaks*, July 1964, 1.

Bibliography

Archival Sources

American Baptist Historical Society, Valley Forge, Pa.

The American Baptist–Samuel Colgate Historical Library, Rochester, N.Y.

Assemblies of God Archives, Flower Pentecostal Heritage Center, Assemblies of God, Springfield, Mo.

Claude Barnett Papers, Chicago Historical Society, Chicago, Ill.

Bentley Historical Library, University of Michigan Library, Ann Arbor, Mich.

Mary McLeod Bethune Council House, National Park Service, Washington, D.C.

Anthea D. Butler Private Collection, Rochester, N.Y.

> Lelia Mason Byas interview by author, Memphis, Tennessee, June 1995
>
> Program of the Church of God in Christ's Thirty-Seventh Annual Women's Convention, 1988

David D. Daniels III Private Collection, Chicago, Ill.

David Du Plessis Papers, Fuller Theological Seminary, Pasadena, Calif.

Sherry Sherrod DuPree Collection (African American Pentecostal and Holiness Collection), Schomburg Center for Research in Black Culture, New York Public Library, Harlem Branch, New York, N.Y.

Sherry Sherrod DuPree Private Collection, Gainsville, Fla.

> Minutes of the Church of God in Christ Convocations, 1919–32

Glenda Goodson Collection, The Center for African American Church History and Research, Lancaster, Tex.

Mattie McGlothen Library and Museum, Oakland, Calif.

Moorland Spingarn Center, Howard University, Washington, D.C.

Raynard Smith Private Collection, Edison, N.J.

Southern Baptist Historical Library and Archives, Nashville, Tenn.

Tennessee State Library and Archives, Nashville, Tenn.

Newspapers and Periodicals

Chicago Defender, Chicago, Ill.
The Christian Hope Magazine
Commercial Appeal, Memphis, Tenn.
The Evangelist Speaks, Memphis, Tenn.

Hope, Organ of the Fireside Schools,
  Nashville, Tenn.
The Ivy Leaf
Lifted Banners, Omaha, Neb.
The Whole Truth, Memphis Tenn.

Printed Sources

Anderson, James. *The Education of Blacks in the South*. Chapel Hill: University of North Carolina Press, 1988.

Anderson, Robert Mapes. *Vision of the Disinherited: The Making of American Pentecostalism*. New York: Oxford University Press 1970.

Austin-Broos, Diane J. *Jamaica Genesis: Religion and the Politics of Moral Orders*. Chicago: University of Chicago Press, 1997.

Baer, Hans A., and Merrill Singer. *African-American Religion in the Twentieth Century: Varieties of Protest and Accommodation*. 1st ed. Knoxville: University of Tennessee Press, 1992.

Baldwin, Lewis V. "Black Women and African Union Methodism, 1813–1983." *Methodist History* 21, no. 4 (1983): 225–37.

Bean, Bobby. *This Is the Church of God in Christ*. Atlanta: Underground Epics, 2001.

Best, Wallace. *Passionately Human, No Less Divine: Religion and Culture in Black Chicago, 1915–1952*. Princeton: Princeton University Press, 2005.

Blake, Charles E., *The Church of God in Christ: Its Organizational Crisis*. N.p., 1965.

Blumhofer, Edith Waldvogel. *Aimee Semple McPherson: Everybody's Sister*. Grand Rapids, Mich.: Eerdmans, 1998.

———. *Restoring the Faith: The Assemblies of God, Pentecostalism, and American Culture*. Urbana: University of Illinois Press, 1993.

Bourdieu, Pierre. *Distinction: A Social Critique of the Judgement of Taste*. Translated by Richard Nice. Cambridge, Mass.: Harvard University Press, 1984.

Bragg, Cynthia Barbara. "The Church of God in Christ: A Religious Institution in Transition." Master's thesis, Iowa State University, 1992.

Brasher, Brenda E. *Godly Women: Fundamentalism and Female Power*. New Brunswick: Rutgers University Press, 1998.

Brekus, Catherine. *Strangers and Pilgrims: Female Preaching in America, 1740–1845*. Chapel Hill: University of North Carolina Press, 1998.

Broughton, Virginia W. *Twenty Years' Experience of a Missionary*. Reprinted in *Spiritual Narratives*, by Susan E. Houchins. New York: Oxford University Press, 1988.

Brown, Pearl Page. *Sewing Circle Artistic Fingers*. N.p.: Church of God in Christ, n.d.

Burgess, Stanley M. *Reaching Beyond: Chapters in the History of Perfectionism*. Peabody, Mass.: Hendrickson, 1986.

Burgess, Stanley M., Gary B. McGee, and Patrick H. Alexander. *Dictionary of Pente-costal and Charismatic Movements*. Grand Rapids, Mich.: Regency Reference Library, 1988.

Butler, Anthea. "Church Mothers and Migration in the Church of God in Christ." In *Religion in the American South: Protestants and Others in History and Culture*, edited by Beth Barton Schweiger and Donald G. Mathews, 195–218. Chapel Hill: University of North Carolina Press, 2004.

———. "Observing the Lives of the Saints: Sanctification and Practice in Everyday Life." In *Practicing Protestants: Histories of Christian Lives in America*, edited by Laurie Maffly Kipp, Leigh Schmidt, and Mark Valeri, 159–76. Baltimore: Johns Hopkins University Press, 2006.

———. "A Peculiar Synergy: Matriarchy and the Church of God in Christ." Ph.D. diss., Vanderbilt University, 2001.

Byas, Lelia Mason, with Jack T. Hunt. *From Priors Farm to Heaven: Bishop C. H. Mason, a Biography of His Life*. N.p.: Hunt Family Publishing Company, 1995.

Cayton, Horace R., and St. Clair Drake. *Black Metropolis: A Study of Negro Life in a Northern City*. New York: Harcourt Brace and Company, 1945.

Certeau, Michel de. *The Practice of Everyday Life*. Translated by Steven F. Rendall. Berkeley: University of California Press, 1984.

Chatter, Linda M., Robert Joseph Taylor, and Rukmalie Jaykody. "Fictive Kinship Relations in Black Extended Families." *Journal of Comparative Family Studies* 25, no. 3 (1994): 297–312.

Chaves, Mark. *Ordaining Women: Culture and Conflict in Religious Organizations*. Cambridge, Mass.: Harvard University Press, 1997.

Chesler, Phyllis. *Woman's Inhumanity to Woman*. New York: Thunder's Mouth Press / Nation Books, 2001.

Chude-Sokei, Louis, *The Last "Darky": Bert Williams, Black-on-Black Minstrelsy, and the African Diaspora*. Durham, N.C.: Duke University Press, 2005.

Church, H. Carlyle, Jr. "The Accommodation and Liberation of Women in the Church of God in Christ." *Journal of Religious Thought* 52/53, no. 2/1 (1996): 77–90.

Church of God in Christ. *From the Beginning of C. H. Mason and the Early Pioneers of the Church of God in Christ*. Memphis: Church of God in Christ Publishing House, 1991.

———. *Minutes of the General Assemblies, 1934–1960*. Memphis: Church of God in Christ Publishing House, 2002.

Clark, William. "Sanctification in Negro Religion." *Social Forces* 15, no. 4 (May 1937): 544–51.

Clemmons, Ithiel C. *Bishop C. H. Mason and the Church of God in Christ*. Bakersfield, Calif.: Pneuma Life, 1996.

Cornelius, Lucille J. *The Pioneer History of the Church of God in Christ*. Memphis: Church of God in Christ Publishing House, 1975.

Cox, Harvey Gallagher. *Fire from Heaven: The Rise of Pentecostal Spirituality and the Reshaping of Religion in the Twenty-first Century*. Reading, Mass.: Addison-Wesley, 1995.

Crews, Mickey. *The Church of God: A Social History*. 1st ed. Knoxville: University of Tennessee Press, 1990.

Dabney, E. J. *What It Means to Pray Through*. c. 1940s. Memphis: COGIC Publishing Board, 1987.

Daniels, David Douglas, III. "The Cultural Renewal of Slave Religion: Charles Price Jones and the Emergence of the Holiness Movement in Mississippi." Ph.D. diss., Union Theological Seminary, 1992.

———. "Live So You Can Use Me Anytime Lord, Anywhere: Theological Education in the Church of God in Christ." *Asian Journal of Pentecostal Studies* 3, no. 2 (2000): 295–310.

Dayton, Donald W. *The Theological Roots of Pentecostalism*. Grand Rapids: Francis Asbury, 1987.

DeBerg, Betty A. *Ungodly Women: Gender and the First Wave of American Fundamentalism*. Minneapolis: Augsburg Fortress, 1990.

Duff, Rose Marie. *The Ethnohistory of Saint's Home Church of the Church of God in Christ, Los Angeles, California*. Sacramento: California State University, 1972.

DuPree, Sherry Sherrod. *African-American Holiness Pentecostal Movement: An Annotated Bibliography*. New York: Garland, 1994.

DuPree, Sherry Sherrod, and Herbert C. DuPree, comp. *Exposed!: FBI Unclassified Reports on Churches and Church Leaders*. Washington, D.C.: Middle Atlantic Regional Press, 1993.

Durrand, Tom Craig, and Anson D. Shupe. *Metaphors of Social Control in a Pentecostal Sect*. New York: E. Mellen, 1984.

Easter, Opal V. *Nannie Helen Burroughs*. New York: Garland, 1995.

Eaton, Grace M. *A Heroine of the Cross: Sketches of the Life and Work of Miss Joanna P. Moore, for Fifty-three Years a Missionary among the Negro People*. N.p., 1934.

Evenson, Bruce J. *God's Man for the Gilded Age: D. L. Moody and the Rise of Modern Mass Evangelism*. New York: Oxford, 2003.

Faupel, D. William. *The Everlasting Gospel: The Significance of Eschatology in the Development of Pentecostal Thought*. Sheffield, Eng.: Sheffield Academic Press, 1996.

Fauset, Arthur Huff. *Black Gods of the Metropolis*. Philadelphia: University of Pennsylvania Press, 1944.

Fulop, Timothy Earl, and Albert J. Raboteau. *African-American Religion: Interpretive Essays in History and Culture*. New York: Routledge, 1997.

Gaines, Kevin. *Uplifting the Race: Black Leadership, Politics, and Culture in the Twentieth Century*. Chapel Hill: University of North Carolina Press, 1996.

Gerlach, Luther P., and Virginia H. Hine. *People, Power, Change: Movements of Social Transformation*. Indianapolis: Bobbs-Merrill, 1970.

Giddings, Paula. *When and Where I Enter: The Impact of Black Women on Race and Sex in America*. 1st ed. New York: W. Morrow, 1984.

Giggie, John Michael, and Diane H. Winston. *Faith in the Market: Religion and the Rise of Urban Commercial Culture*. New Brunswick: Rutgers University Press, 2002.

Gilbert, Earl Jean. "Some Personality Correlates of Certain Religious Beliefs, Attitudes, Practices, and Experiences in Students Attending a Fundamentalist Pentecostal Church College." Ed.D. thesis, University of Tennessee, 1972.

Gilkes, Cheryl Townsend. *If It Wasn't for the Women: Black Women's Experience and Womanist Culture in Church and Community*. Maryknoll, N.Y.: Orbis Books, 2001.

———. "The Role of Women in the Sanctified Church." *Journal of Religious Thought* 43, no. 1 (Spring 1986): 24–41.

———. "The Roles of Church and Community Mothers: Ambivalent American Sexism of Fragmented African Familyhood?" *Journal of Feminist Studies in Religion* 2 (1986): 41–59.

———. "'Together and in Harness': Women's Traditions in the Sanctified Church." *Signs* 10, no. 41 (1985): 687–95.

Gilman, Charlotte Perkins. "Surplus Negro Women." In *Radicals and Conservatives, and Other Essays on the Negro in America*, edited by Kelly Miller. 1908. Reprint, New York: Schocken, 1968.

Goldsmith, Peter. "A Woman's Place Is in the Church: Black Pentecostalism on the Georgia Coast." *Journal of Religious Thought* 46 (Winter–Spring 1989–1990): 53–69.

Griffith, R. Marie. *God's Daughters: Evangelical Women and the Power of Submission*. Berkeley: University of California Press, 1997.

Hardesty, Nancy. "Transatlantic Roots of the Holiness-Pentecostal Movement." Paper presented at the annual meeting of the American Society of Church History, Seattle, Wash., January 10, 1998.

Hardesty, Nancy, Lucille Sider Dayton, and Donald W. Dayton. "Women in the Holiness Movement: Feminism in the Evangelical Tradition." In *Women of Spirit: Female Leadership in the Jewish and Christian Traditions*, edited by Rosemary Ruether and Eleanor McLaughlin, 241–48. New York: Simon and Schuster, 1979.

Harris, Fredrick C. *Something Within: Religion in African-American Political Activism*. New York: Oxford University Press, 1999.

Harris, Paisley. "Gatekeeping and Remaking: The Politics of Respectability in African American Women's History and Black Feminism." *Journal of Women's History* 15, no. 1 (Spring 2003): 212–20.

Harvey, Paul. *Freedom's Coming: Religious Culture and the Shaping of the South from the Civil War through the Civil Rights Era*. Chapel Hill: University of North Carolina Press, 2005.

———. *Redeeming the South: Religious Cultures and Racial Identities Among Southern Baptists, 1865–1925*. Chapel Hill: University of North Carolina Press, 1997.

Higginbotham, Evelyn Brooks. "African-American Women's History and the Meta-language of Race." *Signs* 17, no. 21 (1992): 251–74.

———. *Righteous Discontent: The Women's Movement in the Black Baptist Church, 1880–1920*. Cambridge, Mass.: Harvard University Press, 1993.

———. "The Women's Movement in the Black Baptist Church, 1880–1920." Ph.D. diss., University of Rochester, 1984.

Hollenweger, Walter J. *Pentecost between Black and White: Five Case Studies on Pentecost and Politics*. Belfast: Christian Journals, 1974.

———. *Pentecostalism: Origins and Developments Worldwide*. Peabody, Mass.: Hendrickson, 1997.

Hogan, Lawrence D. *A Black National News Service: The Associated Negro Press and Claude Barnett, 1919–1945*. Rutherford, N.J.: Fairleigh Dickinson University Press, 1984.

Hollenweger, Walter J., and J. A. B. Jongeneel. *Pentecost, Mission, and Ecumenism's Essays on Intercultural Theology: Festschrift in Honour of Professor Walter J. Hollenweger*. Frankfurt: P. Lang, 1992.

Holt, W. M. *A Brief Historical and Doctrinal Statement and Rules for Government of the Church of God in Christ*. Memphis: privately published, 1918.

Houchins, Susan E. *Spiritual Narratives*. New York: Oxford University Press, 1988.

Hull, Gloria T., Patricia Bell Scott, and Barbara Smith, eds. *All the Women Are White, All the Blacks Are Men, but Some of Us Are Brave: Black Women's Studies*. Old Westbury, N.Y.: Feminist Press, 1982.

Hurston, Zora Neale. *The Sanctified Church*. New York: Marlow, 1981.

Jackson, Jerma A. *Singing in My Soul: Black Gospel Music in a Secular Age*. Chapel Hill: University of North Carolina Press, 2004.

Jacobsen, Douglas G. *Thinking in the Spirit: Theologies of the Early Pentecostal Movement*. Bloomington: Indiana University Press, 2003.

Johnson, Clifton H. *God Struck Me Dead: Voices of Ex-Slaves*. Cleveland, Ohio: Pilgrim Press, 1993.

Johnson, Mary Magrum. *Life and Labors*. N.p., n.d.

Jones, Charles Edwin. *Guide to the Study of the Pentecostal Movement*. Metuchen N.J.: Scarecrow Press American Theological Library Association, 1983.

Kerber, Linda K. *Toward an Intellectual History of Women: Essays*. Chapel Hill: University of North Carolina Press, 1997.

Lawless, Elaine J. *God's Peculiar People: Women's Voices and Folk Tradition in a Pentecostal Church*. Lexington: University Press of Kentucky, 1988.

———. *Handmaidens of the Lord: Pentecostal Women Preachers and Traditional Religion*. Publications of the American Folklore Society, n.s. 9. Philadelphia: University of Pennsylvania Press, 1988.

Lincoln, C. Eric, and Lawrence H. Mamiya. *The Black Church in the African American Experience*. Durham: Duke University Press, 1990.

Lindley, Susan Hill. *You Have Stept Out of Your Place: A History of Women and Religion in America*. 1st ed. Louisville: Westminster John Knox Press, 1996.

Little, Sweetie. *Back to Pentecost*. N.p., n.d.

Litwack, Leon F. *Trouble in Mind: Black Southerners in the Age of Jim Crow*. New York: Vintage, 1999.

MacRobert, Iain. *The Black Roots and White Racism of Early Pentecostalism in the USA*. Basingstoke: Macmillan, 1988.

Mason, C. H. *The History and Life Work of Elder C. H. Mason, Chief Apostle, and His Co-laborers*. Compiled by Mary Mason. N.p., 1924.

Mason, Mack C. *Saints in the Land of Lincoln: The Urban Development of a Pentecostal Denomination and the Birth of the Gospel Music Industry*. Hazel Crest, Ill.: Faithday Press, 2004.

McCluskey, Audrey Thomas, and Elaine Smith, eds. *Mary McLeod Bethune: Building a Better World: Selected Essays and Documents*. Bloomington: Indiana University Press, 1999.

McCullom, Pearl Roberts. *Historical Sketches of Pioneer Women of the Church of God in Christ, Inc.* N.p., 1975.

McGlothen, Mattie, ed. *Women's Department Revised Edition of Organization and Procedure*. Memphis: Church of God in Christ Publishing House, 1989.

Mendiola, Kelly W. "The Hand of a Woman: Four Holiness-Pentecostal Evangelists and American Culture, 1840–1930." Ph.D. diss., University of Texas at Austin, 2002.

Miller, A. G. "Pentecostalism as Social Movement: Beyond the Theory of Deprivation." *Journal of Pentecostal Theology*, no. 9 (1996): 97–114.

Moore, Joanna P. *In Christ's Stead*. Chicago: Women's Baptist Home Mission Society, 1902.

———. *The Power and Work of the Holy Spirit*. New York: Fleming H. Revell, 1912.

Moorehead, James H. "The Quest for Holiness in American Protestantism." *Interpretation* 53, no. 4 (October 1999): 365–79.

Morris, E. C. *Sermons, Addresses and Reminiscences and Important Correspondence, with a Picture Gallery of Eminent Ministers and Scholars*. Nashville: National Baptist Publishing Board, 1901.

Morton, Patricia. *Disfigured Images: The Historical Assault on Afro-American Women*. Contributions in Afro-American and African Studies, no. 144. New York: Greenwood, 1991.

National Council of Negro Women Inc. *Women United: Souvenir Year Book, Sixteenth Anniversary*. Washington, D.C.: n.p., 1951.

O'Neal, Gwendolyn S. "The African American Chruch, Its Sacred Cosmos, and Dress." In *Religion, Dress and the Body*, edited by Linda B. Arthur. New York: Berg, 1999.

Orsi, Robert. *The Madonna of 115th Street: Faith and Community in Italian Harlem*. 2d ed. New Haven: Yale University Press, 2002.

Owens, Robert R. "The Dark Years (1961–1968): Leadership Styles and Organizational Types in the Transition from the Founder to the Successors in the Church of God in Christ." Ph.D. diss., Regent University, 2000.

Parham, Charles F. *A Voice Crying Out in the Wilderness: The Sermons of Charles F. Parham*. New York: Garland, 1985.

Paris, Arthur E. *Black Pentecostalism: Southern Religion in an Urban World*. Amherst: University of Massachusetts Press, 1982.

Pleas, Charles H. *Fifty Years Achievement, 1906–1956: A Period in the History of the Church of God in Christ*. Memphis: Church of God in Christ Public Relations, 1956; Reprint, 1991.

Powdermaker, Hortense, Brackette F. Williams, and Drexel G. Woodson. *After Freedom: A Cultural Study in the Deep South*. Madison: University of Wisconsin Press, 1993.

Range, C. F., ed. *Official Manual with the Doctrines and Discipline of the Church of God in Christ*. Memphis: Church of God in Christ Publishing House, 1973.

Robeck, Cecil M. *The Azusa Street Mission and Revival: The Birth of the Global Pentecostal Movement*. Nashville, Tenn.: Nelson Reference & Electronic, 2006.

Roebuck, David G. "Limiting Liberty: The Church of God and Women Ministers, 1886–1996." Ph.D. diss., Vanderbilt University, 1997.

Rooks, Nowlie. *Hair Raising: Beauty, Culture, and African American Women*. New Brunswick: Rutgers University Press, 1996.

Ruether, Rosemary Radford, and Rosemary Skinner Keller. *Women and Religion in America*. 1st ed. 3 vols. San Francisco: Harper and Row, 1981.

Ruether, Rosemary, and Eleanor McLaughlin, eds. *Women of Spirit: Female Leadership in the Jewish and Christian Traditions*. New York: Simon and Schuster, 1979.

Sanders, Cheryl Jeanne. *Saints in Exile: The Holiness-Pentecostal Experience in African American Religion and Culture*. New York: Oxford University Press, 1996.

Sernett, Milton C. *Bound for the Promised Land: African American Religion and the Great Migration*. Durham: Duke University Press, 1997.

Seller, Maxine Schwartz. *Women Educators in the United States, 1820–1993: A Bio-biographical Sourcebook*. Westport, Conn.: Greenwood Press, 1994.

Simmonds, Dovie Marie, and Olivia L. Martin. *Down Behind the Sun: The Story of Arenia Cornelia Mallory*. Memphis: Riverside Press, 1983.

Sing unto the Lord a New Song: Songs of Inspiration, Revelation and Doctrine of the Church of God in Christ from the 1930's to 1950's. N.p.: Gospel in Reach Ministries, n.d.

Smith, Jessie Carney, ed. *Notable Black American Women*. Detroit: Gale Research, 1992.

Smith, Susan L. *Sick and Tired of Being Sick and Tired: Black Women's Health Activism in America, 1890–1950*. Philadelphia: University of Pennsylvania Press, 1995.

Society for Pentecostal Studies and Wesleyan Theological Society. *Purity and Power: Revisioning the Holiness and Pentecostal/Charismatic Movements for the Twenty-First Century*. Proceedings of the Twenty-Seventh Annual Meeting of the Society for Pentecostal Studies in special session with the Wesleyan Theological Society, March 12–14, 1998. N.p.: Society for Pentecostal Societies, 1998.

Stanley, Susie. *Holy Boldness: Women Preachers' Autobiographies and the Sanctified Self*. Knoxville: University of Tennessee Press, 2001.

Steady, Filomina Chioma, ed. *The Black Woman Cross-Culturally*. Cambridge, Mass.: Schenkman, 1981.

Stephens, Michael. "Who Healeth All Thy Diseases: Health, Healing, and Holiness in the Church of God Reformation Movement, 1880–1925." Ph.D. diss., Vanderbilt University, 2004.

Stewart, Walter Sinclair. *Later Baptist Missionaries and Pioneers*. Philadelphia: Judson Press, 1928–29.

Swan, Sallie M. *A Brief History of the Life and Work of Elder B. S. Lyle*. N.p., 1944.

Synan, Vinson. *The Holiness-Pentecostal Tradition: Charismatic Movements in the Twentieth Century*. 2d ed. Grand Rapids, Mich.: Eerdmans, 1997.

Tinney, James. *Black Pentecostalism: An Annotated Bibliography*. Washington, D.C.: privately published, 1979.

Toulis, Nicole Rodriguez. *Believing Identity: Pentecostalism and the Mediation of Jamaican Ethnicity and Gender in England*. Oxford: Berg, 1997.

Truesdell, Leon E., and T. F. Murphy. *Religious Bodies: 1926*. Prepared for the U.S. Bureau of the Census. Washington, D.C.: U.S. Government Printing Office, 1930.

Trulear, Harold Dean. "Ida B. Robinson: The Mother as Symbolic Presence." In *Portraits of a Generation: Early Pentecostal Leaders*, edited by James R. Goff and Grant Wacker, 309–24. Fayetteville: University of Arkansas Press, 2002.

Turner, Bryan S., ed. *The Blackwell Companion to Social Theory*. 2d ed. Malden, Mass.: Blackwell, 2000.

Turner, William Clair. "The United Holy Church of America: A Study in Black Holiness-Pentecostalism." Ph.D. diss., Duke University, 1984.

"The Voice of Mother Robinson: First General Supervisor of Women, Churches of God in Christ, Inc." *The Whole Truth*, February 1968.

Wacker, Grant. *Heaven Below: Early Pentecostals and American Culture*. Cambridge, Mass.: Harvard University Press, 2001.

Weisenfeld, Judith. *African American Women and Christian Activism: New York's Black YWCA, 1905–1945*. Cambridge, Mass.: Harvard University Press, 1997.

Weisenfeld, Judith, and Richard Newman. *This Far by Faith: Readings in African-American Women's Religious Biography*. New York: Routledge, 1996.

Wells, Patricia Casenia. "Historical Overview of the Establishment of the Church of God in Christ." D.Min. diss., International Bible Institute and Seminary, 1987.

White, Deborah Gray. *Too Heavy a Load: Black Women in Defense of Themselves*. New York: W. W. Norton, 1999.

Wiggins, Daphne C. *Righteous Content: Black Women's Perspectives of Church and Faith*. New York: New York University Press, 2004.

Williams, Melvin D. *Community in a Black Pentecostal Church: An Anthropological Study*. Pittsburgh: University of Pittsburgh Press, 1974.

Wilmore, Gayraud. *Black Religion and Black Radicalism: An Interpretation of the Religious History of African Americans*. 3d ed. Maryknoll, N.Y.: Orbis, 1998.

Wilson, Charles Reagan, and William Ferris, eds. *Encyclopedia of Southern Culture*. Chapel Hill: University of North Carolina Press, 1989.

Wolcott, Victoria W. *Remaking Respectability: African American Women in Interwar Detroit*. Chapel Hill: University of North Carolina Press, 2001.

Wood, William W. *Culture and Personality Aspects of the Pentecostal Holiness Religion*. The Hague: Mouton, 1965.

Index

Baptist Church: Southern Baptist Convention, 6; women's organizations in, 6, 15; National Baptist Women's Convention, 6, 26, 41, 42, 54, 61, 77, 121, 155; and sanctification, 7, 19–20, 26–27, 30–31; and Joanna P. Moore, 15; home missionary activities of, 16; and Bible Bands, 25–26; and speaking in tongues, 30–31; and women's role in ministry, 38; National Baptist Convention, 38, 41, 67, 99, 160; and lower-class women, 67; shunning of ecstatic practices by, 73; and education, 99, 100; as cessationists, 170 (n. 52); and women's day, 174 (n. 33)

Barnett, Claude, 108, 124, 142, 177 (n. 14), 179 (n. 17)

Barnett, Ida B. Wells, 24

Best, Wallace, 168 (n. 5)

Bethune, Mary McLeod: and Arenia Mallory, 9, 101, 109–14, 116, 118, 120, 137; religious base of organization built by, 24; and Holiness movement, 109–11; and education, 110–13; photograph of, 111; dress style of, 112; and Saints Industrial School, 112; skin color of, 112; and National Association of Colored Women, 112, 121; and Roosevelts, 114, 121; and National Council of Negro Women, 120–24, 138–40, 153; as National Youth Administration director, 121; and interracial cooperation, 121–22; and Moral Re-Armament (MRA) movement, 122; and Coffey, 123–24; and Women's Army for National Defense, 127–28; and Robinson's funeral, 133; at Women's Convention (1951), 148; retirement of, 153; and conference on black women an children, 178 (n. 48)

Bethune Training School for Girls/ Bethune Cookman College, 112

Bible: on Eli's calling of Samuel, 13; and teachings of bourgeois respectability, 14–15, 19; *Hope* magazine for study of, 15, 18–26, 47; sale of, 18, 22–23; Fireside Schools for study of, 18–20, 169 (n. 18); on body as temple of Holy Spirit, 20, 76, 169 (n. 25); and women's teaching versus preaching, 32, 34–35, 39, 61; on wives' submission to husbands, 33; and convocation, 40; on overseer, 41; on nakedness, 79–80; Jezebel in, 83, 84–85, 175 (n. 18); on premarital sex, 86; on marriage, 92; education through scriptural admonitions, 98–99. *See also* Bible Bands; *and specific books of Bible*

Bible Bands: establishment of, by Joanna P. Moore, 15–25; and leadership by African American women, 16–17, 19, 24–25, 34, 35; and literacy of women, 19, 22, 26, 35, 97; and Lizzie Robinson, 21–24, 31, 34, 35, 47, 53–54; and Baptist Church, 25–26; and Charles Mason, 41; in COGIC, 42–45, 62, 97, 98, 100–101, 115

Bigamy, 92–94, 103. *See also* Marriage; Sexuality

Bishops' Wives Circle, 141

Black church: history of, 6–7; women's participation in, 24; as patriarchal and hierarchical, 24, 169–70 (n. 40); and women's calling to preaching ministry, 32–33; in North, 58–59; and modernity, 115; and civil and human rights in twentieth century, 165; meaning of term, 169–70 (n. 40). *See also* Church of God in Christ; *and specific denominations*

Body: sanctification of, 20, 75–86, 76, 169 (n. 25); as temple of Holy Spirit, 20, 76, 169 (n. 25); purity of, 69; racist view of black body, 75; African cosmology of self and, 84; female body as temple of Christ, 84

Bostick, Daniel, 50, 51, 117

Bostick, Lucinda, 50, 51, 78

Bourgeois respectability, 14–15, 19, 77, 80–81

Brooks, Jerry and Lula, 56

Brooks, Mazy, 70

Broughton, Virginia, 26, 174 (n. 2)

Brown, Charlotte Hawkins, 113

Brown, Lavonia, 127

Buchman, Frank Nathan Daniel, 122

Burroughs, Nannie Helen, 14, 98, 100, 109, 121, 174 (n. 3), 174 (n. 33), 175 (n. 12)

Byas, Lelia (Mason), 71–72, 175 (n. 17)

Bynum, Juanita, 165

Calhoun, Lillian S., 158

Cantrell, Carrie, 139

Carter, Elder and Mother, 71

Carter, Minnie, 78–79

Celibacy, 86, 87, 90, 158. *See also* Sexuality

Chandler, Hannah, 44, 45, 50

Chaves, Mark, 171 (n. 18)

Chicago Defender, 87, 104, 117, 124, 137, 146

Children and youth: Sunshine Band for, 46–47, 62; purity class for youth, 47, 86, 149; and Sunday school, 98; illegitimate children, 158–59

Christian Hope, 115, 127, 129

Christian Methodist Episcopal Church, 6, 34

Christian Right, 165

Church mothers: role of, 2–3, 12, 43–48, 152, 161–62; in COGIC, 2–3, 44–48; and sanctification, 3–4, 67–71; agency of, 4, 12; and power through purity, 5–6; themes of work of, 25; and dress code, 40, 69, 77–78, 81; definition of, 43–44; relationship between pastors

and, 45–46, 48–50, 52–53; church-planting activities by, 50–53, 58–60, 64; and migration of African Americans, 58–64; preparation and selection of, 68–69; and convocation, 71–72; and Lillian Coffey, 152; from 1970s to present, 161–64. *See also* Leadership by African American women; *and specific women*

Church of God, 37

Church of God in Christ (COGIC): origins and founding of, 1, 12, 27; membership statistics for, 2; church mothers' role in, 2–3, 12, 44–48, 152; significance of history of, 6–10; name of, 27, 29; compared with Pentecostal churches, 30; and women's teaching versus preaching, 34–40, 60–61; convocations of, 40, 46, 71–74, 117, 130–34, 145, 149–50, 160, 171 (n. 22), 174 (n. 30); overseers in, 41–42, 52–53, 171 (n. 24); Prayer and Bible Bands in, 42–43, 68–69, 73, 86, 97, 145; Bible Bands in, 42–45, 62, 97, 98, 100–101, 115; and Sunday school, 46–47, 98, 142, 172 (n. 38); fictive family relationships in, 48–50, 57, 66, 108; music of, 49, 65; and church-planting activities by women, 50–53, 58–61, 64; finances of, 53; and migration of African Americans, 55–74; family connections of leaders within, 58, 173 (n. 7); ecstatic religious practices of, 72–73; and education, 96–116; publishing by, 115, 142; and World War II, 117, 118, 119, 126–29, 151; and World War I, 117–18, 120, 129; and pacifism, 117–18, 120, 129, 151; and civic engagement, 117–34; and Mason Temple, 126, 129, 130, 131, 133; social class of members of, 137–38; inner circle of leadership of, 138; media coverage of, 138; turmoil in, after Charles Mason's death, 157, 181 (n. 2). *See also* Church of God in Christ (COGIC) Women's Department; Mason, Charles Harrison; Pastors/preachers; Sanctification

Church of God in Christ (COGIC) Women's Department: establishment of, 2, 9, 41–43; and church mothers' role, 2–3, 12, 44–48, 152, 161; Robinson's leadership of, 4, 7, 35, 39–43, 53–54, 133, 135, 176 (n. 35), 177 (n. 6); Coffey's leadership of, 4, 7, 56, 115, 123, 132, 133, 134, 139–44, 155, 158–61; significance of, 6–10, 165; themes of women's work in, 25; and Bible Bands, 42–45, 53–54, 62, 97, 98, 100–101, 115; Sewing Circle in, 46, 47, 69, 78, 81; and Sunshine Band, 46–47, 62; and purity class for youth, 47, 86, 149; and relationship between pastors and church mothers, 48–50, 52–53; autonomy of, 50, 53; church-planting activities by, 50–53, 58–61, 64; and state overseers/supervisors, 50–53, 161, 175 (n. 24); and migration of African Americans, 52, 54, 55–56, 55–74; bank account of, 53; and education, 98–99, 151; and Home and Foreign Missions Band, 115; and civic engagement, 117–36; and National Council of Negro Women, 123–24, 129, 136, 138–40, 153, 163, 164; and retirement homes, 124–26, 136, 142–43; and World War II, 127–29; and Mason Temple, 130, 131; media coverage of, 138, 146–47, 152–53; demographics of, 140; auxiliaries of, in 1950s, 140–42; promotion of, 142–43; publications of, 142–43; and Home and Foreign Missions Board, 144, 148, 149; and Women's Conventions, 145–53, 154, 160; from 1970s

to present, 161–65. *See also* Church mothers; Church of God in Christ; Leadership by African American women; Missionaries; Sanctification

Church of Christ, Holiness, 29

Church of God, Pillar and Ground of Truth, 37–38

Church-planting activities, 50–53, 58–61, 64

Cities. *See* Migration of African Americans

Civic engagement: and sanctified life, 4–5, 117–34; and National Council of Negro Women, 8, 9, 101, 118, 120–24, 129, 136, 138–40, 153; and Arenia Mallory generally, 9, 122, 124, 129, 136–37; and Alpha Kappa Alpha, 101, 104–8, 113, 118; and World War II, 117, 118, 119, 126–29, 151; and community motherhood, 119–20; and home mission work, 120; Robinson's avoidance of, 120; and Coffey, 120, 123–29, 134, 136; and interracial cooperation, 121–22; and Moral Re-Armament (MRA) movement, 122, 129; and retirement homes, 124–26, 136, 142–43; and Women's Army for National Defense, 127–29, 136; and COGIC convocation (1945), 130–34; symbol of, on *Lifted Banners* cover, 134, 142; and Women's Conventions in 1950s, 150–53

Cleanliness and sanctification, 20, 77, 81, 83

Clemmons, H. C., 93, 176 (n. 42)

Clothing. *See* Dress code; Dress styles of unsanctified

Club movement. *See* Women's club movement

Cobb, Estella, 175 (n. 26)

Coffey, Lillian Brooks: and leadership of COGIC Women's Department, 4,

respectable African American women, 80–81; sermon on, 81; hymns on, 81, 83; photograph of clothing of COGIC women, 82; and white clothing, 82, 83; and Alpha Kappa Alphas at Saints Industrial School, 105–6; and Mary McLeod Bethune's dress style, 112; and Lillian Coffey, 133, 143–44; in 1950s, 141–42; from 1970s to present, 163, 164. *See also* Hairstyle; Makeup prohibition

Dress styles of unsanctified, 78–79, 83, 174 (n. 17), 175 (n. 16)

Driver, Eddie, 61

Driver, E. R., 117

Du Bois, W. E. B., 14, 19, 97, 112

Duncan, Pinki, 99, 100

Early, Lillie, 50

Ebony magazine, 91, 149, 153, 157–60

Ecstatic religious practices, 72–73

Education: Burrough's training school for girls, 14, 98, 100, 109, 174 (n. 3), 175 (n. 12); and Fireside Schools, 18–20, 169 (n. 18); and Bible Bands, 19, 22, 26, 35, 97, 100–101, 115; illiteracy of preachers, 26, 35; and Pentecostalism, 96, 100, 177 (n. 9); of African Americans in early twentieth century, 96–97, 100, 113; W. E. B. Du Bois on, 97; Booker T. Washington on, 97, 98, 100, 109; through scriptural admonitions, 98–99; and Baptist Church, 99, 100; Arenia Mallory's goals on, 109; and Mary McLeod Bethune, 110–13; Women's Convention (1953) on, 151. *See also* Bible Bands; Saints Industrial School

Evangelicalism, 165

Evangelists, 94

The Evangelist Speaks, 142, 161

Exodus, book of, 174 (n. 31)

Faludi, Susan, 165

Family relationships. *See* Fictive family relationships in COGIC

Fasting, 68, 72, 76, 99. *See also* Sanctification

FBI, 118, 120

Feminist and womanist movements, 165

Ferebee, Dorothy Boulding, 107, 153

Fictive family relationships in COGIC, 48–50, 57, 66, 108

Fireside Schools, 18–20, 169 (n. 18)

First Century Christian Fellowship, 122

Fisk Jubilee Singers, 177 (n. 16)

Fisk University, 109

Flagg, Lucy, 75, 83, 175 (n. 16)

Food: and sanctification, 20; at COGIC convocation, 71–72

Ford, Louis, 138

Fundamentalism, 170 (n. 2)

Gambling, 60, 76

Garveyites, 67

Gender roles: of church mothers, 2–3, 12, 43–44, 152; in COGIC generally, 5–6; and ordination of women, 5–6, 25, 37–38, 171 (n. 18); Robinson on, 11, 34–40, 60, 62, 177 (n. 6); and Pentecostalism, 32–33, 35, 37–40, 171 (n. 13); and women's teaching versus preaching ministry, 32–40, 60–61; and biblical admonition on wives' submission to husbands, 33; and protection of womanhood, 33; and sanctity of femininity, 33; and biblical admonition on teaching versus preaching, 34–35; relationship between pastors and church mothers, 48–50, 52–53; and migration of African Americans, 62–63; and sanctified living in urban areas, 66–67; and dress code, 78–79; and sexual purity, 80, 84–85. *See also* African American women; Church mothers; Leadership

nature of, 53; and sanctified body, 76–86; and sanctified marriage, 86–95; and COGIC auxiliaries in 1950s, 140–42; and Women's Conventions in 1950s, 150–53. *See also* Bethune, Mary McLeod; Church mothers; Coffey, Lillian Brooks; Mallory, Arenia; Robinson, Lizzie Woods

Leviticus, book of, 40, 174 (n. 31)

Lifted Banners, 134, 135, 142–43

Light Burners of Africa, 144

Lincoln, C. Eric, 43, 44

Literacy. *See* Education

Little, Adam, 88–90

Los Angeles Sentinel, 146–47, 148

Louis, Joe, 138

Makeup prohibition, 83–85, 175 (n. 18). *See also* Dress code; Hair

Mallory, Arenia: and Saints Industrial School, 9, 93–94, 101–9, 112–14, 118, 136, 142; and Mary McLeod Bethune, 9, 101, 109–14, 116, 118, 120, 137; and Lillian Brooks Coffey, 9, 116, 123, 124, 138; and civic engagement generally, 9, 122, 124, 129, 136–37; birth of, 70; family background of, 70, 137, 138; conversion of, 70–71, 101; marriage and divorce of, 90, 93–94, 103, 176 (n. 42); daughter of, 93, 176 (n. 42); on sanctification, 96; education of, 101; and Alpha Kappa Alpha, 101, 104–8, 113; and National Council of Negro Women (NCNW), 101, 118, 120–22, 124, 136, 140, 153, 181 (n. 22); and Jane Addams, 101, 177 (n. 12); and Charles Mason, 101–2; photographs of, 103, 140, 162; fund-raising activities by, for Saints Industrial School, 104–7, 112, 114, 118, 136; and health care program, 107–8, 113, 153; on goals of church-based schools, 109; media coverage

of, 112–14, 124, 135–36, 137, 152, 177 (n. 14); as race woman, 113–14; White House visits by, 114, 118, 119, 140, 161, 162; and World War II, 120; and Moral Re-Armament (MRA) movement, 122; honors for, 124, 153; and Women's Army for National Defense, 127–29, 136; and airplane crash, 137; at convocation (1951), 149; at Coffey's funeral, 161; in 1970s, 162; death of, 163; and conference on black women and children, 178 (n. 48)

Mallory, Eddy, 70, 137

Mallory, Frank, 70, 137

Mamiya, Lawrence, 43, 44

Marriage: of darker skinned men to lighter skinned women, 85, 180 (n. 2); and upward mobility within church ranks, 86–87, 89; sanctification of, 86–95; arranged marriages, 87, 175 (n. 26); sexuality within, 88–89; difficulties of, 89, 90; sermon on, 89–90; and men as head of home, 90; prohibition of remarriage after divorce, 90–92, 173 (n. 8); and migration of African Americans, 92; and slaves, 92; double marriage (bigamy), 92–94. *See also* Divorce

Martin, Olivia, 93

Mason, Charles Harrison: and COGIC Women's Department, 2, 9, 41–43, 53, 56; death of, 9, 154, 157, 159; founding of COGIC by, 12, 27, 29, 34; and C. P. Jones, 26–27; and Holiness movement and Pentecostalism, 26–27, 29–30; healing experience of, 27; marriages of, 27, 30, 85, 91, 170 (n. 50), 180 (n. 2); and sanctification, 27, 30, 86; education of, 27, 97; photograph of, 28; first meeting between Lizzie Robinson and, 30, 57, 170 (n. 49); and women's teaching role n COGIC, 36–37; and

Lizzie Robinson's teaching role in COGIC, 36–38; and convocations of COGIC, 40, 72, 149; and Lizzie Robinson as overseer of women's work, 41–43; as "father" of church family, 48, 57–58; and finances of COGIC, 53; Lillian Brooks Coffey's relationship with, 56–58, 115, 144, 145, 154, 158, 159, 171 (n. 23); Lizzie Robinson's relationship with, 57; and calling of Johnsons, 60; and women's role in COGIC generally, 62; and healing ministry, 72; as race man, 85, 180 (n. 2); on divorce and remarriage, 91, 92, 173 (n. 8); and Arenia Mallory, 101–2; and pacifism, 118, 129; and Mason Temple, 130; and dress code, 144; and Women's Conventions, 145, 148; parade honoring, 149, 180 (n. 2); home of, 153; racial violence against home and church of, 153; health problems of, 153–54

Mason, Elsie (Washington), 140, 170 (n. 50)

Mason, Lelia (Washington), 170 (n. 50)

Mason, Vivian Carter, 153, 181 (n. 22)

Mason Temple, 126, 129, 130, 131, 133

McCardell, McKinley, 62

McCullom, Pearl, 84–85

McGee, F. W., 81, 138

McGlothen, Mattie, 163

McKenzie, Albertha, 11

McPherson, Aimee Semple, 63

Media coverage: and Associated Negro Press, 108, 124, 132–33, 136, 142, 146–47, 177 (n. 14), 179 (n. 17); of Arenia Mallory, 112–14, 124, 135–36, 137, 152, 177 (n. 14); of Saints Industrial School, 124, 142; of Lillian Brooks Coffey, 135–36, 152, 157–60; of Church of God in Christ, 138; of Church of God in Christ Women's Department, 138,

146–47, 152–53; and radio, 138, 147. *See also specific newspapers*

Megachurches, 7, 165

Memphis Commercial Appeal, 130, 163

Memphis Tri-State Defender, 108, 135, 136

Memphis World, 124

Metalanguage of race, 33

Methodist Church, 29

Methodist Episcopal Church, 44

Michigan Chronicle, 128

Migration of African Americans: and COGIC Women's Department, 52, 54, 55–56; and religious practices of southern migrants, 55, 58–59; and challenges of urban life, 55, 75–76; and church-planting in North and West, 58–61, 64; and church mothers, 58–64; and storefront churches, 64–65, 67, 70, 100; and sanctified living in urban areas, 64–71; and single status of African American women, 65, 172 (n. 48); and fictive family relationships in COGIC, 66; and convocations of COGIC, 71–74; and sanctification of body, 75–86; and dress code, 76–83; and marriage, 92; and aged women, 124

Missionaries: Joanna P. Moore and home missionary activities, 15–16; and Baptist Church, 16; and church-planting, 50–52, 61; appointment of, 73; Home and Foreign Missions Band, 115; foreign missions, 115, 124, 144, 145, 148; Home and Foreign Missions Board of COGIC, 144, 148, 149; home mission work and civic engagement, 120; retirement home for, 124–26; and *Evangelist Speaks*, 142; and Robinson, 144; and Coffey, 144, 145, 148, 149

Mix, Elizabeth, 169 (n. 19)

Moody, Dwight L., 110

Moody Bible Institute, 109, 110

Moore, Joanna P.: and *Hope* magazine,

Pentecostal Gospel Mission (Los Angeles), 63–64

Pentecostalism: and Holiness movement, 19, 27–30; and Charles Parham, 28; and William Seymour, 28–29; and speaking in tongues, 28–31; and baptism in the Holy Spirit, 28–31, 37; and Azusa Street revivals, 29, 62; and Charles Mason, 29–30; compared with COGIC, 30; and women's role in ministry, 32–33, 35, 37–40, 164, 171 (n. 13); and women's right to ordination, 37, 171 (n. 18); familial terms for members of Pentecostal churches, 49; and tent ministries, 52; in urban areas, 67; and divorce and remarriage, 91–92; and education, 96, 100, 177 (n. 9); fundamentalism compared with, 170 (n. 2); illness of leaders of, 170 (n. 45). *See also* Church of God in Christ

Perry, Mrs., 140

Peter (apostle), 172 (n. 34)

Pleasant, W. S., 27

Pleas, Charles H., 41–42

Politics of respectability, 14, 77, 80–81

Powdermaker, Hortense, 4, 176 (n. 40)

Powell, Adam Clayton, Sr., 104

The Power and Work of the Holy Spirit (Moore), 20

Prayer, 68–69, 72, 98–99. *See also* Sanctification

Prayer and Bible Bands, 42–43, 68–69, 73, 86, 97, 145

Preachers. *See* Pastors/preachers; *and specific preachers*

Prohibitions of sanctified life. *See* Sanctification

Prostitution, 60, 76, 80

Pullum, J., 93, 176 (n. 42)

Purity: and sanctification, 5–6, 25, 47, 69; in speech, 47; sexual purity, 47, 77, 80, 84–87, 149; class for youth on, 47, 86, 149. *See also* Sanctification

Racial pride and uplift, 14, 19, 33, 35, 65, 66

Racism, 75, 102–3, 106, 153. *See also* Segregation

Radio, 138, 147

Range, C., 130

Reforming type, 79

Renfroe, Earl, 137

Respectability, 14–15, 19, 77, 80–81

Retirement homes, 124–26, 136, 142–43

Right living, 15, 66

Rivers, Willie Mae, 163

Roberts, W. M., 58, 61, 137, 138

Roberts, William, 137

Robinson, Edward, 48

Robinson, Ida, 38

Robinson, Ida Florence (Lizzie's daughter), 13, 21, 48, 86, 124, 131, 175 (n. 24)

Robinson, Lizzie Woods: and leadership of COGIC Women's Department, 4, 7, 35, 39–43, 45–46, 53–54, 133, 135, 176 (n. 35), 177 (n. 6); and sanctification, 4, 20–25, 30–31, 68, 131–32, 133; on motherhood, 11, 12–14, 133; birth and family background of, 12–13; childhood of, 12–13; daughter of, 13, 21, 86, 124; God's calling of, 13, 23, 31; and mother's death, 13–14; marriages of, 13–14, 15, 21, 48, 87, 90, 124; and *Hope* magazine, 20–26, 47; as washerwoman, 21, 23, 165; and Joanna Moore, 21–23, 31, 133; and Bible Bands, 21–24, 31, 34, 35, 47, 53–54, 97, 115; at Baptist training academy (Dermott, Ark.), 23, 30–31; and education, 23, 97, 98; and Charles Mason, 30, 36–38, 57, 170 (n. 49); speaking in tongues by, 30–31;

expulsion of, from Baptist church, 30–31, 34; and teaching versus preaching role of women, 34–40, 60, 62; strictness of, 39–40, 95; and dress code, 40, 69, 77, 79–80, 81, 143; as general overseer of women's work in COGIC, 41–43; and church mothers, 44–48, 62; goals of, for Women's Department, 45–46; and Sewing Circle, 46, 47; and Sunshine Band, 46–47; travels of, 48, 50, 86, 114–15, 175 (n. 24); and church-planting activities, 50–53; charismatic leadership of, 53; death and funeral of, 56, 132–35, 143–44; and Women's Day, 73; and arranged marriages, 87, 175 (n. 26); and rulings on double marriage (bigamy), 94; and Saints Industrial School, 114–15; and pacifism, 118, 120; on social clubs and lodges, 120; care of, during later years, 124; health problems of, 130–31; at convocation (1945), 130–32; and Mason Temple, 131; and missionaries, 144; writings by, 168 (n. 2); as widow, 176 (n. 35)

Romans, Letter to, 60

Roosevelt, Eleanor, 9, 114, 118, 121, 122

Roosevelt, Franklin Delano, 9, 118, 119, 121

Saints, 66, 73–74, 79, 86, 152. *See also* Sanctification

Saints Industrial School: and Arenia Mallory, 9, 93–94, 101–9, 112–14, 118, 136, 142; and sanctified living generally, 98; founding of, 99; curriculum of, 99–100, 108; and Alpha Kappa Alpha, 101, 104–8, 113, 118; disrepair and impoverished condition of, 102, 104; and Jubilee Harmonizers, 104–5, 112, 114, 119; fund-raising activities for, 104–7, 112, 114, 118, 136; dress code of, 105–6; health project at, 107–8, 113,

153; goals of, 109; and Mary McLeod Bethune, 112; and Lizzie Robinson, 114–15; and Lillian Brooks Coffey, 115–16, 118, 123, 136; library for, 124; promotion of, 124, 142

Samuel, First Book of, 174 (n. 31)

Sanctification: spiritual practices involved in, 3, 66–71, 99; and COGIC, 3–4, 30, 44–45, 47; and church mothers in COGIC, 3–4, 67–71; and Robinson, 4, 7, 20–25, 30–31, 68, 131–32, 133, 143; and agency of black churchwomen, 4, 12, 66; and Coffey, 4, 67, 144, 155; and civic engagement, 4–5, 117–34; and power through purity, 5–6; and Baptist Church, 7, 19–20, 26–27, 30–31; and Pentecostalism, 19; definitions of and differing perspectives on, 19, 26, 47; and Holiness movement, 19, 28–30; and Joanna P. Moore, 19–20; and food intake, 20; and temperance, 20, 24, 25, 47, 77, 160; and health, 20, 25; and healing, 20, 27, 62, 170 (n. 45); of body, 20, 75–86, 76, 169 (n. 25); and cleanliness, 20, 77, 81, 83; on holiness of the body, 20, 169 (n. 26); and *Hope* magazine, 20–26, 47; and Charles Mason, 27, 30; and pure speech, 47; and dress code, 47, 65, 66, 69–70, 76–83, 143–44, 163, 164, 174 (n. 11), 175 (n. 13), 175 (n 16–17); and abstinence from sex, 47, 77; and migration of African Americans, 64–71; sanctified living in urban areas, 64–71; and hair, 65, 69, 83–85, 144, 174 (n. 7); and Saints, 66, 73–74, 79, 86, 152; and consecration, 67–69; and fasting, 68, 72, 76, 99; and prayer, 68–69, 72, 98–99; and tarrying, 69, 99; and makeup prohibition, 83–85, 175 (n. 18); of marriage, 86–95; and education, 98–99; and Arenia Mallory's friendship with

CPSIA information can be obtained
at www.ICGtesting.com
Printed in the USA
LVHW111518050822
725203LV00006B/552